THE SCIENCE OF

Becoming Oneself

T.S.G. Publishing Foundation, Inc.
Complete Line of Torkom Saraydarian's Works
P.O. Box 7068, Cave Creek, AZ 85327 USA
Tel: 480-502-1909 • Fax: 480-502-0713
www.tsgfoundation.org

The Science of Becoming Oneself

First Printing 1969
Second Printing 1976
Third Printing 1982
Fourth Printing 1996

ISBN: 0-911794-26-3 (hardcover)
ISBN: 0-911794-27-1 (softcover)

Library of Congress Catalog Card Number: 71-097402

Printed in the United States of America

Printed by: Data Reproductions
                 Rochester Hills, MI

Published by:
            T.S.G. Publishing Foundation, Inc.
         Complete Line of Torkom Saraydarian's Works
         P.O. Box 7068, Cave Creek, AZ 85327 USA
         Tel: 480-502-1909 · Fax: 480-502-0713
                 www.tsgfoundation.org

Note: The exercises, meditations, and visualizations contained in this book are given as guidelines. They should be used with discretion and after receiving professional advice.

Dedicated to

Rossul M . .

and to

the Youth of All Nations

Om Mani Padme Hum

TABLE OF CONTENTS

AUTHOR'S INTRODUCTION

The keynote of this book is freedom, the revelation and release of the unknown mystery in man, the freedom of lightning!

Those who feel great tension within themselves, those who crave freedom and cannot find it in the "freedoms" they have, are invited to read this book and to live it.

It is written for those who are strong in spirit and fiery of heart. It is written in great suffering, tension, love, ecstasy, and discipline. It is a gift to the youth of the world, a gift to inspire them to free themselves from hand-made chains and prisons.

It is a fire which will inflame the hearts of those who are intelligently looking to the deeper, true layers of freedom.

A young boy, in a moment of madness, tears off his clothing. Naked and standing on a rock, he cries in a loud voice, "Freedom, freedom, freedom!" and then throws himself into the ocean.

In this age, numberless wise fools, daredevils, will tear off their masks, their outworn emotional and mental clothes and, standing pure and clean on the rock of their own being, will throw themselves into the ocean of their essential freedom. This book is written for such "fools." They will know how to approach the Lotus and release the Jewel.

This is the age of release. No longer will the growing energy of freedom in the human soul tolerate slavery of any kind. Like a great flood, the energy of freedom will wash away all obstacles that stand in the way of the new age of release. It is the starlight flood of the Aquarian Age, the energy of freedom, which is flowing down from the mountains and valleys. It is the youth of all nations who will use this energy to create the new culture and the new civilization.

If you are ready to leave your old, worn-out self behind; if you are ready to walk alone with fiery drops falling from your cheeks and with new horizons in your heart; if you are ready to walk over the hot sands of human glamors and illusions and aspire to the fresh air of the high mountains within you; if you are ready to renounce your false ties and your palaces of daydreams; if you are ready to destroy the iron bars of your prisons, you are ready to begin this book and work on yourself. It is written for you. It is an outpouring of a fiery love that is felt for you.

The greatest moment in your life will be that moment when you stand face to face with your SELF. This moment will surpass all joys of the world. It will be your birth, the moment of your greatest awakening, your greatest freedom.

The energy of freedom becomes a path on which the pilgrim of fire travels toward the Source of Fire. He has to take major steps toward his total freedom. With each step, the space in which he lives and breathes becomes larger, wider, until at the end he is in unlimited Space. The seven steps of freedom are the seven techniques of the science of becoming Oneself. Through these seven steps of freedom the Spark returns Home.

Freedom is gained step by step. It is a process of expanding your consciousness into the upper levels of your being to reach "the Jewel in the Lotus." When you have gained this freedom, you will experience true love, you will enjoy true beauty and goodness, and your life will be a radiant service for humanity. You will be a shining star in the ocean of the blue Space, your Cosmic Home.

OM MANI PADME HUM

PREFACE

Space is the source from which everything proceeded.

Space is a living, conscious, ever present, ever existing ocean of electricity. It is the *Presence.*

Space visualizes, wills, and meditates; the idea condenses, becomes objective, and we have the manifested universe.

Space inhales, and the forms gradually melt away like a piece of ice in the ocean. Nothing remains but Space.

Space is unity. The Cosmos and all existence are as bubbles in Space.

Every single atom in manifestation has Space within. That portion of Space is the Real Self in any manifestation. That portion of Space is the source of Law, Love, and Light. It is the Inner Core of any atom, man, Solar System, and Cosmos.

Space is one. It has no need to communicate — it is communion itself. Bodies have need to communicate with each other — but not Space, not the Space within each of us, because in our inner Space we are one with the whole Space.

This is the space age, and man is flying toward Space, toward his Mother. In reality he is not moving in space; he is in the process of realizing his Infinity and unity with Space. Every degree of progress in space is a step forward to man's Inner Essence. Every step in conquering space is a process of extending our inner Space or putting away the walls of illusion separating us from Space. To conquer Space does not mean to go from one place to another; it means to eliminate the walls of ignorance within us.

Man is a drop of Space, crystallized, illusioned, and apparently cut off from his Source. He is bottled energy — Space in the atom. He has to be released. *We have released the atom; we are going to release man from his prison.*

Our own space is the limit of our consciousness; our space extends as far as our awareness goes. To conquer space means to have more space of awareness, to be more simple and pure. To conquer space means to extend our presence deeper, higher, and face our true *Selves.*

The space age into which we are entering with our spaceships and rockets is the external picture of the happenings in inner Space within man and humanity as a whole. We are sending lines of communication to the moon, to Venus, to the sun. In the inner Space, also, man is bridging gaps and shores which for so many centuries were left unbridged. Man is now able to communicate more easily with his Central Fire, with the Source of his Life, Love, and Light in his inner Space; thus he is able to fly toward more Space.

It is interesting to note that Space is motionless, ever present, but the materialized side of Space is active, in motion, and transitory. So it is with us. Inner Space is without activity, without emotion, without thinking. Inner Space is above the illusions, glamors, and maya; but our bodies, emotions, and minds are active. True peace, true bliss, and true joy are the characteristics of inner Space. Thus we find that those who approach their own Essence are peaceful and simple; they are in joy and bliss.

Space is "the One in Whom we live and move and have our being," as spoken by the old sage, Ephimiades.

There is only one energy that can conquer Space, and that energy is Love. Love is Space changed into pure electricity. It is the only means by which man can step out of his limitations and enter into his unlimited Space heritage, into his Infinity.

Hatred is extinction of Space, extinction of Love, extinction of Life. Wherever Space is extinguished — whether in our hearts, in our minds, in the Universe, or in Cosmos — there is suffering, limitation, death.

Space is Light. Space is Love. Space is Power. Space is Life.

All evolution is a process of overcoming and becoming Space. *The Real Self of man is Space.*

As from a burning fire a thousand sparks of similar nature and character come out, so too, O gentle one, from the Unchanging One come out manifold beings, and these merge into IT again.

II MUNDAKA UPANISHAD
Chapter I, verse I

Chapter I

TOWARD FREEDOM

... Age-long identification with the form side of life is not easily overcome and the task ahead of the disciple is a long and arduous one but one which promises eventual success, provided there is clear thinking, earnest purpose and planned scientific work.[1]

The process of evolution is beautifully explained in the story of the Prodigal Son who received his share of inheritance from his Father, then journeyed to far-off lands where he squandered his wealth in riotous living. While tending swine and suffering great deprivation, gradually the memory of his Father's home dawned in his consciousness, and he pronounced the most poignant statement ever recorded:

I will arise and go to my Father.

As he approached, the Father rushed forth part way to embrace him. The progress of humanity or of an individual begins when man starts to raise himself and walk toward his Real Self. Our Father is our *Self.* The long road that separates us from our Father seems to us so far, as far as the farthest star, but actually it is closer than our eyes.

The reason for this illusion is that throughout the ages we — the Real Father in us — have identified ourselves with the form side of life, and we have lost ourselves in the running water of transient forms. This can be explained if we take the process of sleep as an example. Note how your active consciousness gradually becomes more distant, sinking deeper and deeper into apparent nothingness. In that stage of sleep it seems as though we do not even exist. So it is with the Spark, the Father, Who gradually loses Himself as he identifies with coarser and denser

---

[1] Bailey, Alice A., *Glamour: A World Problem*, p. 265.

matter — until one day He stands on the pole directly opposite His Real Being.

The lowest point of identification is reached when a man cannot distinguish between himself and his form. He exists as a living form. Then, gradually, he perceives that there is a difference between his form and other forms. Following this recognition of the physical form, he develops the emotional nature and later the mental nature. As his mental nature develops, he realizes that he is a separated being.

After long ages of experience, this sense of separation increases and forms a permanent state in his consciousness. This permanent state of separation becomes a dominating factor, a governing factor, an "I." For a very long period this "I" is worshipped. During that time it becomes the central pivot of the life of the man; he sacrifices everything to save and keep that "I." It is the idol behind which there is the true God, but identification with it is so real that the man never thinks beyond it. It is, for him, a life preserver in the ocean of existence. He thinks that he will be lost forever if he loses the idol, the little self, the "I." There comes a time when the Inner Lord begins to move, and gradually the power of the idol lessens; the small lives of man's nature — of his physical, emotional, and mental vehicles — respond with a new vibration.

Centuries pass. The man cultivates his physical plane life and makes it a beautiful garden. He cleans the muddy and agitated waters of his emotional world, purifying his motives, his thoughts, his words, and then turns his face toward his Father's Home. He is now willing to tread the Path consciously. He must walk for ages and ages until the Father is seen and at-one-ment is achieved.

To tread this fiery way, he learns and uses *the science of becoming oneself.* There are three main steps involved in this science.

The first step is the step of doing good, through which the inner influences increase and new integration and fusion occur among the vehicles. The man tries to be an agent of goodwill, and in all his acts, feelings, and thoughts he tries to express Goodness, Beauty, and Righteousness as far as he is able to do so. This is creative living — the way of service.

The second step is the step of facing up to the facts about himself. He holds all expressions under survey and tries to find the *why* of all his reactions and responses on the three levels of his being. He analyzes his thoughts, his emotions, his actions, and he tries to find the urges and motives behind them. He does not do these things as some introspectives do, identifying themselves with their inner and outer states — as he analyzes, he views himself impersonally, and thus cultivates within himself the attitude of a detached observer. When he succeeds in observing himself impersonally, he tries to view others and all events with the same impersonality.

Through this process he discovers the pseudo-rulers in his subjective and objective worlds and gradually decreases their number, until eventually the observer himself becomes the sole ruler of his being. This means simply that the man is no longer the victim of his physical urges, of his emotional waves, or of his different thoughts and momentary tendencies. He tries to face himself at every turn and attempts to unmask every activity and every state of being which pretends to speak or act in the name of the True Self. Here the man becomes a duality. There is the objective world and the one who rules it, but the latter is not yet a clear-cut figure.

Ages pass, and the observer gradually distinguishes between himself and the physical body. Now he thinks and assumes that he is the emotional man. In the next step he leaves behind the physical body and emotional states as *not-selves* and identifies himself with the mental world. Here he lives for quite a long time, identifying himself with many different states of being, until one day he surpasses his mental world too and becomes a deeper being, a deeper observer on a higher plane. This is called "the path of detachment" and "the path of facing oneself" upon every turn of life.

The third step is the science of bridge building. This bridge building becomes a conscious process when the man lives on the mental plane. It has three progressive stages:

1. Concentration, Meditation, and Contemplation
2. The Science of Impression
3. The Technique of Indifference

The first stage is very important and forms the foundation for the entire work of bridge building. We can build nothing in our inner or outer world without scientific concentration, meditation, and contemplation. The science of becoming oneself is a great science and the greatest goal of humanity. When a man starts the bridge building process, it is evident that he sees a high peak which challenges all that he has and is. He realizes that he cannot jump there in one step, but that he must build numerous bridges and paths, even space ships, to reach the peak which may turn out to be a star.

Through scientific concentration, meditation, and contemplation the man builds many bridges and different lines of communication between the inner world and the mental plane. He ceases to be the slave of his threefold personality (his physical, emotional, and mental natures) and frees himself to live in the unlimited world of spiritual development.

Through intense discipline he controls his mind; he cleans it and sets the gamut of the mental plane into activity. This is the result of concentration and focusing. Then he tries to extend the bridges between the mental and the spiritual world through scientific meditation. In reality, scientific meditation is a technique to fuse the spiritual and mental worlds. It gradually changes and becomes contemplation, "which is the source of inspiration and illumination." In this stage man "becomes a static point of concentrated contemplation" and enters into "that silence which enables him to tap the divine Mind, wrest God's thought out of the divine consciousness and to *Know*."

Still the star shines in the deep blue sky beyond the mountains. The man finds that to reach it, he must use not only the mental, love, and intuitional substances but also another kind of substance called *the energy of the will*. This energy is the answer of the Father to the invocation coming from the Son. The building of a new and higher bridge has begun, using this will energy. It expresses itself as the divine Purpose, as the divine Plan, and as creative, pure ideas.

On the path of his high journey, the man is sensitive to the impressions coming from the Center where the Will of God is known, from the Center which we call the Heart of God, and from the center which we call *humanity*.[1] By means of this threefold bridge, he communicates with the highest spiritual Source

---

[1] See *The Great Invocation*, p. 304.

and becomes impressed by the divine Plan and the need of humanity.

And so, from stage to stage the disciple passes, going from light to light, from perception to perception, from force to energy, from personality focus to soul integration and, then, from soul to spirit, from form to life. He has explored all the avenues of knowledge; he has descended into the depths, into hell and into the valleys; he has climbed the mountain top of initiation and from there has swung out beyond space and time; he has lost all self-interest and is a focussed point of thought in the mind of God.[1]

He stands as a pillar of light in humanity. He is in the world, but not of the world. He can now repudiate, refuse "to be identified with anything save the spiritual reality." He is now the *Jewel in the Lotus*, a liberated man. This sublime state is beautifully given in an old writing:

The fivefold one hath entered into peace, yet walks our sphere. That which is dense and dark now shineth with a clear pure light, and radiance poureth from the seven sacred lotuses. He lighteneth the world, and irradiateth the nethermost place with fire divine.

That which hath hitherto been restless, wild as the ocean, turgid as the stormy sea, lies quiet and still. Limpid the waters of the lower life and fit to offer to the thirsty ones who, groping, cry of thirst.

That which hath slain and veiled the Real for many lengthy aeons is itself slain, and with its death the separated life is ended. The One is seen. The Voice is heard. The Real is known, the Vision glimpsed. The fire of God leaps upward into a flame.

The darkest place receives the light. The dawn appears on earth. The dayspring from on high, sheds its bright beams in hell itself, and all is light and life.[2]

In the secret brotherhoods of the Orient, this science of becoming oneself was given through the mysteries of initiation.

---

[1] Bailey, Alice A., *Discipleship in the New Age*, Vol. I, pp. 772-773.

[2] Bailey, Alice A., *The Light of the Soul*, p. 419.

Plato, who was an initiate into the mysteries, wrote: "The design of the mysteries is to lead us back to the perfection from which, as a principle, we first made our descent."

There were initiation temples "where the mysteries were most sacredly guarded and kept secret." These temples were found in India, Greece, South America, and in many other locations on the earth. The purpose was always the same: to lead the Prodigal Son to his Home, to his Father.

Christ, the Son of God, openly expressed for us the process of initiation in His life, from Birth to Resurrection, through seven great dramatic events:

> The Birth in Bethlehem
>
> The Baptism in Jordan
>
> The Transfiguration
>
> The Renunciation
>
> The Revelation
>
> The Decision
>
> The Resurrection

Through these seven initiations, Christ demonstrated to us the means through which a man can gradually approach his own Essence and be one with his Father, which is his essential Self. These seven events are given here in religious terminology, but actually they are scientific and, more importantly, they are psychological processes of spiritual growth, development, unfoldment, and detachment.

The whole process of the mysteries of initiation is the process of meeting Oneself and becoming Oneself. On that level only an Initiate can truly say, "I and my Father are one."

Chapter II

BENEVOLENCE

To give is a divine attribute. The inexhaustibility of giving is found in varying degrees in all of nature. But fire is the element in which giving is most apparent. The very principle of Fire is transmutation and constant giving. Fire cannot exist without the sacrifice of giving; likewise the fiery seed of the spirit exists through giving. But the sacrifice is a true one only when it has become the very nature of a man.[1]

The word "benevolence" is composed of two words: bene and volence. Bene means *well* or *good*; volence means *to will, to do*. It is an act of benefaction or an act of goodwill. Benevolence, benefaction, or goodwill is an act or activity by which you express your inner goodness through your thoughts, feelings, words, or actions.

Man in his essence is a drop of goodness. It does not matter where he is or what he is; he is still a drop of goodness in his essential being. He may act wrongly from the viewpoint of others. He may have wrong feelings and distorted thoughts. But behind these distortions and aberrations there is the essential goodness in the depth of the human soul.

Sometimes man is like an enslaved king. His enemies have chained his hands and feet, and he is unable to act as a king — to use his authority, his royal will. He is chained like a puppet in the hands of his enemies. Psychologically many people are in this same position. They are slaves to their habits, vices, and subconscious urges; slaves of their bodies, emotions, and even of their minds; slaves of their religious or political doctrines and dogmas. They are virtual slaves. If, however, the chains are

---

[1] Agni Yoga Society, *Fiery World I,* par. 546.

broken and they are released from such bondage, you will see that there is a splendid beauty in them, a radiant goodness.

Christ said to love our enemies, for behind their masks there is goodness. There is the Spark of God within them. We love men for the goodness in them and because very often, "They know not what they do." If a man does anything against good, even intentionally, it still does not mean that he is evil in his innermost essence. It does mean that he is *chained*, aberrated, and that distortion exists somewhere in his mechanism.

The sun still shines behind clouds, smoke, and dust storms. It is always there in its splendor and beauty, but if searched for through these obstacles, it seems to be lost, to not exist. Take away the dust, take away the smoke, the clouds, and you will find the sun unchanged, beautiful, and glorious. The same is true of man. We may say that evil people are sick people. Sometimes their sickness is contagious and incurable for a long period of time.

In our world we know that ill will is widespread; evil works are everywhere. Gossip, hatred, jealousy, and crime are common; people are trying to find solutions to these individual and social problems. Psychosomatic medicine, psychiatry, and other psychological and medical methods as well as religions are being used in the search for a means to heal individuals, groups, and even the masses of people. But most of the searchers are looking for the key where it is not kept. The key is in man himself. The panacea is the Inner Man, the real Essence of man, the Real Self. Try to release this Essence, and you can gradually solve all problems.

This Inner Essence is Goodness itself. It is Fire; it is Light; it is Love; it is Power; it is Beauty and Bliss; it is Life itself! It is the source of all our highest inspirations. We know about the stupendous energy of the atom. We have released the atom. Now it is time to release the Fire in man. Imagine how humanity will be expanded when this Fire is released! It will be the new age of the Spirit, the "Spiritual Age" about which all true seers of the ages have dreamed and spoken.

  ... The Fire of Benefaction creates the most beautiful transmutations.[1]

---

[1] Agni Yoga Society, *Fiery World I*, par. 28.

... If each one filled with goodness would sow it with every touch! What a myriad of beneficent sparks would be sent out into space.... [1]

... One must sow good with each glance of the eye and each touch. [2]

How can one release this Fire? How is one to release the good in man, the goodness which is his true essence? The answer is: Teach children and men everywhere *the science of doing good.* Teach them how to think about the good, how to feel the good, how to speak about the good, how to live and express the good.

When they begin to release the Inner Fire, their life and environment will gradually change. This current of fiery energy will heal all psychological cleavages in man, in the family, and in nations. The mind of man will gradually receive increased light; the heart of man will slowly change and become a powerhouse of love and radiance; the body of man will be healthy, shining, and strong. This fiery energy will wash away all thoughtforms, illusions, and glamors which are poisonous and cause disorders in the nervous system, the glandular system, and in the whole life of man.

A small act of benevolence, a small act of goodwill, releases a beam of Light from the Inner Core, from the fiery Goodness in man. This Light works miracles in man and in his social relationships. It starts an inner clearing process and produces a healing energy which washes away all causes of suffering, pain, and misery.

... Striving toward Good avails itself of all higher paths.... Thus, the streams of Light conquer in limitless cosmic action. [3]

There are two very important injunctions given by two wise people. The first one says: "Man, know thyself." The second one says: "Man, be thyself."

We can know ourselves by *being* ourselves. The shortest, wisest way to be oneself is to express oneself, to radiate one's Real Self, one's Inner Essence. This true expression of the

---

[1] Agni Yoga Society, *Heart*, par. 407.

[2] Ibid., par. 410.

[3] Agni Yoga Society, *Infinity II*, par. 326.

Essence is known by many names, but fundamentally they are the same. It is Goodwill, Benevolence, Sacrifice, or Service.

One of the master minds has said:

> ... *service is the scientific mode, par excellence, to evoke spiritual integration and to call forth the resources of a divine son of God.*[1]

Every good thought, every act of goodwill, and every word expressed from the heart shorten the distance between our two selves: the small self lost in the illusions and glamors of the world; the other Self, found in the blue sky of joy and bliss.

Our destiny is to release ourselves and to be our Selves. Only by this path are all beauty, joy, progress, and the health of humanity created.

---

[1] Bailey, Alice A., *Discipleship in the New Age*, Vol I, p. 269.

Chapter III

THE SCIENCE OF DOING GOOD

There is a trinity about which the ancients spoke reverently and by which they tried to live their lives. That trinity is Goodness, Beauty, and Righteousness.

In every act of Goodness we must have Beauty and Righteousness. In every act of Beauty we must have Goodness and Righteousness. In every act of Righteousness we must have Goodness and Beauty. These three cannot be separated.

Essentially, man in himself is a trinity. He is essentially a drop of Cosmic Fire. This Fire or Spark expresses Itself as Goodness, Beauty, and Righteousness, or in other words, as Will, Love, and Light.

The inner, Central Fire wanted a mechanism through which to express Itself, and so, magnetically, the Fire attracted millions of tiny lives to Itself and from them built three vehicles: the physical, emotional, and mental vehicles. The Central Fire holds them as a unit throughout Its cycle of expression; It sustains them as a mechanism of communication between the outer and inner worlds or between the objective and subjective worlds.

The Central Fire, the kernel of man, is a powerhouse of Light, Love, and Power. It is the source of life for the vehicles and even for the surrounding world. But often, due to lack of integration and alignment, there is very weak communication between the Central Fire and the three vehicles: the physical, emotional, and mental bodies. This lack of alignment and integration is the real cause of all psychosomatic illnesses, psychological disorders, and of course of all our personal and social problems. The basic method for healing these cleavages, disorders, and problems is to release the energy of the Divine Spark within us, to increase the vitality of our physical body, to increase the love energy in our emotional nature, and to increase the light in our mental world.

To accomplish this we may use a very simple technique. We have within us a fountain of Light, Love, and Power. Somewhere near this fountain is the small garden of our life with trees, flowers, and many living things. To keep our garden alive and healthy, we bring to it water of Light, Love, and Power from our inner fountain. The garden is our life, our environment.

The first step is to start with our physical environment. We sit alone, quietly, and think, "Do I know of a man, woman, or child who is in need?" Perhaps after a few minutes we will remember that one of our friends or neighbors needs a pair of shoes, a book, a suit, a car, or a radio. We say to ourself, "Does this person really need it? Yes. Do I have enough money to buy what is needed? Yes, I do! I will buy it and give it to the one in need." The second step is to buy the item decided upon. The third is to give it to the person in the nicest and most considerate way. When we perform an act such as this, we feel that new energy starts to flow and circulate in our mechanism; we experience deep joy, new strength, and new peace.

What exactly did happen? We may say that through this act of goodwill, a tiny current of life energy came down to our mechanism from the Central Fire, and on the way it washed away some obstacles and established feeble communication between the Central Fire, our vehicles of expression, and our environment.

Any time you feel depressed, alone, and neglected, just perform a deed of goodwill with no expectation of return. This is a real science and cannot be learned except by doing it. From such expressions of goodwill you will learn how to act in a selfless way with an impersonal attitude. You will learn how to approach people, how to come to know them, to feel with them, enabling you to better meet the real need. If you continue to use this technique over a long period of time, the channel of communication between your Real Self and your personality will become wider and deeper, and you will be ready to take the next step.

Sometimes you cannot help others financially; often they do not need it. Perhaps they need only your smile, your pleasant words, sweet songs, music; sometimes they need only your presence, your silent presence. You begin to give your smiles and words to those who truly need them. In giving them joy, you feel that your own inner joy increases; in giving words of peace and comfort, your inner peace deepens; you come closer to your Inner Fire and closer to the Inner Fire of the ones whom you are helping. Gradually you notice that your emotional and physical problems are lessening and often disappearing because the vitality and love energy are dispelling the fog, the mist, the clouds in your emotional world. The Central Fire is pouring forth its healing rays into your mechanism, aligning and integrating it.

You cannot, however, stop here. You must add another step: the work of goodwill on the mental level. This work involves the giving of your light to others by helping people to solve their own problems through a process of education and enlightenment.

There are times when people need not know what you are giving. We often receive energies of love and light without ever knowing their source. Some of our friends think about us and send their deepest love and compassion. We are helped; we gradually overcome our depression, our sorrow, and our trouble because of prayer-like thoughts and love waves which have been projected toward us by our friends, husband, wife, or parents.

Suddenly a beam of light shines in our darkest hour. The light gives us courage and leads us to the door. A true friend is thinking about us. He is sending his courage, his love; he is feeding our Inner Fire to help us overcome the obstacles, whatever they are. This is also a kind of giving by which we are opening the inner doors so that our love and pure thought can pour through and thus increase the inner communication with our Essence. To attain this height, we must work toward it gradually.

The simplest way to start is to teach something to someone who needs it. You may teach orally, through letters, writings, creative articles, books, and even through your thoughts. Here the real *science of doing good* begins. Before we can be of real help to others, we must learn:

- Not to impose our ideas, opinions, and thoughts upon anyone but to respect the freedom of others.
- How to clothe our ideas to reveal their greatest beauty.
- How to find the level of our friends so that we will not harm them by giving them more than they can assimilate.
- To speak or write only the *truth*. We should never taint our teaching with lies, great or small.
- To approach people with deep and sincere love, a love that penetrates the heart of your brother and unveils his woes.

As you continue your good work on the mental plane, planting lights, bringing enlightenment and illumination, you will notice that the light in your own mind is increasing tenfold, and a new energy of love, light, and joy is circulating through your brain, through your heart, and throughout your nervous system.

Thus, year by year, the communication and relationship between your Central Fire and vehicles of expression will increase. Proportionally they will align, integrate, and fuse with the Inner Light. This fusion will express itself as acts of goodwill, sacrifice, and love; as creative living; as radiant health. Through such expressions and through our efforts to bring enlightenment to others, we heal ourselves physically, emotionally, and mentally. This is the simplest way to make contact with our life-giving Spark.

It was because of this that Christ said to His disciples, "It is more blessed to give than to receive." This is divine sharing. If you transmit a spark to a friend or even to a stranger, your fire increases many-fold. In the process of clearing physical obstacles, of dispelling glamors, deep-seated emotional problems, and of removing illusions from the minds of people, the act of goodwill must take place on the three levels simultaneously.

Try to remove an obstacle in another person on any level, and you will discover that you are removing a corresponding obstacle in yourself. We cannot do anything to anyone else without first doing it subjectively to ourselves. Likewise, whenever we act physically, emotionally, and mentally against the Good, the Righteous, and the Beautiful, we build a wall between ourselves and our Inner Essence. In so doing we invite psychosomatic illnesses, physical complications, and ill health in general on three levels.

To live a radiant life, we must return to our Source and become one with our Real Self, which is the Central Fire within us. Doing good on the three levels of human endeavor is the path leading us back to our Father's House.

EXERCISE ONE

Take a few minutes in the morning before you start your daily work. Sit quietly, relax, and say:

> *The sons of men are one, and I am one with them.*
> *I seek to love, not hate;*

I seek to serve and not exact due service;

I seek to heal, not hurt.

Then think of someone whom you might help today. First consider physical plane help, perhaps helping someone financially. Try to meet a real need on the physical level. This should be done without any expectation of return. Remember what Christ said:

Take heed that ye do not your alms before men to be seen of them.... When thou doest alms, let not thy left hand know what thy right hand doeth. That thine alms may be in secret.[1]

You need not necessarily give money; perhaps you can do some work for someone; you might cut the grass for an elderly neighbor; you might baby-sit for a friend who needs your help at that moment. Try to be of service to someone every day for a whole month. If you do this, you will find that miraculous energies begin to be released from your inner fountain. A new life will open for you, and a healing power will strengthen your body, your heart, and your mind. When you return from your work in the evening or at the time you retire, quickly review the day mentally; see the attitude and feel the joy that the person felt at the time of your help. Before you sleep, say the following prayer:

Lord, lead my step there where I am needed.

On the next day, repeat the same actions. Spread good deeds all around you, in your office, your factory, your school, your home. Sometimes it may happen that you feel no inner joy; do not look for it. Decide to help someone and do it. This is an art.

In using the science of doing good technique, you need two-way detachment. It is important to:

1. Detach yourself from the one whom you are helping. Do not expect thanks, smiles, or any other form of return. Just do the deed for the sake of "goodness," and then try to find another one to help.

2. Detach yourself from your inner sensations, judgments, happiness, or any other feelings you may have. Let pure love flow from your heart and express itself as material plane help.

---

[1] Matthew 6:1-4

Many people help their friends with expectation of return for their service. Later, if there is no response of any kind, they feel resentful, unhappy, and often develop some animosity toward the one whom they have helped. We hear people say, "I helped him many, many times in this way or that way, but he was never grateful; he even became my enemy." Actually such a man did not help because behind his act there was not an impersonal motive; there was expectation of some kind of recognition. Help given with such a mixed motive will automatically create a secret refusal from the heart of the one we would help.

The giving of gifts to our friends on different occasions should carry the same impersonal motive. Originally it was an act of goodwill. You met your friend's need, but gradually this high concept of meeting the need changed into formality and eventually became a compulsory act. You may find that you now take a gift to him because you feel compelled to do so. Although you know that he does not actually need it, you also know that he will feel badly if you do not give him something. The same holds true in the sending of hundreds of Christmas or other greeting cards. It is good if you are meeting a real need on the physical, emotional, or mental level, but it has no meaning if you are forced to do it, or if you are considering what your friend will do or think if he does not receive the card or gift. In all our gifts and cards we must put our sincere love, our impersonal love. We must send them not with expectation, not mechanically, but with real love and with honest intention to meet the need.

Sometimes people bribe even themselves just as they try to bribe God with prayers. There are people who give money just to make themselves "feel good," and for days and days they feel happy because they have given a few dollars to someone, perhaps to a "gambler." We must use discrimination; we must know the real need and the weight of our help. On the path of doing good, we will also gradually learn whom to help and how to remain detached. Only by such an impersonal attitude does the Inner Light shine forth and flood our whole being with joy and blessings.

We are concerned with the release of the Inner Fire, but even this must not be our main motive at the time we are helping. The chief factors which move our hearts are: first, the sense of oneness; and second, the understanding of the true need of the subject. We must feel that the needs of others are our needs, but our help must not paralyze them; on the contrary, it must lead them into action. We must remember to base our own actions on the invocation which we say each morning:

The sons of men are one, and I am one with them....

They are our brothers and, in a sense, they are ourselves. Only upon such concepts can a new civilization begin and a new age dawn in the hearts of men.

It is sometimes possible to put juvenile delinquents back on the right track by teaching them the *science of doing good* through a special educational program. When they begin to learn this science through their own experience, they will gradually change and may even become the most distinguished benefactors of their race or humanity.

We cannot release the sense of responsibility in others unless we first lead them to discover a real need and then a method for meeting that need. It is interesting to note that we see first the shortcomings of others, and we are quick with our criticism. If we can help others instead of criticizing them, we will begin to see our own needs and use our mind to meet them. Thus, when our troubled young people learn to use this technique, they will gradually wash away the obstacles that are responsible for their delinquency, no matter in what area of their mechanism the obstacles may be found; they will be able to release their inner and constructive Fire. Therefore, teach your children to do good at home, in school, in the world, and wherever they can, and they will never become delinquent.

You may use this same method with those who are hostile toward you. Find ways to let them help you, and their hostility will decrease or vanish completely.

The following poem by Lena Stearns Bolton beautifully summarizes this chapter:

I want to do one kindly deed each day
To help someone to find a better way.
I want to lend a hand to one in need
Or find some lonely stray that I may feed.
I want to sing for someone a loved song
To give them courage when the road is long.
If just one smile of mine can lighten pain,
Then I shall feel I have not lived in vain.

Chapter IV

BROTHER'S KEEPER

EXERCISE TWO

For the second month, again choose a quiet spot in your home or in your garden. After relaxing your body and calming your emotional and mental natures, read the following words very slowly, with deep concentration:

> ... *Oh, there is a Love which fears nothing, which is greater than life and greater than death. I am that Love. There is a Love which knows no limit, which is everywhere, which is in the presence of death, and which is all-Tender even in the Terrible. I am that Love. There is a Love which is Unutterably Sweet, which welcomes all pain, which welcomes all fear, which drives away all sadness, which is wheresoever thou dost search for it. I am that Love. Oh, I am the very Essence of that Love. And, O, My own Self, I, that Love, am Thine Own Self, My nature is Love! I am Love Itself!* [1]

After thinking or meditating upon these wonderful words for a few minutes, close your eyes and try to think of someone to whom you can give *love*. You may express your love through acts of goodwill, as explained in the first exercise, or you may express it through words and thoughts. There are people who need encouragement, a few words of appreciation, a single, sincere smile, or a handshake. Love is the highest healing energy; love increases within you when you give it to those who are in need of it. There are many people who are thirsty for love. Elderly people, people who feel rejected, those who are ill, and those who have lost relatives or friends — all are in need of love.

Choose one person each day and radiate love to him by spending some time with him, visiting with him, or by writing to him. We grow spiritually by loving others. Our understanding

---

[1] Alexander, F.J., *In the Hours of Meditation*, p. 26.

31

deepens, our sense of responsibility becomes keener, and our whole being grows stronger and healthier when our love energy is released from our inner fountain of Life. Personal and social problems are known by many names, but if we think deeply about them, we discover that most of them are the result of the lack of love.

Love energy clarifies your thinking, calms your emotions, lessens tensions, lightens your body, fills your heart with joy, gives you power of endurance, and washes away those emotional states which are the cause of many health problems. You experience this healthy current of love when you let love flow from your heart and soul to others. This technique is truly the science of loving. Through it we learn *how to love without identifying ourselves with the problems and personalities of others.*

Your love will be a light which helps a man to find his way. Your love will be sweet music which calls forth the best within the man. Your eyes, your voice, your words, your manner will evoke a power, an energy, a new courage, a new hope. It would be unwise for you to solve or attempt to solve any man's problems, but through your love you can help him to become stronger, clearer in mind, more courageous, and better able to solve his own problems *with his own hands*, and to walk his way *on his own feet.* He will feel that you have no expectation of return for the love you give. Your love will be directed only to his inner being — not to his circumstances, affairs, problems, and conditions.

There are times when a person is unable to receive help or inspiration *from within* unless someone gives him love. Love opens the doors of inspiration and energy. Your love will tell him that you have great faith in him; that you have great visions for him; and that you are confident that he will be able to solve his own problems.

It is important not only to know how to love, but it is also important to be aware of the sensitive condition of those people who are in mourning, in depression, in sorrow and grief. Very often they are in a hypnotic state, and any suggestion of yours goes to their inner mind and becomes a post-hypnotic suggestion. For this reason it is wiser to talk very little and never to make direct suggestions. At times it is better not to speak but merely to embrace them and stay with them in silence. Let them talk, if they wish, as you listen. Quite often their depression or sorrow will decrease or vanish altogether as a result of your silent presence. Do not identify with their sorrows; be spiritually indifferent, but be radioactive in your love. Children, too, may need your love given to them through play, quiet activities, or in other ways suitable to their level. The act of goodwill must be extended to the three levels of human life: physical, emotional, and mental.

There are many ways of showing love. One of the most beautiful and effective ways of expressing love is being grateful to those who have helped us on any level. Some people never express gratitude but take our help for granted. This must not change our love for them. We must realize that people who are incapable of being grateful are like those who eat much food but cannot digest it. The healing energy of love increases as it is passed to another, and another, and so on, continuously. Its current must not be blocked anywhere, in any way.

Respect for others is another way of expressing love. It not only releases your love, but it also releases the love of the one with whom you are interacting. We must not expect gratefulness or respect from others, but we ourselves must show it; we must express it.

Many times, in certain situations, we can express our love even when the subject is not present. Suppose you are sitting with several friends. One of them expresses a dark or harmful thought about one of your friends who is not present. Your first duty as a student and practitioner of love is to protect your absent friend without hurting the one who is doing the harmful work. Harmful, ugly expressions in a group create points of dislike in each person present. This undermines the health of the body, heart, and mind. It must be erased immediately with delicate and wise action. Any harmful word or gossip is like poisonous water which the gossiper drinks first and then gives to you and your friends to drink.

We show our love also when we protect someone who is under attack and whose rights are endangered in some way. On such occasions, heroes are born! If the protection is for a nation, national heroes are created: heroes who voluntarily dedicate and sacrifice their lives to lead their nations from darkness into light and to open the door to a new freedom, a new way of life. This achievement is the result of love energy accumulated age by age and released in a time of great need.

Do this exercise for one month and keep a daily record of your deeds of love and your experiences with them.

Chapter V

TOWARD PURITY

EXERCISE THREE

In the third and fourth months your exercises are deeper, more beautiful, and more effective. The third exercise includes the previous two, but it goes far beyond them.

Step One

Again choose a place in your home or garden and relax your whole body, calm your emotions, and quiet your mind. Enjoy this relaxed state for a moment and then read the following:

> *Seek not, Oh twice-blessed One, to attain the spiritual essence before the mind absorbs. Not thus is wisdom sought. Only he who hath the mind in leash, and seeth the world as in a mirror can be safely trusted with the inner senses. Only he who knoweth the five senses to be illusion, and that naught remaineth save the two ahead, can be admitted into the secret of the Cruciform transposed.*
>
> *The path that is trodden by the Server is the path of fire that passeth through his heart and leadeth to the head. It is not on the path of pleasure, nor on the path of pain that liberation may be taken nor that wisdom cometh. It is by the transcendence of the two, by the blending of pain with pleasure, that the goal is reached, that goal that lieth ahead, like a point of light seen in the darkness of a winter's night. That point of light may call to mind the tiny candle in some attic drear, but — as the path that leadeth to that light is trodden through the blending of the pairs of opposites — that pin-point, cold and flickering, groweth with steady radiance till the warm light of some blazing lamp cometh to the mind of the wanderer by the way.*
>
> *Pass on, O Pilgrim, with steady perseverance. No candle is there nor earth lamp fed with oil. Ever the radi-*

ance groweth till the path ends within a blaze of glory, and the wanderer through the night becometh the child of the sun, and entereth within the portals of that radiant orb.[1]

After reading these lines, close your eyes and imagine that you are standing high upon a mountain. Look around you in your imagination and try to see the trees, flowers, birds, rivers, and other wonders of creation. Do not hurry; take your time. Then, raising your arms (in your imagination), bless the world, bless humanity, bless all living creatures, the trees and flowers, saying very slowly:

May the divine Love, Light, and Beauty be our daily breath and thought, and let Light, Love, and Power restore the Plan on earth.

After saying this prayer, imagine for a few moments a golden light pouring out from your heart and head, flooding the world.

Step Two

Imagine a small, blue star at the middle of your brain. Gradually make it grow larger and larger until you are sitting in the center of a large wheel of blue light. Let your emotions, thoughts, organs, and body be flooded with that blue light. Then imagine the blue light becoming smaller and smaller until it is again a tiny blue spark in your head.

These two steps will help to clean your mental and emotional worlds of various negative and limiting forms of vibration, making them ready for the flow of inner, fiery energy.[2]

Please know that it will be a long time before you will be able to do these exercises as effectively as is expected, but do not be discouraged. Go forward inch by inch, step by step, trying each day to control a greater part of your nature. Your purpose is to extend the power of your Inner Lord over your vehicles, and this takes time. At first your physical and emotional bodies will show signs of rebellion, but keep trying, and one day they will be your obedient servants. The fire which purifies and builds the vehicles burns slowly.

---

[1] Bailey, Alice A., *A Treatise on White Magic*, p. 121.
[2] Caution must be taken not to exceed the limit of 2-3 minutes.

Step Three

You will now analyze your prayer, word by word, to discover the whole meaning and implication of the two main clauses:

May divine Love, Light, and Beauty be our daily breath and thought, and let Light, Love, and Power restore the Plan on earth.

Allow yourself ten minutes to search the deeper meaning of these words. You will then be ready for the fourth step.

Step Four

Imagine that you are sitting on the same mountain. Visualize three rays of light coming from the blue sky to your head, flooding your mind with the energy of Love, Goodness, and Beauty. Hold your body, emotions, and mind under the flow of these energies and imagine that your whole being is becoming a transparent light which is radiating Love, Goodness, and Beauty to the whole of humanity. Then project these three light rays to your home, your church, your club, or any organization in which you work, flooding them with the energies of Love, Goodness, and Righteousness.

Following this, slowly remember where you are sitting and slowly open your eyes. Remain silent for about ten or fifteen minutes. Your exercise is over. These steps, as explained above, help you to purify your mental atmosphere of crystallizations, wounds, and negative thoughts. The result will reflect upon your physical body also, making it more energetic. It will take time and perseverance, but gradually results will appear as you continue with your exercises.

In a short time you will notice that your mind is better able to penetrate any form, symbol, book, lecture, ritual, or expression and come in contact with the world of meaning. Gradually your thinking will throw out all prejudices, all limiting crystallizations and reach freedom. This does not mean that you will lose all your cherished ideas, ways of thinking, faith, or doctrine; it means that you will see in them the parts that are closer to Righteousness, Beauty, and Goodness; you will see the same qualities in those faiths, doctrines, or religions which you had previously thought to be wrong. Thus the world of meaning and significance will stand wide open for you. Only such consciousness can approach the higher creative energies and bring them into the world of men.

When people approach the creative, fiery world without due preparation, they can be hurt. They invite psychological problems and other troubles for themselves as well as for others. When one approaches the subtler energies of the inner Spark, potent energies are released from the Spark. These energies, passing down through the mental atmosphere, degenerate when mixed with unhealthy thoughtforms, crystallized attitudes of mind, and negative waves. At the same time they stimulate these unhealthy thoughtforms and create strong, powerful urges in the inner world of a person. The individual finds, to his surprise, that instead of approaching the higher concepts, ideas, and the spiritual world, his thinking and behavior have degenerated, and he is a victim of forces coming from his desire world and of separative forces in the form of selfishness, greed, hatred, jealousy, and so on. He tries desperately to oppose and control them with his higher aspirations. Here you have the inner conflict, the guilt complex, and the cause of psychological and nervous breakdowns. "Every kingdom which is divided against itself will be destroyed."

It is important that the work of preparation be carried out in the three worlds of personality: physical, emotional, and mental. When these three are cleansed, coordinated, integrated, and fused with the higher world of Light, Love, and Power, there is no danger in touching the creative Fire within yourself. Thus we can see the necessity of cleaning from the mental and emotional atmosphere those vibrations which are egoistic, selfish, separative, and destructive.

This cleaning process must take place in your daily life to guard and protect your thoughts, imagination, and speech. If at any time you notice a negative action within, check it at once and try to transmute it with positive energy. Suppose that, through an old habit, you start to speak evil of a man. Immediately try to recall the fact that you are a pilgrim on the Path, and slowly change the direction of your conversation; begin to speak of the best qualities in that same man.

You may use this same technique when you are thinking negatively, judging, condemning, or hating. Concentrate your thoughts upon noble things so that your thoughts will grow and become greater. If you emphasize evil in others through your speech or thought, you will not only increase the evil in them but also in yourself. Christ said: "Do not fight against evil; even bless your enemies." There is a great wisdom in these words. Another great Teacher tells us:

> *The best thing is to destroy the germs of base thoughts, which are more infectious than all diseases.*[1]

> *... Formerly, one was responsible for action; later the significance of the word was understood; and now it is time to know the conflagration of thought. It is better to learn silence and purify one's thoughts.*[2]

In olden days teachers used to emphasize the importance of silence, because one who keeps silence in his daily relations and speaks only needed words not only develops a deep sense of discrimination, but he also purifies his emotional and mental worlds.[3] Those who are trying to cleanse their minds must practice *harmlessness* in all their activities and reactions.

The human being is like a huge workshop. Hundreds of machines are running; hundreds of men are working at different duties. There are various relationships with other factories and offices. There is the manager and there is the owner. In our case, the owner is the Spark, the nucleus of Light, Love, and Beauty. He has the plan. The purpose of the whole workshop is to work out that plan as a harmonized unit and, in so doing, be a mechanism for the expression of Goodness, Beauty, and Righteousness.

---

[1] Agni Yoga Society, *Leaves of Morya's Garden II*, p. 80.

[2] Ibid., p. 109.

[3] See Chapter XIX, *The Meaning of Silence*.

Chapter VI

HARMLESSNESS AND DETACHMENT

EXERCISE FOUR

In this chapter we are going to learn the exercise of harmlessness and try to make it a permanent guiding light in our life.

> *... Study your daily conduct and words and thoughts so as to make them utterly harmless. Set yourself to think those thoughts about yourself and others which will be constructive and positive, and hence harmless in their effects. Study your emotional effect on others so that by no mood, no depression, and no emotional reaction can you harm a fellow-man. Remember in this connection, violent spiritual aspiration and enthusiasm, misplaced or misdirected, may quite easily harm a fellow-man, so look not only at your wrong tendencies but at the use of your virtues.*[1]

The exercise of harmlessness must be carried on all through the day, keeping your consciousness awake to all expressions and inner activities. Every evening before you retire, sit for about ten minutes in your place of peace and silence, and review your life for that day to discover whether or not you have been harmless to others:

- in your thoughts
- in your speech
- in your emotional reactions
- in your activities

As you think back through the day, it is important that you assume the position of a detached observer. Visualize yourself as

---

[1] Bailey, Alice A., *A Treatise on White Magic*, p. 101.

someone other than yourself and observe all expressions of this other person to find where he could have been more harmless. Do not criticize him or condemn him; simply study his behavior toward others with divine indifference. This procedure is an art and should be performed in an artistic way. By so doing, you will gradually discover that your inner Real Being is essentially good, and that this inner Being is something other than the personality that thinks, feels, and acts. When you have reached this state of detachment, you can transmute all undesirable vibrations and use them for better ends.

Harmlessness is the "destroyer of all limitations" — limitations found in your mental vehicle, your emotional vehicle, and in your life and relationships on the physical level. It cleanses all vehicles of expression and lets in the pure light of divine consciousness. To be harmless means to live a life flooded by the inner goodness. Goodness purifies, integrates, transmutes, and leads to the mountain of Transfiguration.

In doing the evening review on harmlessness, it is important to know how to deal with what we discover in our observation. As time passes, you will find that you express many harmful words, emotions, thoughts, and attitudes. Your first inclination will be to try to change them. This is wrong. Never try to change your ways forcefully; just continue to review them and see them as they are. There should be no violent change. The change must start in the inner levels of the mind and gradually come about without pressure or forcing. Change is inevitable, but it must come as the result of your inner achievement and detachment.

When we were children, we had our toys. Most of our faults and vices are like toys to which we are still attached. We must continue to grow until the day when our "toys" no longer hold any attraction for us. We will accomplish this through natural and gradual development. We must always consider the necessity of a period of adjustment to new kinds of energies and inner states. It is for this reason that we say *just observe*; observe carefully and learn all about yourself, but do not become excited. Be calm and indifferent as though you were observing another person. This will bring clarity of mind and vision. With clarity of mind and vision, your inner Light will gradually clear the clouds and fog from around and within you.

EXERCISE FIVE

This exercise, *the exercise of detachment*, deals with the basic steps leading to our inner heritage. It is divided into three parts.

Part I

Part I should be used for the first month, changing the object of your exercise every day, moving gradually from those in which you are slightly interested to those with which you are identified. Use the following procedure:

In your private room, relax your whole body, your emotions, and your mind. Look at your furniture for a few minutes and then say:

"This is my furniture. These are my books. This is my room. All the things in this room are mine because I am using them. Someday they will be old and I will throw them away, or I will be old and pass away and leave everything that belongs to me. When my physical relations with them are broken, they are no longer mine; so this must mean that they are not mine, but that they belong to the part of my being which is other than my real Essence. What is that part of my being which belongs to the world, to my home, to my furniture? It is chiefly my physical body."

Here, raise your hand in front of you and look at your fingers. Open and close them. Look at your fingernails, the veins, the hair on the back of your hand, and then say:

"This is my hand, but I am not my hand. The hand belongs to me. I use it. It is like a piece of furniture, a piece of living furniture. It is part of my body. My body is a piece of living furniture. It is not 'me.' I may use it. It is my car, my vehicle. It is a fine, complicated bridge between the world and me."

At this point, step before a large mirror for only *one minute* — no more — and look at your feet, body, hands, head, face, and eyes. Then, looking at your body as a whole, say:

"This is the body which I am using. The real 'Me' cannot be seen."

Following this, sit on a chair, close your eyes, and look inside your body. Using your imagination, visualize your organs, your glands, your heart, your stomach, your intestines, your lungs, and then your brain. After only a few minutes of this visualization, say silently:

"All these organs are parts of the body; with the body they will disintegrate and become elements. They belong to the physical world; I am merely using them as my mechanism of contact and expression. I can cause them to work better and serve me longer."

This exercise may be used in thinking of living things as furniture. Your dog, your cat, pet birds, any living creatures which are close to you, you may consider to be your properties, your possessions. Friends, relatives, and family members may also be thought of as your "furniture" when you are using this exercise of detachment. You must be aware of the fact that they can disappear at any time. They do not belong to you. You do not have the power to use and keep them for yourself. Whenever you identify yourself with others, it is impossible for you to keep yourself detached in your relationships with them. You cannot have basic serenity and stand firm in your own being when you become a plaything of change.

Sometimes you may feel at one with others and share their problems, emotions, and thinking. But this sense of oneness on the physical, emotional, and mental levels is an illusion. You are one with them in your Higher Being, in your Essence. Recognition of this fact leads you on to harmless living and impels you to fulfill your duties and responsibilities to them. But this must always be done without identification and always from within the stronghold of your Being. Thus you will be led into more freedom and into deeper joy because the farther you are able to detach yourself from the form side of life, the deeper you will be able to go into your inner Being, which is essentially joy and bliss.

The above exercise must be performed carefully and faithfully for an entire month.

Part II

Part II of the exercise on detachment will be used for the second month. The instructions are as follows:

Close your eyes, and think of a possession that is very dear to you such as a movie projector, a house, a car, a watch, a book or manuscript, and so on. Then, in your imagination, stand back away from it and destroy it in any way you wish. After you have seen it destroyed, in your imagination sing a song of joy and happiness and then say:

"It is not 'Me.' I know that my Real Self cannot be affected, even though the article is actually destroyed or taken from me."

Choose different objects as you do this exercise throughout the month.

Part III

In the third month you will be using the next exercise on detachment which is more advanced. Please follow these instructions:

Each day for the first fifteen days, sit quietly in your room for ten or fifteen minutes, close your eyes, and imagine a funeral service. See yourself lying in the coffin, with your dear ones and hundreds of other people passing by. Let them take your body to the crematorium and burn it; let them throw your ashes to the winds. See how they cry, how they feel. Watch them and listen to them as they speak. Use your imagination to make everything as real as possible. In the beginning as you start this exercise, you will find some inner resistance, but slowly it will become easy to do.

For the last fifteen days choose a dear friend, then a relative, a family member, perhaps your husband, wife, or children and proceed in the following manner:

Think of how many times the person has passed away and through what kinds of death. Imagine one of his deaths, and dramatize it in every detail. Think also about his present body, and imagine what will happen to it in the next one or two hundred years.

This last exercise includes both emotional and mental detachment about which we will speak in lessons to follow. It is a basic fact that every time you detach yourself on any level, you increase your control there; you increase your Light, Love, and Power on that level.

These exercises are life-long exercises. First we use them for three months to create a conscious detachment from our physical body, from our home, and from the world. This detachment gradually deepens, and there comes a day when we no longer identify ourselves with the body or with various objects. This gives us a deep sense of freedom, but at the same time it gives us a new and deeper way of enjoying our objects. We become freer in our social relationships. Our sleep and relaxation become deeper and more sound, and our nervous system receives more nourishment than ever before.

There is, however, one important point concerning this exercise about which a few suggestions must be given:

Age-long identification with the body and with objects and violent separations from them have left strong memories in our inner world. At the time we are doing the exercises, some of these memories may recur or become stimulated and cause inner irritation, discomfort, fear, depression, or sorrow. If such feelings do occur, it means that the exercises are doing their clearing work. We can make no real progress until we burn the impressions coming from our former lives and until we learn, through detachment, to become masters of our physical body, our feelings, and our thoughts. The impressions that we are dealing with are very real. They were registered upon us in various ways at the time we left our physical body in several different lives. Each time we left our physical body, each time a beloved one or a possession, precious to us, was taken away, we were strongly impressed. Some of these impressions are very dark. They are often responsible for our many psychological or mental disorders. They may create nervous and glandular difficulties. They may also be the cause of social upheavals. Dark impressions may be stimulated and affect our consciousness in many ways, but we cannot pass to higher dimensions until we rid ourselves of them.

By doing these exercises we release these impressions and lessen their strength and effect or annihilate them completely. By doing these exercises we also eliminate the pressure of our mental waves which are sometimes concentrated upon one particular area of the body. Our mental waves are very potent energies which stimulate or even paralyze that part of the mechanism upon which they are constantly concentrated. These exercises eliminate this pressure, establish equilibrium, and give the body a chance to breathe freely.

Harmlessness is the process of radiation of the Inner Glory. The radiation increases gradually as the inner obstacles are removed through the exercise of detachment. We can gain no real knowledge about ourselves and about the technique of becoming ourselves unless we work diligently in our inner laboratory through sincere observation. Our main objective is to be a real, detached observer. When we have achieved this objective, the rest will come naturally.

Chapter VII

NOTES ON DETACHMENT

We may think that to detach ourselves means to hate, to ignore, to divide, to separate, to stand aloof, or to be cold and rough toward a given object. These are not signs of true detachment. True detachment is a Soul attitude, a function carried out on the Soul plane rather than on the physical, emotional, or lower mental planes. Actually you are not detaching your true Self from anyone or anything. You are detaching your Self from the inertia of the body, from the glamors of your emotional world, and from the illusions of your mental realm. You are also detaching your Real Self from the objects with which you were identified only through inertia, glamors, and illusions.

With detachment you are dis-identifying yourself but not separating. You are releasing yourself from the control of identification. When you have achieved detachment, you are no longer conditioned and controlled by the inertia, glamor, and illusion of objects. You are free. Detachment means freedom. It means a truly self-determined attitude.

In true detachment your spiritual identification deepens and widens on the spiritual side of an object. At the same time you identify less and less with phenomena until, eventually, you are able to see the object as it is, free from your personal, mechanical reactions and free from your imposing, forcing will of the lower self, expressed in many ways. According to your degree of success in detaching from any object, your soul love increases, your light becomes brighter, your will stronger, and your joy deeper. Attachment makes you smaller; detachment makes you greater.

When you are truly detached, the personality factor of the object does not disturb or control you. The inner reality, the core of his being, becomes the important factor to you, and you help to release that beauty by detaching your self from personality reactions, inertia, glamors, and illusions. In detachment you are not ignoring the Real Man; you are ignoring the illusion, the appearance, and you can see more clearly than before because you are not caught in the net of personality reactions. Detachment changes the nature of your relations with the object. Since your relationship is no longer based on your personality reactions nor on the other's personality reactions, you are not mechanical in your behavior toward him. You are awake and conscious, and your approach is a soul approach.

Detachment eliminates personality conflicts and friction between objects. You recognize and can accept the freedom, the existence of the object. In detachment you cease to use others for your own selfish interests. You recognize each existence as important to the great Plan. In the process of detachment you become aware of the Law of Karma, and you see clearly the way in which the Law works. You seek the highest good for the object; you learn not to interfere with the karma of others. In so doing you help them to increase their inner Light, and you give them courage to live the best life possible for them.

Detachment leads you to Soul infusion. Eventually you find the path leading to your True Self, and you become one with that Self. Actually the process of detachment is the process of *becoming oneself.* Gradually you detach yourself from all that is not the Self. When you reach the stage of becoming your True Self, you are one with creation itself but without the limitations of its inertia, glamor, and illusion. Thus detachment is the process of at-one-ment. In detachment man leads himself from the transient to the unchangeable, from the unreal to the Real.

When you have learned the process of detachment, you become magnetic. Truly magnetic people are those who are really detached persons. They have not become personality magnetic, but *Soul magnetic.* A truly detached person has achieved the ability to do the right thing at the right time and in the right proportion.

The existence in which you live is a part of you. All is one. The process of detachment is the process of realization of this unity. Only on such a high level of awareness can you free yourself from

1. separation
2. the concept of property
3. the illusion of "mine" and "yours"

4. your anxieties and worries

Thus your sense of responsibility grows deeper and higher. Detachment helps you to understand the purpose of the Great Being "in Whom we live and move and have our being."

Impersonality is another term for being detached. A detached person is an impersonal person. Impersonality is a state of consciousness which is above the physical, emotional, and lower mental levels and which functions upon the Soul levels. A detached person is a person who is in the process of becoming himself. Detachment is not a level but a continuous negation of imprisonment and an urge toward *spiritualization or liberation.*

Chapter VIII

THE SEA OF EMOTIONS

Our emotional vehicle is like a chaotic mist around our physical body.

> *... It is not light, or starry or clear. It is apparently impenetrable disorder, for it is the meeting ground of forces.*[1]

Our emotional body is a part of the emotional body of humanity and of the planet. Imagine how these three must act and react upon one another. The emotional vehicle is a field through which pass electrical-magnetic forces and currents such as attraction and repulsion. It also resembles a pool which reflects the many and varied emotional states of the surrounding world.

The centers of sensation are located in the emotional body which acts in three directions:

1. It receives vibrations from the physical world through the physical senses. In this body the impact changes to sensation, and thus a man becomes conscious of the world around him.

2. It is sensitive to the emotional waves, moods, feelings, and desires which originate in the man himself.

3. It is a direct link with the intuitional world and can be a pure channel for love energy from the intuitional level.

Because of its stage of development, most of humanity is polarized in the emotional world. Our emotional world is like a pool of water, and the self of man is often like a reflected moon which identifies itself with each wave of emotion. This self floats upon the water, and every wave gives to it a different shape, a different form. Because of the fact that man is identified with every emotion he experiences, it is very difficult for him to detach

---

[1] Bailey, Alice A., *A Treatise on White Magic*, p. 221.

himself from his emotions or the emotional world and to observe the changing waves of that world with non-identification, with detachment.

This does not mean that it is impossible to create a break between the observer and the emotion. We can do this by raising our consciousness to a higher level and from there controlling the emotional department, holding it to its proper function. The emotional body relates us to the physical world, to humanity, and to the inner sources of man. The question is how to organize the body, how to raise its substance, and how to make it a clear channel for intuitional love energies.

If the emotional body is not in a healthy condition, we find the following:

1. All impressions that come from the outer world through the five senses are translated incorrectly and bring forth wrong reactions.

2. All energies coming from higher levels degenerate and are used to strengthen negative emotions.

3. All surrounding emotional waves enter the body and create new agitation there.

Following are the results of the above action:

a) Negative emotions are formed in the emotional vehicle.

b) The physical body is burned in the fire of negative emotions, causing nervous and glandular problems.

c) The mind cannot think clearly and gradually becomes the slave of negative emotions. Psychosomatic illnesses appear, bringing with them dark consequences.

In ancient times teachers were not allowed to impart the Teaching to those who had not passed through emotional purification. The symbol of the emotions was the heart. The Teaching held that the heart should be pure before it could approach the divine Light and Beauty which descend from the intuitional level.

Whenever we wish to speak about higher truths, we must be cautious about the emotional condition of our listener because any truth can degenerate in a muddy pool of emotions. Because of the imparted truth, the power of negative emotions found in our listener may increase tenfold and make the person more dangerous than before. Christ warned of this danger when he said

> *Give not that which is holy unto the dogs; neither cast you your pearls before swine, lest they trample them under their feet and turn again and rend you.*[1]

If in an extremely negative condition the emotional body is stimulated and energized by higher energies, the negative emotions found in the body become magnetic and attract similar emotional waves from other people in the surroundings. They put great strain upon the physical body, affecting the nervous and glandular systems in particular. It is possible that they may even destroy the physical body immediately.

The emotional body also responds to the impact of thought coming from one's own being or from the minds of others. It is like a sensitive musical instrument upon which every wind plays a different melody and creates different vibrations and responses.

The emotional body is the battleground of man and of the race. It is here that the first great battle is bitterly fought. On this battleground are both negative and positive forces. Negative forces come from the lower nature and from accumulated past experiences; positive forces come from the higher sources of the Soul or the Intuitional Plane. Conflict rages between these two forces on the emotional plane. The student of the Ageless Wisdom cannot move on until he finishes the battle and stands detached from emotional complications instead of losing his ship's helm and floundering upon the stormy sea.

Of these two forces, the negative represents the will of all that is selfish, separative, involuntary, and leading to darkness, inertia, and matter; the positive represents the divine Will, leading to the Good, the True, and the Beautiful. Through the first force, or will, all negative forces in individual man, in humanity, and in the world can act and fight. Through the second force, all positive energies try to express themselves, to transform and transmute, to evolve and develop everything they touch. The mind can be an agent of both positive and negative forces. The emotional body is like the sea, while the mental body is like the wind. The two are so closely connected that any motion or any change in either of them affects the other.

---

[1] Matthew 7:6

It is impossible to win the battle on the emotional plane if we do not stand apart from it on a higher level, the level of the mind. We can fight against the evil army only if we hand the command to the Inner Lord. The Inner Lord can fight upon the emotional battlefield only through the forces and energies of the mind.

Examples of negative forces on the emotional plane are:

hatred	resentment
depression	antagonism
self-pity	avarice
jealousy	feelings of meritoriousness
fear	irritation
bitterness	hurt feelings
anger	feelings of injustice
envy	lustfulness

and all their relatives, friends, and grandchildren.

What important steps can we take to eliminate the enemies of our progress?

The first step is *observation*.

The second step is *dispassion and nonidentification*.

The third step is *transmutation*.

Through these three steps the emotional body can be purified and become a clear mirror, reflecting outer, inner, and higher worlds. It can change into a channel of Love, Light, and Beauty and become a fountain through which the life-giving waters of the Aquarian Age may pour.

Let us begin with the first step, *observation*. What are we going to observe? We are going to observe ourselves, starting with emotional reactions. We will try to see ourselves as we are, how we react and feel under different conditions when relating to people and events. It is important to remember that in the act of observation there is no criticism, just indifferent observation. In the beginning it is difficult to acquire an indifferent and neutral attitude, but this is the objective toward which we are working. Until we are indifferent, we will not be able to see things within ourselves as they actually are. To observe means to receive a photographic picture of events taking place within us, within our emotional world.

Thus the first step in learning all about ourselves is simply to observe. When someone is trying to hurt you with words, observe yourself, and discover what is going on within you. Do not search for reasons and results; simply observe. Observe steadily, and see your emotional reactions. There are many names given to these reactions and responses. Watch for them at different times and under many different circumstances. Do you have fears? What are they? How do they start, and how do they fade away? Observe them when they are present. Do not create them, but observe them as your agitation recedes and you come out of your emotional mood.

Continue watching, and you will find that hundreds of currents cross your emotional world in one day. Do not try to stop them. Observe them, and identify the reaction or response. This is jealousy; that one is self-pity; this response is hatred; this is avarice; this new reaction is irritation, and so on. In due time your observing eyes will begin to notice more subtle currents, more subtle connections, reasons, and results. When the time comes that you begin to see yourself as you are, you will note that, gradually, you have been divided into two poles. One pole is acting — your action in any situation — and the other pole is observing. It is not easy to observe oneself. It takes training and work, but when, in spite of this, you learn the art of observation and practice it regularly, you will feel great release and great joy.

The second step in eliminating obstacles which are hindering your progress involves *dispassion* and *non-identification*. Through observation the Inner Man has begun the process of detaching himself from emotional states and outer events. He ceases to identify with them, and he notes that all emotional upheavals are only surface ripples, resulting from different winds that pass, and from inner and outer currents. He recognizes and understands deeply the effects of negative emotions, how they originate, how they develop, and how they can be eliminated. He also notes that when these negative emotions are observed, they lose their power. When the Inner Man refuses to identify with them, they melt away as patches of clouds in a blue sky. The moment a man identifies with his negative emotions, he becomes an instrument of destruction and cleavage in the hands of these emotions. To control our negative emotions, we must not supress them nor try to destroy them; we must refuse to identify with them. Only thus can we annihilate them.

Observation and non-identification are two important steps leading us toward conquering the emotional sea. This conquest will not be meaningful unless that sea is transmuted into a higher level substance, a substance which has the capability of becoming in tune with its higher correspondence, intuitional substance.

Transmutation is the third step in clearing your path for progress. It is the result of observation and detachment. When the Inner Man has succeeded in detaching himself from physical and emotional identification through observation, he becomes radioactive, magnetic, and fiery. The fire slowly burns the lower energies, drawing them upward. Thus begins the process of transmutation. First the glamors of the emotional world melt away, and the emotional body is purified. The outer, negative currents create no response in it because it is now in tune with the beauty of Nature, with the inner harmony of the Universe, and it continuously radiates compassion, love, and attraction. We cannot reach this high point of achievement in a few years. It necessitates continuous observation, detachment, and transmutation over a very long period of time.

We must remember that our emotions are not wall pictures or names. They are energies; they are substantial. Jealousy is a kind of force, a toxic force. Fear, depression, or envy are all toxic forces. They are special forces which take special forms within our atmosphere and attack special organs. We project these poisonous forces through glances, our voice, words, motives, and many other modes of expression. We cause them to flow out and do their destructive work.

We all have a very subtle envelope of energy around us called the *aura*.[1] It is an extremely sensitive protective film surrounding our physical body like an electromagnetic field which shields us, receives impressions, and sends out currents of energy. It includes the health aura, the etheric body, the astral or emotional body, and the mental body. The aura can be poisoned, crystallized, or agitated. It is affected not only by the outer currents, but also can be strongly affected by the inner streams of force that flow out from our mind, our heart, or as words from our mouths.

There are two kinds of energy currents. One is destructive and the other is constructive or creative. When a current of ill will, jealousy, or hatred is directed to our aura, the aura is affected,

---

[1] Read *Cosmos in Man* by H. (Torkom) Saraydarian, pp. 63-70.

though we often do not feel it because of the insensitivity of our nervous system. Later, however, we feel weak, depressed, or melancholy because the destructive current has poisoned our aura, weakening it by crystallizing or paralyzing some part of it. To protect ourselves from such negative currents which are so abundant today, we must shield ourselves with love energy, energy of truth, sincerity, faith, and courage. When we build a shield of these positive, constructive energies, no evil current can penetrate our aura and cause us trouble, nor can it create in us weakness, ill will, low desires, and negative attitudes. Doubts, insincerity, lies, and fears wound and crack our aura, creating open doors and windows for the entrance of negative currents.

When the aura is protected with fiery love energy, it becomes a sensitive apparatus for the currents of love, beauty, rhythm, peace, and harmony. Christ said, "The bread that I will give you is heavenly bread, and whosoever eats it never dies." At another time, when He was on the Mountain of Temptation, Satan said to Him: "Command that these stones be changed into bread." The Lord said, "Man does not live by bread alone, but also by the word of God."

In these two instances we see clearly that there are two kinds of bread, or food. One is to nourish the physical body, and the other is to nourish the subtle bodies. For example, all art expressions are food for our emotional and intuitional bodies. Knowledge and truth are food for our minds. Higher spiritual ideas, divine Will, and laws provide another kind of food for our higher bodies. These foods are in the form of vibrations, impressions, currents, and energies that come and enter our aura, where they are assimilated according to our achievement, purity, and service. They come from different sources: from our advanced friends, teachers, Masters, groups, and even from extra-planetary sources. Thus it is easy to understand that love is a heavenly food. Compassion, courage, and truth are divine foods which, if given to a man at the right time, will feed his aura, enrich it, harmonize it, and release some fires that are latent there.

In olden days when people spoke of vices and virtues, they were talking about two kinds of energy. They were speaking of energies that are destructive, harmful, or poisonous and energies that are creative, constructive, and beneficial. The point that must be emphasized here is that poisonous currents or forces first cause the disintegration and ruin of a man's aura. Then, when these energy currents or forces are expressed by him, the destructive work is carried on within other people, groups, and nations.

We may think that only microbic diseases are contagious, but this is a fallacy. Negative emotions, evil thoughts, poisonous currents are also contagious and will spread faster and bury themselves deeper. The spreading of germs of some illnesses can be prevented through medical means, but it is difficult, if not impossible, to prevent the germs of hatred, jealousy, ill will, envy, greed, and many other potent negative forces from spreading. When they penetrate your aura, it cannot be disinfected until you burn them out with you inner Fire of Love and Righteousness.

Our aura is a chemical laboratory in which most of the work is performed automatically. Any impression that strikes it is changed, assimilated, or thrown out. Here again we are given the key to the words of Christ, "Do not cast your pearls to the swine, lest they trample them under their feet and turn again and rend you."

This is exactly what happens when you direct high level energy to men who are like swine — those people filled with hatred, jealousy, fear, and negative emotions. Your pure current penetrates a man's aura, loses its love quality, and becomes an energizing force which stimulates his wounds and his many weaknesses; the man becomes worse than before. Thus it is clear that any energy entering into the atmosphere of a man will be conditioned by the state or chemistry of that atmosphere. Love energy will create bitter hatred if the chemistry of the object is contaminated with negative elements. The opposite is also true. Great hatred and misery change into outpouring love and compassion if the object is elevated to high levels. The same is true in regard to humanity and the planet when planetary, extra-planetary, or extra-systemic energies come in contact with our planet and humanity.

It is important to form groups of people who are advanced enough to assimilate these high voltage energies and bring them down to the level of the average human being, where they can be used as beneficial, healing, illuminating energies. Hence it is important to watch our contacts and relations with others, to watch our words, our conversations, and even our facial expressions.

Throughout the month we must read and reread this chapter, trying to put into practice the three lights given: observation, non-identification, and transmutation. There is no special exercise, but we must try to keep our observing mind ever alert and watchful for what is happening within and around us.

This is a lifetime instruction; an instruction which will open for you the way to self-knowledge, to self-transmutation, and to resurrection toward your Real Self.

Chapter IX

THE STORMY SEA

... How could one attain the highest state, attain refinement of consciousness, without spiritual labour?[1]

As a man progresses toward Himself, he passes through three great areas of discipline and exercise. He often wanders about in these areas, never once seeing a guiding light, but the pain and the pleasure gradually lead him out of one field into another.

He wanders for long ages in the deserts of the physical plane in ignorance, blood, and pain. Then gradually he passes into the emotional sea, and his great and difficult journey begins in the waves of that vast and stormy sea. As we have said, this is an ocean of mirages and glamors, a sea of deep sorrow and pleasure. It is a wild and stormy sea which can engulf you at any moment, a sea upon which you cannot find any sign of permanent guidance, and upon which you lose yourself hundreds of times. There are moments when you simply give up your journey and throw yourself to the wild waves of emotions, mirages, and glamors.

Occasionally, through the mist, you see some bright stars shining, but the next moment they are lost to you. You hear voices from the higher world, but the voices change into the roaring of the waves as they beat against the shore. You, the pilgrim, are like a piece of wood floating upon the waters.

It takes the pilgrim many ages to cross this great ocean. Gradually he builds stronger muscles, better boats and ships, and one day he steps onto the fiery land of the mental plane. The mental plane, too, has its problems, obstacles, and difficulties. In coming lessons we will discover how to cross this plane, but our challenge now is to cross this emotional sea and make it possible for our Inner Christ to walk upon its waters without sinking. Our main task is to organize our emotional body, the boat. We cannot rid ourselves of a vehicle, nor can we control it until we organize

---

[1] Agni Yoga Society, *Fiery World III*, par. 37.

and transmute it to the highest degree. We cannot control our physical body if it is not healthy, pure, and full of vitality. The same is true of the emotional body; we can control it and detach ourselves from it if that body is pure, calm, and developed.

It is impossible to bring the mental vehicle under full control of the Soul, the Inner Lord, if that body is not integrated, highly developed, and disciplined. We can detach ourselves and observe mental modifications or activities if we stand higher than they. This cannot be done until the mind has developed its full potential.

In olden days advanced people knew that the way to purify and organize the vehicles was to place them under severe discipline. Such discipline was known by many names. It was called penance, repentance, fasting, or mortification. Later the true significance of these words was lost, and many people caused much suffering and pain to their bodies, thinking that this was necessary for the good of their bodies and souls. This practice was prevalent in ancient times, especially in the early centuries of Christianity and up until medieval times. It was generally called "mortification." The original purpose of this discipline was to cleanse the physical, emotional, and mental bodies of those impurities which were preventing integration, soul infusion, and spiritual radiation, but the practice was exaggerated and carried too far. It became a retarding force for many ages and led to extreme suppression or violent inhibitions which acted upon the bodies, causing dire complications. The purpose of discipline is not to kill the vitality of any vehicle. On the contrary, the purpose is to develop that vitality and direct it into proper channels, or to transmute and sublimate it.

If you have excess energy in any body, there are three things you must know:

1. Why and how that excess energy came to be there.

2. How you can use or spend it in constructive and creative ways.

3. How you can sublimate and transmute it to a higher level.

Energy suppressed in any vehicle becomes a center of trouble there. It gradually releases itself through nervous or other disorders if it is not expressed or sublimated. Hence, the main intention of right discipline is:

- To organize the vehicles.

- To integrate the vehicles or bodies and thus establish right communication, right relationships among them.

- To transmute the energies of the vehicles into their corresponding higher vehicles.

EXERCISE SIX

In this exercise we will learn *how to organize the emotional vehicle*. Instructions are given in five parts.

Part I

The following steps will bring potent results if they are performed in the right way. At a specified time, sit in your room and play recordings of classical music from masters such as Beethoven, Johann Strauss, Mozart, Handel, Tschaikovsky, Gomitas (especially his church music), Sibelius, Wagner, and so on. Start with soft melodies, and gradually move to such great pieces of music as Beethoven's *Eighth Symphony* or Wagner's *Parsifal*.[1]

Close your eyes and relax as you listen to the music. Take a few deep breaths. Imagine that you are sitting near a blue lake, a calm, clear lake at a high elevation. Look around you. See the beautiful trees and flowers. See the colors, and far off in the distance see a high, blue mountain. Then take another deep breath.

Next visualize a little girl with a lighted candle in her hand, approaching your back. See her standing three feet behind you, holding the candle at your solar plexus level and blowing the flame (without extinguishing it) toward your spinal column and upward to your head. Visualize the flame reaching your head and forming a golden halo around it. Then see your whole visualization magically disappearing.

Do this exercise very slowly, timing it so that your visualization will have disappeared at the conclusion of your recorded musical selection. Then remember who you are and where you are. Rub your hands together. You have finished the exercise.

If you are not satisfied with the music you have chosen, keep changing it until you find the kind that gives your mind clear visualization and awakeness.

---

[1] We highly recommend *A Touch of Heart* (CD) and *Infinity* (audio tape) as well as other music by Torkom Saraydarian.

This exercise should be done once each day for two weeks. In the beginning your imagination may be weak, but continue in your endeavor until your visualizations become clear. We learn to do by doing.

Part II

In the second part of exercise six you again listen to great music. In your imagination go to your favorite place in nature. Sit and relax for a few moments, then slowly rise and take a walk. As you walk, visualize a low, orange colored cloud. Enter into the cloud and imagine that your whole body is slowly disappearing, dissolving, and you, as a flame, are crossing through the cloud. When you emerge from the cloud, stand as a flame, breathe deeply, and imagine that while breathing, a beautiful light-body is forming around you, and a very beautiful physical body is materializing. After this visualization is over, listen to the music until it ends. Do this exercise for at least four weeks before you start the third part.

Part III

Again, listen to fine music. In your imagination go to a place you like and visualize dancers performing to the rhythm of the music in a beautiful dance production. Do not try to recall group, folk, or ballet dances with which you are familiar. Try to create a new fairy-like dance in which many graceful figures move magically about, gliding, swimming, or perhaps flying. Dig deep into your imagination and bring forth the most beautiful combinations possible of color, light, and form. You may begin with simple, single step dances and gradually build them into more complicated and intricate dances in which many different performances go on simultaneously within one large frame. Do this exercise for at least four weeks, and end it as you have ended the others.

Part IV

The fourth part is somewhat different. Play the music. In your imagination go to your special place in nature, and after relaxing your whole being, imagine two birds fighting. Let them fight fiercely, pulling at each other's feathers, pecking, and clawing each other, causing ugly, bleeding wounds. Witness this scene until the music ends, trying not to express any emotion; be an observer, an indifferent observer. Visualize this situation only once.

On the second day imagine a similar scene of action in which two animals are fighting. Follow the same procedure of feeling indifference.

On the third day imagine a woman starting ugly gossip about someone you love, about someone you hate, about someone to whom you feel indifferent. Listen quietly, calmly, with a detached attitude.

For the next two months, each day imagine a dramatization of a negative emotion from the list given on page 56. When you have finished the list, start again, and this time you, yourself, will participate in the dramatizations. For example, in your imagination, be angry. Do anything that an angry person might do. Watch yourself as if you were watching someone else; observe yourself as if you were a different person. Then take part in a drama as a jealous man, as a man of hatred, a man of fear, a depressed man, an insulted man. Use the whole list and create dramatic scenes, powerful dramas with you as the star performer — but remember, you are to observe *him*, without attachment, with no feeling of identification. If at any time you feel identification, go through it again and again until you are able to observe with indifference, with detachment. It will be many months or years before your emotional vehicle is cleansed of negative emotions. When in your daily life you notice a special negative emotion, work on it during your exercises, but do this on a gradient scale, first projecting it upon birds, animals, children, adults, and then upon yourself.

Part V

This part will be performed in the same manner as the others through the use of music, imagination, and the place of quiet and relaxation. Following the suggested steps, choose some object, and try to *admire* it. Gradually you will find the deeper meaning of admiration.

First admire the music. Secondly, admire a flower, a tree, an animal, a lovely scene, or anything that is very beautiful. Thirdly, try to worship something or someone. Then try to elevate yourself to the plane of the object you are worshipping. Create so great a beauty in your imagination that you genuinely admire and worship it. Think about divine heroes, great leaders, a genius, and awaken within yourself a sense of deep appreciation, admiration, and worship. You may do this in highest creativity with music, literature, synthetic art, or it may be done in the very simplest way.

During all these periods of exercise, which may take five months or five years, you must observe yourself continuously in your daily life. Whenever you have been negative, when you have expressed negative emotions, go to your private room or special place and reenact that experience, but this time reverse the situation by substituting positive expression for negative expression. For example, you were with a group of people. Hearing some unpleasant criticism about yourself, you felt hurt, depressed, and you uttered a few negative words. To clear away the negative reaction, find an opportunity to be alone and imagine experiencing the same event; but this time, instead of feeling hurt and depressed, feel elated, joyful, blissful, and bless the one who voiced the negative criticism. The same procedure should be followed with other happenings and with many different negative experiences. Thus many of your suppressed emotions will come to the surface and will be washed away.

All these exercises will help to highly organize your emotional body. In a short period of time you will feel a new energy flowing through your being. You will be more magnetic, optimistic, tolerant, joyful, and healthy, and you will radiate a spirit of understanding, tolerance, and love.

During this period it is important to exercise severe discipline in speech. The spoken word is closely connected with the emotional body. One who can control his speech can also control and organize his emotional body and thus facilitate control of his mental body. The disciplining of our speech is a thinking process.

> *It is well to speak little; better still to say nothing, unless you are quite sure that what you wish to say is* true, kind, *and* helpful. *Before speaking, think carefully whether what you are going to say has those qualifications; if it has not, do not say it.*[1]

Evil, negative speech rends the emotional body and brings into it burning energies, resulting in toxic conditions. Negative speech inflames the state of the emotional body, causes ill health to the physical body, and obscures mental vision. By controlling your speech you gradually gain control of your emotional body, your mental body, and so your physical body. In every word you utter there are many energies involved. There are vibrations of the

---

[1] Krishnamurti, J., *At the Feet of the Master.*

voice, emotional energy, and mental energy. We are conditioned by what we express. Christ said:

> *It is not what goes into the mouth of a man that makes him unclean and defiled, but what comes out of the mouth; this makes a man unclean and defiles him.*[1]

When we express mental, emotional, and physical energy through our speech in lies, gossip, fear, or other negative emotions and thoughts, we defile ourselves. Our expressions become living parasites in our mental and emotional atmosphere; they condition the free circulation of emotional, mental, and vital life energies; they also build and present a picture of us as we are. On the inner side we are known by what we build through our speech. We *become* what we speak. This is a form of identification with our emotions and thoughts. In the *New Testament* we find:

> *For by your words you will be justified and acquitted and by your words you will be condemned and sentenced.*[2]

By identifying ourselves with any emotion, we come under the domination of that emotion; by disidentifying ourselves from our emotions, we dominate them.

The secret behind these exercises and disciplines is detachment, disidentification, transmutation, and sublimation. A major result of our work to organize and sublimate our emotional body is a gradual and natural coming forth of our innate creativity.

> *... How can one be isolated from the entire cosmic creativeness when man is the creative fulfiller of the Cosmic Will! One should therefore develop in oneself consonance with the Higher Forces, for without striving to consonance there is no creativeness.*[3]

> *Each creative step is the affirmation of great battles.*[4]

> *...It is correctly pointed out that love is a guiding and creative principle. This means that love must be con-*

---

[1] Matthew 15:11

[2] Ibid., 12:37

[3] Agni Yoga Society, *Hierarchy*, par. 72.

[4] Ibid., par. 320.

scious, striving, and self-denying. Creativeness requires these conditions.[1]

... Love is the leading creative principle.[2]

To cultivate the seeds of creativity, choose any one of the many branches of art and try it. It is not important whether or not you create something great; the important factor is that in your endeavor to that end, you will start a small stream of energy coming down from higher levels of your consciousness and expressing itself on the emotional and physical planes. When creativity begins to flow within you, you will find that gradually all your lower forces are sublimated, becoming creative energies on higher levels. You will find, too, that love and compassion fill your heart.

When your emotional body is organized and purified, it turns into a bridge between your intuitional plane and your life. It is through such a purified emotional vehicle that the energy of intuition pours down, bringing with it a sense of great devotion, a sense of direction, and a sense of discrimination.

The exercise in creative expression will help to develop the divine energy of *Will*. Will energy is the beam of light coming down from our inner Divinity and gradually coordinating, harmonizing, integrating, and fusing our vehicles with the Plan and Purpose of our inner Divinity, thus making us the expression of the inner Reality. Throughout our vehicles, Will energy builds the bridge to lead us to what we essentially are. It is the energy of detachment and non-identification. At the same time, it is the main energy which leads us to unity with the whole.

Sometimes it happens that people are overpowered by a violent negative emotion which carries the body, the mind, and the "will" in the wrong direction and uses them for blind, devastating purposes. Under these conditions, people harm one another, kill one another, start wars, and all that should be used for good is used as fuel to feed the flames of war. When such is the case, it is too late to check the flow of negative emotions and to quiet the battle cries of the opposing forces. Thus we can see the great necessity for controlling the slightest negative emotion, the

---

[1] Agni Yoga Society, *Hierarchy*, par. 280.

[2] Ibid., par. 281.

smallest fire, always remembering that you have the power to control because you are the Inner Lord.

The Indweller of the body is never born, nor does It die. It is not true that, having no existence, It comes into being; nor having been in existence, It again ceases to be. It is the unborn, the eternal, the changeless, the Self. It cannot be killed, even if the body is slain.[1]

... the Dweller in the body can attain immortality when It is indifferent toward pain and pleasure, and It is not affected by them.[2]

In these two verses is the story of evolution. We suggest that you memorize them and recall them whenever you detect the slightest sign of negative emotion within yourself.

Our intention in giving these exercises is not to teach you to fight against negative emotions but to help you learn to create conditions in which the birth of negative emotions will be an impossibility.

---

[1] The *Bhagavad Gita*, 2:20, translation by H. (Torkom) Saraydarian.
[2] Ibid., 2:15

Chapter X

THE FIERY WORLD

The past two chapters have dealt with the emotional world of man. Several exercises were presented to help in the purification, control, and transmutation of the emotional vehicle. If the student followed the instructions carefully, he probably discovered that in the performance of the exercises relating to the emotions, he used his mind, too.

The emotional body cannot be controlled by the emotional body itself. A higher level force must be used to control it and to do the purificatory work. The mental body resembles the air or the wind. In the *Bhagavad Gita* we find:

> *... The mind ... is restless, turbulent, forceful, and unyielding. To control it is as hard as to control the wind.... but by practice and by detachment it can possibly be controlled.*[1]

The emotional world is like the waters of the stormy sea, and the mind is like the atmosphere above it. They are so closely inter-related that any motion in one affects the other.

We are chiefly identified with our emotions, our emotional world. Our main task is to detach ourselves from our emotions, to observe them with indifference, and then to transmute them to their higher counterparts. The same technique is used in the mental world. We are not the mind; we *use* the mind. It is like a servant who obeys the command of the Inner Man, the Inner Lord, the Source of all good. Our work is to cleanse the atmosphere — our mind — of clouds, mist, haze, and violent winds so that the sun can shine in all its glory, in all its beauty and light. Thus is the inner Good released.

To radiate conscious goodness and beauty through the mental world, we must know ourselves upon the mental plane itself.

---

[1] The *Bhagavad Gita*, 6:34-35, translation by H. (Torkom) Saraydarian.

Indeed, we must learn to face ourselves on every plane of existence. We must know ourselves as physical beings; we then surpass this stage and know ourselves as emotional beings; again, we move to a higher level and know ourselves as mental beings. Here, on the mental plane, we must not pause too long because the Real Man is not the mind. He is higher than the mind. Sooner or later the detachment process begins, and the man again loses his familiar, comfortable level and travels to a higher altitude. He is predestined to find himself and will not be satisfied until he finds his True Self, until he becomes his Self.

The physical brain is the switchboard of the mind, and the mind is simply a vortex of energy currents. The *Thinker* is not the mind as some believe; It is the Dweller within the body. The mind serves as a bridge between the Thinker and the brain. The Thinker clothes His ideas in the substance of the mind and acts upon the physical plane through the physical brain and nervous system.

The mind is a most complicated organism of very fine substance, composed of seven degrees of density. The lowest level, the seventh, is the densest plane. The highest level, the first, is the least dense, being composed of very subtle, very fine substance. Each plane is sensitive to corresponding vibrations. These vibrations come from many possible sources: from human, planetary, universal, or cosmic sources.

Not every man has a developed, organized mental equipment. Most people do not have a seven-level, organized mind. They have only a cloud of mental substance around their heads. The mist gradually becomes organized, and slowly the first clear color appears; then the next level is organized, the next and the next, until the atmosphere surrounding the man's head is a rainbow-like aura with seven streams of energy radiating through it.

Mental substance is a particular substance in space which man gradually attracts and makes his own. At first he attracts the coarsest substance; then, as his development continues, he adds to it higher level substance, until he has the seven-level rainbow about his head. This process requires an extremely long period of sincere effort and steady work, but slowly man weaves the beautiful garment of his mental body.

Many people use the terms consciousness, mind, intelligence, and intuition synonymously, but they are in error. Each of these terms has its own different and distinct meaning. The mind is not consciousness; it is an instrument, a sense, an organism used by the Inner Man to build relationships. The following graph shows the degree of consciousness or awareness in relation to the seven planes or levels of the Cosmic Physical Plane.

Degree of Consciousness or Awareness

LIGHT

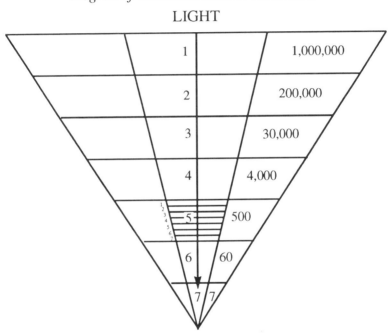

Explanation:

    a) The inside triangle, numbered 1 through 7, symbolizes the seven sub-planes of the Cosmic Physical Plane.[1]

    b) Number 1, the divine sub-plane, is the highest, the subtlest.

    c) Number 7, the physical sub-plane, is the lowest, the coarsest.

    d) Number 5, the mental plane, is divided into its seven levels or grades of substance.

---

[1] See p. 131.

e) The outer triangle symbolizes the field of consciousness; the figures on the right indicate the degree of consciousness or awareness as related to the seven sub-planes.

f) The arrow intersecting the triangle is the Arrow of Light descending from the Divine and Monadic Planes to the dense physical plane. This is the light of consciousness and awareness, the "Knower of the Field."[1]

As the human soul progresses from one level to another, or as its consciousness expands progressively, it causes the tiny lives of its vehicles to progress also. Each of our bodies — physical, emotional, and mental — is composed of billions of tiny lives. These tiny lives are of different orders or rays; they have different rates of vibration, radiation, and unfoldment. For example, the average man has a mental body formed chiefly of fifth grade substance, of lives that belong to the fifth order of development. As the human soul progresses, it influences the tiny lives and they become more radioactive, more sensitive; they take an "initiation" of their own and enter into the fourth order of substance, then into the third, the second, and eventually into the first order of mental substance. The first, or the highest lives of any plane, are called *atomic lives*.

When we have reached that stage in which our bodies are formed of first grade atomic substance, our whole personality becomes a soul-infused entity because of the transmutation and initiation of the lower lives of our being into higher level consciousness. As the human soul is progressing, so are the "souls" of the tiny lives progressing from one level to another. This is the way in which transformation occurs and transfiguration of the personality vehicle is accomplished.

The same is happening on the cosmic level. As the planetary Life is progressing and taking initiation, all tiny lives are progressing and taking atomic, human, or super-human initiations. As they initiate, their "consciousness" expands and their light increases.

- On the physical plane the light is very dim. It is the consciousness of the atom and the cell.

---

[1] See the *Bhagavad Gita,* Ch. 13, translation by H. (Torkom) Saraydarian.

- On the emotional level it is the light of sensitivity. Its light is distorted in the glamors, agitations, and depth of the sea.

- On the mental level true consciousness begins. The seventh, sixth, and fifth levels are called *lower level consciousness*. The third, second, and first levels are known as the *higher* or *abstract mind*, the *superconscious mind*, where the light is much brighter.

- On the fourth level is the *conscious mind*, the analytical mind. Here man begins to live a conscious life; as he raises his level, he becomes more and more conscious.

At the time of individualization, man was already using mental levels up to the fourth, the conscious mind. He began to experience self-consciousness when the substance of the Lotus was placed there in the mental body.

The fourth mental level, the conscious mind, functions differently in three stages of development. It acts:

1. As the slave or the vehicle of blind urges on the three lower planes, when man is in the early stages of development.

2. As an independent unit, using or controlling the lower levels of the mind, when man is on the path of liberation.

3. As the receiver of inspirations coming from higher levels, when man begins to build the Rainbow Bridge between the lower and the higher mind.

The seventh, sixth, and fifth levels of the mind are known by many names. Together they form a unit called the *subconscious mind*[1], the *reactive* or *lower mind*; it is closely connected with the "mental unit." It is the mind that plays a role in hypnotism and in building up mental complexes and engrams.[2] These three levels (7th, 6th, and 5th) make up the switchboard of the autonomic nervous system, which controls the functions of the visceral organs. It is because of this fact that hypnotism or the aberrative

---

[1] See Saraydarian, Torkom, *The Subconscious Mind and the Chalice.*

[2] Engram: Any moment of greater or lesser "unconsciousness" on the part of the analytical mind which permits the reactive mind to record; the total comment of that moment with all percepts. Hubbard, L. Ron, *Dianetics*, p. 438.

contents of the lower mind can control the body and create psychosomatic illnesses.

The lower mind is the place where illusions are found. Illusions are distorted impressions. When a great idea, revelation, or a vision penetrates into the sphere of a mind that is full of low level thoughtforms and restless with conflicting urges, it degenerates and forms illusions. Illusions are distorted realities, distorted facts.

In the average man it is the three lower levels of mind that control all his expressions. He is chiefly the victim of his illusions and engrams, and until they are cleared away or erased, man cannot enter into the light of reality and live a truly sane life. When a mind has no illusions, engrams, or posthypnotic suggestions, it is a sane mind, provided that the brain mechanism is not damaged.

It is in this area that most psychoanalysts and confessors do their work. The illusions, engrams, complexes, distorted pictures, or thoughtforms are touched upon and brought out into the light of the conscious mind, where they are seen as they are in reality.

The Soul, the Ego, or in occult terminology, the Solar Angel, dwells on the three higher levels of the mental plane. It is the Thinker. It is not the man. It is the bridge between the reflection and the Real Self. The reflection comes into being when the combined Light of the Monad and the Solar Angel strikes a lower sub-plane and creates an "I" there. The Soul is not the reflection. It is the Thinker. It produces light and consciousness through the mental substance. Your light depends upon your degree of consciousness. If your "bulb" is 25 watts, you have light equal to 25 watts. If it is 1000 watts, then your light is equal to 1000 watts, and so on. Consciousness or awareness is light. It gradually becomes brighter and brighter as man passes from level to level until it eventually illuminates the whole field. This is the process of awakening, the process of the expansion of consciousness.

In the process of retracing its steps to its true Source, the reflection slowly merges with the Thinker, the Soul, and a mystic marriage takes place. Man becomes *one* with his Solar Angel and sees the path leading to his true Home. At this stage, he has become a living Soul, radiating Love and Beauty, Light and Sacrifice. He no longer belongs to his family, nation, or race. He belongs to the whole of humanity. He cannot remain at this level, however, because before him opens a new horizon which will lead him toward intuitional awareness, atmic awareness, monadic awareness, and eventually cosmic awareness. As he ascends toward these higher levels, his consciousness and awareness increase. As he enters into soul consciousness and intuitional awareness, the Plan of the Hierarchy opens to his admiring eyes. When he enters monadic awareness, the purpose of the great Life unveils Itself. Thus man passes from glory to glory, until he merges with his True Self.

It is a fact that the reflection, the human ego, the human "I" cannot think, does not think; it only reflects. True thoughts are streams of energy coming from the Inner Lord, the Solar Angel. As they flow through the mental plane, they create new ideas, urges, drives, and aspirations. The lower mind clothes them in forms and modifies them in accordance with its purity and unfoldment. As a musician plays upon his violin, so the Inner Lord plays His thoughts through the mind. All thoughts created by the Inner Lord are pure and in accord with the evolutionary Plan.

How do evil thoughts come from a man if the thoughts of his Inner Lord are good, true, and beautiful in their nature? To answer this question we can say the following.

The real thought is a projection of the Inner Lord: Goodness, Love, Righteousness, and Beauty. It is a river flowing from an underground lake and giving life to nature. As the lofty thought projected comes in contact with a man's mental substance, it creates forces that can be translated into art, religion, science, and leadership. It then passes through the emotional atmosphere, where it is clothed in a new color and form according to the contact and type of the emotional and physical world in which the man lives. In the soul of every man there is an individual and universal *plan*. Thoughts are used in the building process of bringing that *plan* into materialization.

There are many apparently evil thoughts which are in essence the most pure thoughts. They seem to be evil because of their destructive quality or because of their high voltage. For example, the thought of Galileo concerning the revolving of the earth was an evil thought to the clergy at that time in Rome. The teaching of Christ was evil to the priests in the synagogues. In short, to build a new house, replacing an old one, you must first use your thoughts destructively and then constructively.

Evil thoughts originate in several ways:

1. Evil thoughts do not come from the Inner Lord. Most of them are the result of impressions gathered in our unconscious moments and later act as commands. They block the light of our consciousness and run our machine against our inner will. The actions of most criminals fall into this category.

2. Evil thoughts may result from being possessed by an incarnate or a discarnate mind which is completely aberrated.

3. At times our emotions take over and use our mental mechanism to create selfish, negative thoughts which may lead us into taking some action which we would not otherwise have taken.

Returning to our original idea: real, true thought is pure; it is universal; it is cosmic. It is the radioactivity of the Inner Lord. If we use the higher levels of the mind, our thoughts will be charged with more electricity. They will be more creative and pure, corresponding to the original impulse of the Inner Man. When we use the lower levels, thought becomes coarser and coarser, until upon the lowest levels it degenerates and is used as food or energy for negative emotions and physical drives.

So-called evil people can generally be likened to hypnotized people or machines. Their lives are run by automatic reactions. Such persons are to be found everywhere in all areas. Many of them hold responsible positions in governments and in colleges and universities throughout the world. Whatever they do is the result of reflex action. They are good mirrors. Their minds reflect the thoughts and intentions of others and work under the direction of those thoughts and intentions. The waves of daily living carry their boats haphazardly from one place to another.

Most people are not living according to their own will but according to push-buttons placed in their own psycho-field, their inner field of sensitivity. These push-buttons, or let us say the commands which the switches activate, direct all their thinking, feeling, and acting without letting them know what is going on inside. A man may think he is free, but actually he is not a free individual. He is the slave of the commands put into his psycho-field. He has no choice other than to obey them. People speak of freedom, free nations, free actions, and free speech. How can there be such freedom if people are bound within themselves, imprisoned by the commands recorded in their inner world? Truly, they are fighting mainly to protect the freedom of their inner insanity, of their inner slavery.

What are these commands or hypnotic suggestions? They are recordings which act as forceful urges when in any way restimulated. They are registered as blind urges and commands under circumstances in which we are not conscious because of a physical pain or accident, because of emotional stress and pain, because of a state of extreme happiness or excitement, or because we are in grief, depressed, or suffering the loss of a loved one. For example, when a wife loses her husband, at that moment she is more or less in an "unconscious state," and impressions can be registered as inner commands. They are also registered as forceful urges or commands each time we commit an act of evil, an act against our conscience, against the good of any creature. A man who kills someone, steals something, or lies is at that moment in a relative state of unconsciousness, and his gates are open to hundreds of devils — in other words, to posthypnotic suggestions.

We become unconscious to some degree when we enter into a dark emotional state called hatred. When we feel hatred for someone, some mode of activity, or a certain doctrine, we shut off the consciousness center within us and immediately register all the negative points that we so strongly dislike in that person, organization, or government. For this reason, those who hate gradually change and begin to imitate the methods, the kinds of activities, and the ideas of the one or ones for whom they feel hatred. We find, however, that they now place different labels on the methods, ideas, and activities and offer various excuses for adhering to them. Thus they build in themselves a second, mechanical nature and further complicate their lives because they have made themselves more prone to blind urges and drives.

Christ advised us not to hate but to love, to use our reason in searching for the truth because when we hate, we plant within ourselves the ugliest qualities of our enemies and close our hearts to the good in them.

What happens if we hate some high level person, ideology, or organization? Hatred prevents a person from seeing the good in anyone or anything. It brings out all that is ugly, destructive, and harmful. If such negative things are not already there, the one who hates creates them in his imagination, and he becomes hypnotized by his own creations of ugliness. The outcome is that he is fighting against himself.

Results are entirely different when we love, because in true love a man is conscious to the highest degree. He loves his enemy, but he does not try to copy him. Instead he tries to find the best way to change him into a friend or to lift him up toward beauty and light.

When your emotional department is in agitation, whether positively or negatively, every word and action will pass into your lower mind as a potential posthypnotic suggestion. It is for this reason that the great Masters of Mind and advanced thinkers of the race always emphasize the need to be awake and in peace. To be awake and in peace, you must have the ability to see things as they actually are and to be conscious on the higher mental levels. When our emotional nature is agitated, the part of the mind that registers the commands and puts them into action is working. When you are wide awake and conscious, this area of the mind is inactive, so whatever you see, hear, taste, touch, or smell becomes pure experience for you. Your experience can be used for creative purposes to enhance your survival on different levels.

All contacts made in your unconscious moments or in moments of psychological sleep go deep inside and become blind urges that control your life against your true will. We think we are thinking; we think we are feeling; we think we are acting as we wish to act. But the fact is that we are thinking, feeling, and acting not according to our own wishes but according to what has been thrust into our lower mind, our reactive mind. Since most people in the world are psychologically asleep, you can well imagine the number of commands they are gathering daily and to what degree such people are puppets of their blind inner commands.

Viewed from a higher level, people are sleepwalkers. They are fighting; they are creating; they are loving; they are hating; they are working; they are coming and going. Whatever they are doing, thinking, or feeling, they are performing as if in sleep — as unconscious creatures or puppets hung on strings and manipulated by commands, by hypnotic suggestions. It means nothing that some of them are creative or directed toward higher goals; these worthy endeavors could easily be blind commands planted during unconscious moments.

There are those who believe that because a man is thinking on a high level, he is performing a conscious act, but this is not necessarily true. Even his higher creativity or great aspirations could be impressions put into his lower, reactive mind when he was in an "unconscious state." When such people express themselves, the slightest pressure or obstacle can divert their direction and raise or awaken new drives, hidden deep within their inner world — drives that can work against their adopted creative direction or high aspiration. Consequently they are divided, confused, and frustrated. Inner failures or frustrations are caused in this way. It happens not from the outside but from inner conflict. The conflict is caused by opposing forces, which in this case are hypnotic commands; suggestions planted in us and now fighting against each other.

We find reference to these facts in classical literature. For example, in one of his letters, Saint Paul says:

For the good that I would I do not; but the evil which I would not, that I do. Now if I do that I would not, it is no more I that do it, but sin that dwelleth in me.... O wretched man that I am! [1]

This great apostle found the law of mind and discovered also that, "... it is no more I that do it, but the *sin*...." Here sin refers to an inner blind urge or command which is controlling him against his will.

In the literature of the mystics they also speak of temptations and of how sometimes they are unable to resist tempting thoughts and urges. These dark periods through which the mystics passed were known as the "dark night" of the soul. It was a time when the "evil" in them was reigning. They were aware of this fact but could do nothing about it. When they were cleansed of these sins, when the inner commands or hypnotic suggestions were cleared away, they entered into pure consciousness or awareness which is called *illumination*. Jesus was in this state at the time of His transfiguration, and Buddha experienced it at the time of His illumination under the blessed tree.

We may ask, "Is there a way to rid ourselves of these inner commands?" Yes, there are many advanced methods or even esoteric methods which can be used to erase them completely or to

---

[1] Romans 7:19, 20, 24

weaken them until they become paralyzed and ineffectual. Such methods involve *observation*. We must learn to observe carefully whatever we are doing. This is extremely important, and the reward is very great.

First step. Observe yourself from 10:00 to 11:00 in the morning, and discover what your thoughts, your words, your feelings, and your actions really are. Think and find the motives behind them. It is most important to *find the motive*. Gradually you will begin to see that you do not really know why you acted, felt, or spoke the way you did. When you discover and realize this, it will be easier for you to know and understand that you are mechanical, that you are somewhat like a puppet. It is often very comical to find out about ourselves. When you know about mechanical expression, the opportunity is yours to gradually awaken yourself and cease to be mechanical. This is self-observation.

Second step. Use confession, which means to observe yourself in the mirror of your expression. Confession is observation, but you are not observing yourself as your *self*; you are observing from the standpoint of your expression. You are seeing yourself in the light of your mode of expression and the content of your expression, the meaning which it carries.

To begin, go to a person whom you trust, and speak with him about your thoughts, your feelings, your deeds, your actions, and your behavior. Even though he may not evaluate your expressions, you will be able to see yourself more clearly than before, and this being, to some extent, a conscious act, the inner commands will gradually decrease until one day you will see yourself as you are.

In confessing to others, you must not ask for an evaluation, suggestions, or advice. In olden days people used to go to the river or the woods and make their confession in a loud voice to Nature, which is a living entity. This practice is sometimes better than confessing to a person who appreciates, analyzes, and often solves your personal problems. No true listener judges from what he hears because he knows that most of the things said or done by the subject were expressions of inner commands. Thus we can see the reason why all Saviors of humanity emphasize forgiveness. How can you judge a man's actions or punish him if he is acting in his sleep? Jesus said at the cross:

Father, forgive them, for they know not what they do.

An awakened man never performs evil actions, never hurts anyone because man is essentially good.

In confessing to another, one faces oneself as one is. One divides oneself into two: one who is doing, acting, or speaking and one who is *observing*. The important thing is not the confession. The important thing is the observer within the confessing one. The main duty of the listener is not to analyze the subject, the meanings of the confessed things, but to *listen* and ask a few questions to make the subject continue to confess as far as possible, as detailed as possible. By questioning the listener can make the subject face or observe himself better and more deeply.

The confessing one must be helped to see himself as he is. This is the main purpose. If the man is badly shocked because of what he did, the observer will know that it is an emotional agitation and will try to raise him up to the mental level, where the problem will be taken in a sense of responsibility and in cool reasoning.

In confession the important thing is what one did to others, not what the others did to him. What the others did is mostly a reflection of what he did to others. Make him face his motives, the urges behind all his expressions. Unveil him to himself and show the phases of his personality and its various colors of which he was completely unaware.

Here again a most important point should be observed. The confessor must know that his real essence is Goodness, is Beauty, is Righteousness, and all his expressions that are not in tune with Goodness, Beauty, and Righteousness are basically the faults of his personality, of his physical, emotional, and mental mechanism.

We may say that when the human mind is working in its optimum range of clarity, it is an integrated, seven-dimensional mechanism. In its gradual development it passes through three distinct steps which have seven stages.

First step:

- In the first stage the mind works through impulses coming from the physical world and from the physical body.

- In the second stage the mind works through impulses coming from the lower levels of the emotional world.

Second step:

- In the third stage the human mind responds chiefly to commands picked up in its unconscious moments, moments of great excitement.
- In the fourth stage the mind passes through a learning process. It registers whatever is given to it or forced upon it. In most schools and universities the students are found on this level.
- In the fifth stage the mind begins to register subtle thoughtforms or thought waves from space. It thinks and acts according to the thought waves it registers. This process is sometimes called "inspiration," through which people speak or create artistically, but actually it is still a mechanical performance, not true creativity. Most artists are on this level with the veil of ignorance still hanging over their true nature.

Third step:

- In the sixth stage the mind begins to discriminate between the incoming currents of mental energy or thought currents; it chooses the highest and the universal thought waves to express in its activities.
- In the seventh and last stage, the mind registers the thoughts of the Inner Lord. At this point man truly thinks for the first time. He is now a real creator.

On these three steps or seven stages, the Inner Thinker or Lord is present, but He is not free to act through the body except in rare instances or flashes. As the man grows and the mental plane becomes more organized, these flashes from the Inner Lord are more frequent. Most of them are lost and die in the mist and darkness of agitation and turbulence in the lower levels. Gradually the mists clear, and the flashes become stronger and more dominating. When the Thinker dominates the mental plane, the man is a true creator or a genius. He works on the first, the highest subplane of the physical, emotional, and mental planes with no obstructions on his path.

On the lower mental levels the incoming thought-currents and events not only are reflected by the mind, but also, through the law of association, they change into something quite different. An original incoming thought associates with many different incoming thoughts, and a mixture is the result. Sometimes a strong, important thought can assimilate tens of weak ones and use them as fuel for its course. A man whose mind works in this way acts, writes, sings, and thinks as a mirror, and the Inner Man is in deep sleep.

Our brain is like a photographic plate. The vehicle of light is the sevenfold mind. The ideas or thoughts are objects planted in the mental sphere. The density of the light-mind and the purity of the mental atmosphere condition the clarity of the picture upon the brain. Thus, if the light is not of high quality, if the intermediate space is not free from interfering thoughtforms or coarse vibrations and static, the projected idea or thought wave will never be clearly pictured upon the brain, and the true message will be lost. Sometimes it happens that we receive a warning from our innermost center, which may manifest as conscience or intuition, but it flashes for only one second and dies under the attack of negative waves and vibrations.

It is important that we clear and purify our mind and build our brain cells of higher plane substance. It will then be possible for the Inner Dweller to project a thought, an idea, and it will come down greatly enhanced by the richest content of each level through which it passes. To clear these lower layers of the mind, we must exercise observation, detachment, and transmutation on the mental plane; we must try to keep mental silence for short periods of time. When we understand that our thoughts are different from our minds, we will eventually learn to detach ourselves from our thoughts and create new and higher level thoughts. It is our thoughtforms that condition our state of being; the outer conditions of our lives are the direct result of our thoughts. Through our routine thinking, we create a chain-like process, a deep groove in which our wheels turn and spin. We must do something to change this course if we wish to travel upon a higher level.

Highest creativity occurs when a disciplined and highly developed mind is held in a moment of deep silence by the Inner Lord, while a new idea is projected on the mental screen. There it is grasped, completely assimilated, charged, and vested with the needed electricity, matter, and form. Every high-voltage idea that comes into the atmosphere of the mind is transformed according to the time, the need, and the achievement of the man. It becomes intellectualized, formulated, and crystallized and is used in his daily relationships. This much is inevitable, but man should build a bridge over which he can pass from the form side of the idea to its energy side, thereby expressing the idea more completely.

Every mind is a laboratory with chemicals and elements of its own. The incoming ideas or thought-currents can be completely assimilated, thus enriching the contents, whether high or low. They can be taken in as they are and reflected back, or they may undergo a chemical change. For example, a thought current of lead may change into the substance of gold, or a current of gold may become lead; it may even become poisonous gas, due to a toxic substance present where it is received. Thus again we are reminded not to throw our pearls to the swine.

It may also happen that — through certain contacts, breathing exercises, or the use of some drugs — a current of high energy flows down from higher levels and sources to the lower levels of the mental plane. If there are any evil or negative thoughtforms on the lower levels, they become highly charged and stimulated, affecting the corresponding glands and organs of the body. This *overstimulation* is the cause of many tragic events in families, groups, nations, and in the world as a whole. This may happen not only to an individual, but at times a church or a nation can be controlled by such overstimulation, creating great upheavals in the life of the planet. It can express itself through physical disease, emotional storms, or mental illusions, carrying with it a powerful force to dominate.

Many people have been ruined by coming in contact with high voltage ideas or merely with highly developed individuals. The first and most important sign of overstimulation is an increasing egotism or selfishness. A person begins to build an image within himself and then starts to worship it. If the overstimulation continues, he goes deeper and deeper until one day he becomes a tyrant in his home, his church, his group, or even his nation, providing he can find enough people to support him. He is blinded like the man who stares at a very bright light and then loses his vision for a while. The man who cannot digest high level ideas and who has in his atmosphere many evil thoughtforms becomes the victim of these thoughtforms, which flow like a flood down the mountain.

All mental exercises, self-observation, concentration, meditation, and contemplation tend to cleanse, purify, and transmute the mental substance and atmosphere, increase sensitivity in the brain cells, and build a small number of bridges in the mental world.

In the following paragraphs some mental exercises are presented.

EXERCISE A.

The first exercise deals with observation. We intend to find ourselves by detaching ourselves from those pictures, glamors, and illusions with which we have identified. Detachment is a direct result of careful observation. Hence our main work for a few months or a few lives is observation. What are we to observe? We are to observe our mental reactions, our different states under a variety of conditions and events. Our mind, with all its modifications and idiosyncracies, is the most precious book or source of experience in our possession.

By observing our mind, distinguishing its levels, activities, and reactions, you will gradually free yourself from the lower levels of the mental plane and perceive the lower levels from a higher viewpoint. This practice will eventually lead you to the chair of the successful observer. It will lead you to higher and higher levels until the time when you are completely free from the domination of the mental body and its automatic, mechanical functioning. Observation is the basic path; careful observation without criticism, without self-condemnation, without self-pity, without identification; cold, clear observation to learn to know the how and why of the activities of the mind. Each observation will open a new door to information about yourself. All added information will open the observing eye wider, and the day will come when you will realize that you are not the mind, that you are not a bird in a cage of mental reactions — you are a liberated observer.

How and what should you observe? Observe, for example, in many different situations, that you are not the mind, that you are something other than the mind. Do this observation carefully and note it in your diary. Try to discover just how you did this observation and on what occasions. By doing this you will see that your mind is a very strong mechanism, and that it often controls you completely. Although you may be under its control, you will note that there are parts of the mind or thoughts which you can, in some instances, handle, stop, use, or reject. This may surprise you, but it will also encourage you in your expedition into your mental world.

You will discover, also, a close relationship between your emotions and thoughts. Observe how they control or reject each other, how they agree or disagree. In ancient times it was written, "As a man thinketh, so is he." Through observation you will see how your thoughts condition you, your daily relationships, and even your physical body. When you have reached this point, you will begin to think of *how to change your inner world* so that you are able to have a better life, better living conditions. However, before you can do anything about the inner world of your emotions and thoughts, you must come to understand that not only your inner world conditions your life, but also that the great Life with Its innumerable relationships affects you greatly, and that every moment creates changes in your thoughts, moods, and inner states. When you realize this, when you truly understand how the two worlds act upon each other, you may begin to think and make decisions to change your inner world. The first step, then, is observation: careful, patient, scientific observation.

EXERCISE B.

The second exercise in building bridges in the mental world is the process of detachment on the mental level. Begin by trying to detach your mind from the influence of your environment, from your physical body reactions, and from your emotions. Focus your consciousness in the mental world. You will find that the mind itself is an agitated sea. Try to withdraw yourself deeper into your innermost center to quiet the mental sea and to reach the deep silence within you. Here, in this center of silence, there is not the slightest ripple or wave of thought.

This process will take five or ten minutes, not more. In the beginning two or three minutes are sufficient. You will find that this endeavor is a difficult task, but you will note that by doing it, you are learning unexpected things about your mental mechanism which cannot be learned from a book or a person. This will encourage you and will increase your interest in yourself and your progress; you will work more diligently, and eventually you will begin to sense the joy of real detachment. When this joy is tasted, the rest will be easier for you.

You cannot have inner growth and radiation if you do not isolate your inner world from outer influences. We are told that the inner chamber of the Great Pyramid, the King's Chamber in the center of the pyramid where deep silence reigns, is protected by huge, massive stones. There stands the Initiate. Symbolically we have the same chamber of silence within ourselves, and there we must stand. Christ spoke of the inner chamber when He said:

> *But as for you, when you pray, enter into your inner chamber and lock your door, and pray to your Father who is in secret, and your Father who sees in secret shall himself reward you openly.*[1]

This chamber is the point of silence within us where is found our Father, our True Self. The path that leads us to that higher chamber is deepening detachment from the three worlds or, in other words, a deepening silence, a deepening peace. This is what we are seeking to attain — detachment in silence and peace. While you are working to accomplish this, you will notice that thoughts will come and go like patches of clouds or like shadows, but you will never allow yourself to hold them in your mind. You will simply observe them with no interest; they will hold no attraction for you. As you continue with your exercise, you will note that the thoughts become stronger and stronger, returning again and again, as if determined to attract and hold your attention. But if you persevere, they will eventually fade away completely, leaving you in deep silence and peace. These thoughts may come from any sensation, from your emotional world, your mental world, or from past memories, but your aim is to find a place of peace within yourself and never to falter even though strong waves of thought attack your shores.

When you have learned to detach yourself from your own emotional and mental worlds, you will have mastered the first important step toward controlling yourself under any condition and in any event. People sometimes resemble a lake into which muddy rivers or all kinds of influences flow. The picture changes when you learn to detach. You then resemble a beautiful, clear mountain lake, and from you hundreds of streams flow down the

---

[1] Matthew 6:6

mountain to spread Life, Light, and Love. You receive your power from the sky of your inner universe; you are a dispenser of the "living waters."

This exercise in detachment will bring other beneficial results. You will find that, in proportion to your success in achieving detachment, your consciousness will become clearer; you will gradually become more wide awake in everything you do. Being awake and alert is important on our path. Too often we do things mechanically. We are absent in our activities. One moment we have an article in our hand, the next moment we do not know where we put it! We search and search, until finally we find it by accident, indicating that we were in a kind of sleep at the time of the action; we were not totally conscious.

Continued daily use of the detachment exercise will also increase your attention span. Try to be conscious in everything you do. You will be surprised to find that you were not "present" in most of your activities. You may have read many books, but you remember nothing about them; you forget names and streets; you do not remember where you put your key, your hat, and so on because your mind was dominated by a persistent thought, feeling, or the influence of a memory with which you were identified. You were not really yourself; you were not independent. Half or perhaps ninety percent of you was lost in the mist. For example, you are listening to a lecture and you see a pretty hat on the person in front of you. It takes you back in memory to a picnic, to a dance, to a party, to a love, to tears, to sorrow — and then slowly you bring yourself back to the lecture. You listen for a few minutes and again you are carried away through a new door. When people later ask you about the lecture, you will probably give one of the following impressions: "I liked the lecture, but I did not understand most of it." "Oh, it was so sad. I wanted to cry." (This was because of your memories, not because of the lecture.) "He didn't really say very much." (This was because you heard only parts of it when you brought your attention back.)

The detachment exercise will eliminate this absent-mindedness, and you will be "present" in all your activities not as a doer but as an observer. This is an important point. There are two kinds of absence. One occurs when you are attached to and lost in a thought, in a memory, while you are doing some specific thing. The other is that time when you are completely identified with what you are doing. In both cases the observer is absent. By using this exercise you will learn how to free yourself, how to be yourself in any situation or experience. Most people of the world are asleep. They do not have their own independent attitude, their own judgment, their own observation. They are deeply hypnotized by the propaganda and advertisement machines, by life itself, and they live in a foggy consciousness. They resemble a monkey who tried on hundreds of eyeglasses and at last threw them all away saying, "These glasses do not show things as I am used to seeing them!" A few minutes later he tried again, saying, "But which one was mine?"

Detachment exercises will focus the light of your consciousness on whatever you *are* at that moment and will unveil to you a part of your self which is other than identification. Thus it is a ladder leading to your Real Self.

These exercises should be done while you are active on the three levels of human endeavor, but to facilitate the process of *detachment on the mental level*, you may use the following exercises:

1. Sit quietly, relax, close your eyes, and enter into silence. After a few moments try to recall an idea that controls you, a thought that persues you, a memory or an experience that never leaves your mind free.

   Choose one of them, and examine it carefully in your inner world. Create a picture diametrically opposed to it, and then burn both of them in your mind. For example, you have in your mind a picture. In that picture, a friend or a loved one is lying in a coffin. The church, hymn singing, the priest, the burial, the tears, the sadness, the memories are all parts of the one picture. Now create another picture. The same friend or dear one is sitting with you in a garden. Everyone is happy. Music, dancing, kissing, happiness are all in the picture. Make it seem real. Construct these two pictures in your mind for a few days or for a few weeks if necessary. Then, in your imagination, hold the two pictures face to face and burn them. At first it will be almost impossible to do, but gradually you will succeed in carrying out the burning process. Then you will be free from the dominating influence or effect of the pictures.

2. The same procedure should be used with a doctrine or dogma. Create the opposite and then rid your self of both. Do not reason as to which is right or wrong. The important thing is to detach yourself from both of them and use one or the other *only* if it helps you *to reach your goal*. Use it as a tool that can be discarded when the goal is reached or when a new tool is created. It will be impossible, however, to use the new tool unless you are detached from the former one.

3. After a while you learn how to work with mental substance. You learn ways of changing or working out crystallized thoughtforms in this substance of the mental plane. For example, you have an enemy whom you hate intensely. It would be difficult to change that man to his opposite pole, a loving man or a friend, but you can try by following these suggestions: Think of him as he is, an enemy. Then look at his clothing and say: "He has a very nice suit. He always dresses neatly. He has beautiful hair and a handsome nose. Let me joke with him. See, he smiled! You know, he is not a bad man. He is stupid. He is ignorant. He does not realize what he is doing to 'anger me.' I have no bad records in my background, in my life. He is bad, wicked... but I think he may have a few good things about him. Maybe someday he will realize his mistakes and I can accept him as a friend. I really do wish he could be my friend instead of my enemy. I will try to imagine how he would look to me if he were my friend. If he becomes my friend, he will listen to me; he will embrace me; he will bring me gifts; he will be sorry for being my enemy and will apologize. He will always be with me. He will sing for me. I will dance and be happy. Everything will be forgotten, and we will have full understanding."

By using this technique, you will be able to form the opposite pole without creating much opposition from your emotional and mental worlds. By creating an opposite picture, the strength of your dominating thoughtform decreases and eventually falls to zero. You can deal with your mental fears and worries in the same way. When you have learned to create the opposite, you can handle your problems as a master handles his tools. From this point on, all your obstacles become possibilities, giving you knowledge, wisdom, and energy. To be rid of control by inner states and outer events means to become more yourself, to be more what you essentially are. To the degree that you detach yourself from your not-self, to that degree you release more Light, more Love, more Power. This is the goal of detachment.

EXERCISE C.

The third exercise for building mental bridges we will call demobilization for lack of a better term. Each of us has an ego, a false "I," a false master. Sometimes it is formed of physical desires, emotional demands, or mental furniture. We have the idea that we cannot survive if we do not protect that "I" at any cost. This idea has a long history. It has been with us throughout centuries and centuries. We could not have grown and become creative without it. However, the use of this idea was greatly changed first when man loved a woman deeply, and then was willing to fight for his children and family. It reached a third stage when it changed to the idea of fighting for his race. The next change will be made when the idea forces us to fight for all humanity. It will not stop there. There will follow a fight for the survival and liberation of all living creatures, of trees and flowers, of every living thing.

Most people are not yet in the second stage. They are married; they "love" their partner and children, but they are not yet able to forget themselves. They simply cannot do it! They are not ready to suffer or die for their children, for their race, for their nation, or for humanity unless they are forced to do so. Most people are still in the first stage of worship — worship of the "I," the separate human ego, a point of identification on any level. Another interesting aspect is that, if they do fight for their family, for their nation, or for humanity, they fight only to assure their own survival, the survival of their ego. To put away and destroy this huge obstacle on the way to becoming oneself, we must start by practicing the great and advanced exercise of demobilization of the human ego. It is not an impossible task, but it takes time and conscious effort. A great sage tells us:

> ... *The spirit limited by the idea of isolation cannot create in step with the pulse of Cosmos.*[1]

---

[1] Agni Yoga Society, *Infinity II*, par. 393.

> *Precisely the beauty of Cosmos brings selflessness
> closer into the consciousness.*[1]

Following is the procedure for the exercise of demobilization of the isolated consciousness, or human ego.

1. In your imagination go to a special place at the seashore or in the mountains. Close your eyes, relax completely, and think about the great space, extending beyond our galaxy, beyond hundreds and thousands of suns and galaxies. Think about Cosmos and then about Space. Imagine that you are sitting on one planet of a galaxy, looking through limitless space at our planet where you exist. Think who you are and what you are in comparison to endless space and in comparison to limitless time. There are suns whose light reaches us in tens of billions of light years. Try to think about such time and space. Then think about an insect, a flower, an animal, a bird, a man, a planet which is a mere particle of dust in space. Examine your problems from the viewpoint of Cosmos. As the joy of Infinity fills your heart, say:

   > *O Thou, Who givest sustenance to the Universe,*
   > *From Whom all things proceed,*
   > *To Whom all things return,*
   > *Unveil to us the face of the true Spiritual Sun,*
   > *Hidden by a disc of golden light.*
   > *That we may know the truth*
   > *And do our whole duty,*
   > *As we journey to Thy sacred feet.*

   The last line calls our attention to the endlessness of the Path upon which we must travel, which we are traveling, and which we will travel for years and years, life after life, for centuries and centuries throughout limitless time, until we reach the "sacred feet," until we come in contact with Him consciously and recognize Him as the Source of our essence.

2. Close your eyes and relax again in your special place where no one will disturb you. Imagine a high mountain. Sit on the grass and feel yourself changing into a rose bush. This will take time. Do not be discouraged if you

---

[1] Agni Yoga Society, *Leaves of Morya's Garden II*, p. 139.

are not able to change yourself suddenly into a bush of roses. Work slowly. Begin by imagining that your hands and fingers are becoming the branches and twigs; your head is becoming a large rose in full bloom; your body becomes the main branch or stem; your feet are the roots. Try it, and with no tension or strain you will succeed in changing yourself into a large and beautiful rose bush. When you have mastered the above technique, go deeper and see the green of your leaves, the closed buds, the opening rose with its lovely color, its fragrance, bees coming and going, a soft, gentle breeze, and other mountains far in the distance. When you can imagine these things vividly, it will be easy for you to change yourself into anything of your choosing.

In your next sitting, try to change yourself into a bee, a real bee; live the next five or ten minutes of your life as a bee. At other times try changing yourself into a beautiful rose, and imagine that a man is picking you from a bush; discover what your feelings are as a rose. Change into a lovely bird or a lively horse. Then, as a bird, imagine a man shooting you and feel the agony of the dying bird. Change to a horse. A man is beating you; try to feel the pain as the horse. Using your imagination, do these exercises as deeply and realistically as you can. Each one should be done for fifteen minutes once a day. You may repeat them for a week if you wish.

After you have passed through these exercises, try to do the following. Think of a man whom you know well, and be that man. Try to think and behave the way he does. Imagine a prisoner, and be that prisoner. Imagine a soldier, and be that soldier. See yourself fighting in the jungles, in the deserts, and so on. Think of a man who has brought about a great change in society. Be that man. Imagine how society is rejecting you, attacking you, perhaps even killing you. Imagine that, as that man, people are burning you. Try to feel the flames. See and feel the excitement of the crowd; feel the flames consuming your body as it turns to ashes. Think about people who suffer. Feel their suffering. Then join them in happiness and joy. Be many different people; be your family, your race, your group; be humanity, be the universe, and try to be Space.

If you perform these exercises regularly, with sincerity, you will find that the crystallized point of the mental station, which we call the human ego, will be shattered. A new, more inclusive center will manifest itself in you; a center which brings the feeling of being at-one with all humanity. You will discover that the deepening of your understanding will be related to your success in the demobilization process. You will find that as you demobilize your human ego, proportionally your horizon of understanding will become wider, deeper, limitless. You will understand people, animals, trees, and flowers. You will sense the Life in them, the Life which is one with the Life in you. You will understand their full meaning as you repeat these words:

> *The sons of men are one, and I am one with them.*
> *I seek to love, not hate;*
> *I seek to serve and not exact due service.*
> *I seek to heal, not hurt.*[1]

You cannot find yourself until you lose your little separated self and unite with the greater Self.

3. To end this period of demobilization, try to do the following exercise for two weeks. Visualize yourself entering into the sun and gradually melting away, evaporating. A flame of pure blue light still exists as your essence, as you. When you reach the center of the sun, visualize that essence becoming one with the fiery kernel of the sun. To be the sun means many things, but here in this exercise as you visualize yourself being the sun, try to give light to all planets in the system; try to give *life* to all kingdoms, mineral, vegetable, animal, and human. Try to realize that it is your Light, your Power, your Love that makes them grow and express themselves. After being the sun for five or ten minutes, slowly emerge, breathe in the sun, and, by visualizing, form a new fiery body, a beautiful body filled with Light, Love, and Power.

Gradually these exercises will destroy your limitations, the prison walls that exist in your inner world, and they will open the door to freedom. Freedom cannot be realized by making yourself

---

[1] *The Mantram of Unification.*

the center of your universe, the center of your family, group, church, community, or nation. Freedom is realized and achieved by freeing yourself from the walls which keep your human ego crystallized and blinded by its own light, and by identifying your *essence* with the essence of the whole.

SUMMARY OF INSTRUCTIONS:

1.   Please read this chapter as often and as attentively as possible.

2.   Use the exercise on *observation* for three months.

3.   On the fourth month, start the exercises on *detachment* and use them for five months.

4.   Follow the *demobilization* exercise previously given in this chapter under steps 1, 2, and 3:

   Step 1 should be carried out for at least three weeks.

   Step 2 should be carried out for the second three weeks.

   Step 3 should be carried out for a period of two weeks.

   Following the eighth week, repeat all three of these demobilization exercises for the next eight week period.

5.   When you have learned to use observation, detachment, and demobilization, carry on with these three processes throughout your lifetime.

Chapter XI

THE PRINCIPLE OF CONFLICT

Dissatisfaction is a quality of the Subtle World. In it can be discerned eternal motion, for without this motion it is impossible to advance in the higher worlds.[1]

There are many people in the world who become discouraged when conflict occurs within their families, churches, groups, or in their nation as a whole. They immediately conclude that everything is in danger, and that the best thing for them to do is to withdraw, attack, pass over to the stronger side, or merge into inertia. If we analyze the situation, we will find that conflict starts when:

1. A new energy, idea, or thought clashes with the old, obsolete one which resists and tries to perpetuate itself.

2. People feel dissatisfaction with the current conditions in economic, social, religious, or scientific fields. This dissatisfaction occurs when a man or group surpasses the level which the time and condition present.

3. An advanced person enters into our ranks and disturbs the calm, peaceful waters in which we are floating innocently or sinfully. We find in literature of olden days that great disciples and saviors were often called troublemakers. This is found to be true in every age.

Conflict does not, however, take place only in a family or in a group of people. It takes place also *within ourselves*. Conflict starts within a man as a result of spiritual thirst or as the result of the call or influence of his spiritual nature. He is then divided between the inner and outer worlds, between material and spiritual paths. Conflict flares up within him and continues until one side or the other of his nature is victorious.

---

[1] Agni Yoga Society, *Heart*, par. 164.

We must remember that the dark forces have their obsessed members everywhere, and that it is their duty to isolate and dishonor light bearers through confusion, indecision, doubts, and lies. They are especially active when a purer light begins to build its fountain of service. They even attack embryos before birth if they see that the coming babies are destined to be leaders of light.

We can discriminate between *conflict* and *attack* if we study the motives behind them. We have conflict if a higher force is trying to create better conditions and circumstances, destroying crystallized hindrances. We have *attack* if limiting, materializing, isolating, selfish, and dark forces are trying to destroy the source or the agent of light through organized gossip, propaganda, or other dark and devious means.

If you open the pages of history, you will find that no great, advanced person ever lived who did not have attacks made upon him by the dark forces. These forces are sometimes awakened and organized in a given place because of the coming or existence of a leader of Light. His high level presence automatically stimulates the evil around him, and the battle begins. But the wise one is not shaken; he uses every arrow thrust toward him.

... Blessed be the obstacles, they teach us unity and resistance.[1]

... All the winds serve the miller to produce a better flour.[2]

No new idea, invention, or leader comes to the world of men without creating opposition, suffering, and labor. Hundreds of light bearers, geniuses, died upon the crosses of hatred, jealousy, and misunderstanding. Hundreds were burned, excommunicated, or crucified. But the centuries which followed proved that they were the most powerful benefactors of the human race. The obstacles and attacks, instead of weakening them, became the main fuel for their upward victory.

We find an example of this in the *Bible*. In ancient Palestine there was a pool, and once each year the Angel of the Lord came down and agitated the waters. At that time, sick people hurried to the pool to throw themselves into the water, for tradition held that the one who entered the water first would be cured. Besides its

---

[1] Agni Yoga Society, *Heart*, par. 401.

[2] Agni Yoga Society, *Leaves of Morya's Garden I*, par. 272.

literal interpretation, this happening has a symbolic meaning. When the "waters" of a human condition, situation, idea, or emotion are agitated, a healing power is released for those who, instead of experiencing antagonism and violent reactions, are able to respond and unify with the healing current.

Conflict may occur on any one of the three levels of human life. It may occur on the mental plane, where ideas fight against each other. If all sides are sincere and free from mechanical influences, gradually the best solution emerges through long, dedicated research work and meditation. Conflict may happen on the emotional level, where emotions and feelings war against each other until the cool light of the intellect interferes and the golden Path is revealed. Conflict may occur on the physical level in the form of revolutions, riots, or wars.

In each case of conflict, two main energies are fighting against each other. One represents the old attitude, the other the new; or one represents the energies of freedom and the other the forces of darkness. History bears out the fact that the forces of Light are always victorious, and that new cultures and civilizations are born as the result of conflict. These changes are the result of new energies coming from the depths of the human soul.

Conflict accomplishes the following:

1. Old forms, attitudes, ideas, and old ways of thinking and acting become clarified and rise to the surface. People begin to use their minds.

2. It separates darkness from light and eventually eliminates darkness, providing there are enough people standing for light.

3. New ideas and new ways of thinking and acting emerge and, as a result, civilization eventually changes and human life adjusts itself to the progress of the times.

4. It awakens the good in many hearts and organizations and integrates these forces which will lead the man, the group, the church, and humanity toward higher dimensions.

5. It produces detachments and renunciations, which have great significance in the progress of any individual, church, or nation. The way of progress is a continuous process of detachment and renunciation from the lower and identification with the higher. However, if this identi-

fication lasts too long, it in itself becomes an obstacle on the path of progress.

6. It leads to liberation and to deeper service. Is it possible to progress without conflict? Human history shows us that it is not, but it is possible to raise the conflict to the mental plane and gradually adjust life to the new light received through the conflict. For example, suppose a man uses too much alcohol. One day, through the advice of friends or from bitter experience, he realizes that he should not drink. Now the conflict starts between the *habit* and the new decision or wish. The conflict continues and the man gradually begins to see things more clearly. This inner illumination strengthens the forces of freedom in his soul, and eventually he is emancipated from his bad habit.

The same is true for a church or group. The group or church may be running smoothly; everything is being properly taken care of, but suddenly trouble starts. An attack is directed toward the leader, one of the members, or against a given decision. The organization is agitated; conflict is on the way. Gradually both sides collect themselves and make their attitudes clear. When both sides have prepared their attack, then gossip, talk, politics, hatred, jealousy all become active. The church or group is under a severe test. Eventually the members begin to see themselves as they are. Their intentions and the tactics become clear. When the battle cools down, they look *above* to see the principles upon which their group or church was formed; they look *below* to see whether or not they are acting according to the teaching embodied in those principles — the teaching which they have been receiving throughout the years. Thus for the first time the conflict furnishes them with a true picture. They are presented with an opportunity for new progress, if they are able to face the issues and make the necessary adjustments.

The same holds true for nations and for all humanity. Progress is the result of conflict. Progress resembles the fire through which transmutation occurs. Conflict offers us the opportunity to surpass our limitations, to awaken, and to take the side of the progressive forces of Light. In one of his books, a Master says:

> *... The time is not yet, but a great awakening is in process; men, however, will only see correctly when this Principle of Conflict is properly evaluated as a spiritual*

necessity and is used by humanity as an instrument to bring about emergence from the wrong controls and principles.[1]

It happens sometimes that students of wisdom become crystallized in their mental nature; they reject any new explanation or approach to the light. When a student limits himself to one approach, he ends his progress. A great Teacher warns us:

Let your horizon be wide, my brother, and your humility great — ready to accept and assimilate any idea which is approved by your intuition or heart.[2]

The way of progress is like climbing a mountain. There is much resistance, but each step takes a man higher and higher toward the peak. Each step in meditation takes him into deeper wisdom and wider experience, but at the same time the pilgrim faces greater resistance from his body, from his emotions, and even from his thoughts. Still he continues. Each step is a problem. No man can go forward without solving his problems. The problems sometimes change their shapes and forms, but essentially they are the same unsolved problems. When a problem is solved, it disappears, and a greater one appears. This time it may not seem as great to him, because each time he solves a problem, he increases his energy and wisdom, and the proportion remains the same. To the degree that our pilgrim moves toward the peak, to that degree does his horizon gradually enlarge, and his sense of proportion and relativity develop. He breathes in purer and finer air, and the noise of the lower levels lessens and dies for him. Each higher step that he takes brings him closer to the Source of Light. His horizon is his heart's compassion; it becomes deeper and deeper, wider and wider — until it encompasses the whole universe.

The air which he breathes on higher and higher levels is the plane of consciousness into which he enters and through which he passes into deeper and higher states of consciousness. Actually such a man does not have to climb to the peak of the mountain. *The mountain is in his soul.* He can start to climb toward the highest peak of being only by using his mind and his Inner Light. To meditate means to breathe in the world of thoughts and ideas. As he penetrates deeper into the world of his higher being, he

---

[1] Bailey, Alice A., *The Rays and the Initiations*, p. 606.
[2] The Tibetan.

brings finer energies down to the outer world, down to his mechanism, and gradually he changes his vehicles of expression, his environment, and the world. This is the meaning of service.

Day by day, year by year, he climbs higher up the mountain within himself; proportionally he changes the substance of his vehicle and the state of his environment. A man breathes through his nose and lungs, but he also breathes emotionally and mentally. He who lives on a high level of the arts and of knowledge cannot live in a poisoned emotional and mental atmosphere. He must have purer air to breathe. This pure air for his inner, spiritual lungs can be found on the higher levels of culture and wisdom. All these things can be achieved through conflict. In its true light, *conflict is the process of transmutation of forces into energies — lower into higher.* It is the process of pushing away the walls of ignorance behind which we live. It is a change of polarity from south to north. A true light bearer is a person who grows through conflict. He will create conflicts and tension if they are not present. One of the Master Minds says very beautifully:

> *It is necessary to become as accustomed to battle as to daily labor. One should understand a battle not only as a test of excelling in strength but also as a source for the accumulation of energy.... Hierarchy does not mean the steadfastness of repose, but steadfastness in the midst of battle.*[1]

---

[1] Agni Yoga Society, *Hierarchy*, par. 233.

Chapter XII

THE CHALICE AND
THE SEEDS

We increase our expression of goodness to the degree that we approach our Inner Being. To the degree that we express goodness, we come closer to our own essence. Thus those individuals who are filled with goodness are known as the benefactors of mankind and are recognized as being divine and holy. It is true; they are divine and holy because they express their own Divinity, which is the goodness within them. Know then that you become your True Self in proportion to your expression of goodness.

All religions emphasize the act of doing good, of being full of Light and Love. All these expressions mean the same thing: release the Divinity within you; release that Divinity, the Flame of Life, that Goodness which is living electricity, through all your expressions.

We have learned much about the mental plane. This chapter will explore the subject in greater depth. The mental plane with its seven sub-planes, is like a cloud around your head and body. Gradually as your *consciousness* unfolds, and as your experiences become richer, the mental plane organizes itself, and seven colors appear, one for each plane. These colors slowly become clearer, and you notice a vortex of energy which in esoteric literature is called a *mental unit*. Then, just as the moon emerges out of a mist, a point of light begins to appear on the higher sub-planes. This is called the *mental permanent atom* or *seed*. The development of the mental plane continues, and one day there can be seen a faint outline of a Chalice. Centuries pass; the Chalice becomes clearer and clearer, with rare beauty of fiery colors and the radiation of twelve streams of energy. More centuries pass, and the time comes when the Dweller in the Chalice is released and passes into cosmic evolution.

What are the permanent atoms? We are told that the genes in the human body are "hereditary determiners." They condition the development of an individual and the characteristics of the body. They are transmitted from generation to generation. Thus a gene is the living or permanent record, the nucleus of the body which is kept in successive generations, slightly changing and modifying according to the combination of the parents. The important point is that the gene contains a record of all past characteristics, and it will be the seed of the future body. Therefore the characteristics are not lost, although they do undergo changes due to the pressures of education, environment, daily living, and other influences.

This may be true in regard to the physical body, but what about the "hereditary determiners" of our emotional or mental bodies or states? In esoteric psychology they are called *permanent atoms*, *seeds*, or *stones*. We have six permanent atoms: one physical, one astral, two mental, one buddhic, and one atmic.[1] All our experiences on these levels or planes are registered in these permanent atoms or seeds, whether we are conscious or unconscious of the impressions.

The mental permanent atom registers all mental experiences, all mental impressions. In the emotional permanent atom all emotional experiences and impressions are registered. The physical permanent atom registers all physical level experiences and impressions. Our permanent atoms are like "memory cells" or storage rooms, in which is stored all that we have done or expressed and all that has been impressed upon our three levels of human endeavor.

All that we do physically and all that happens to us on the physical level enters into the atom or seed and forms a complex record. Even our "unconscious" experiences are registered in our physical, astral, and mental permanent atoms. The mental unit registers only when we are *not* in an "unconscious" state of mind. In our conscious states we are impressed largely by what we do, feel, and think, but in our "unconscious" moments we are impressed by what others do to us. The body eventually perishes, but the permanent atoms remain in the subtler vehicles. Then, when an individual begins to prepare for another physical expression, another birth, the physical permanent seed, working through the etheric centers, builds the etheric body according to

---

[1] One of the mental permanent atoms is called the "mental unit." Please see Saraydarian, Torkom, *Thought and the Glory of Thinking.*

the content of the seed, and around the etheric body the physical body is built.

The emotional permanent seed contains all our emotional reactions and impressions, conscious or unconscious. Long after we leave our physical body, our emotional body dissolves, but all our emotional life experiences are registered in the seed, and each registration is a conditioning factor in the seed.

The mental body lives longer than the physical and emotional bodies, but the time comes when it, too, goes through a process of disintegration. The permanent seed, however, contains all life experiences and impressions of the mental life. When the human ego prepares to return to physical plane life, the mental seed and the mental unit will vibrate; the building of the mental body will begin and proceed according to the recorded "notes" of the mental seed.

All three bodies are built in this way, according to the content of their permanent atoms or seeds. It must be stressed here that the bodies or vehicles are not built at once; the building is a gradual process. As the physical body achieves its maturity, the emotional body continues on toward its maturity; the mental body continues to develop even after the emotional body has reached its maturity.

Thus we have in our temple permanent records. They are like the "Book of God" in which everything is registered. Our whole life is primarily conditioned by the contents of these atoms or seeds. Not only do the physical, emotional, and mental bodies grow from these seeds, but also their future qualities, their potential, the possibilities for development are determined by the seeds.

We react, we are impressed, and we express according to the quality of our instruments. We cannot see a distant star with a toy telescope. We cannot play a symphony on a trumpet — we need other and refined instruments. The seeds furnish us with whatever we have put into them in the past, plus current experiences. In brief, they condition the range of our sensitivity, the range and quality of impressions, and the form and extent of our expression on the three levels of human endeavor. In the permanent atoms we find our complete past with its good and its bad records. All that we have been in the past is in those seeds, and from those seeds will grow our *future*. The past conditions the future. Thus we may say that our past and our future are in the seeds.

We cannot change the past, but we can change the future in the present by living a conscious life and planting good qualities in all three of our permanent seeds. Wrongs done intentionally on the mental plane in our past lives are there. If by some means they are stimulated and released, they will come down slowly, express themselves in our emotional and physical bodies, and affect our lives in many ways, with many forms of problems.

We must consider also that the contents of the seeds is not always negative. On the contrary, you will find in them the best that you gave to your family, your friends, and your nation. These are the seeds which condition your well-being upon the three planes. They are the flowers, the water, the food, and the energy for your long journey back to your True Self.

The degree of development of your three bodies is recorded in these seeds. When you are ready to take the three vehicles for your next life, they will continue in their development from the point where they left off in your past life. Suppose your physical body reached a level of twenty-five degrees in development. The next time it will start its development at the twenty-fifth degree level. The same holds true for the development of the emotional and mental bodies.

There is a very important point to be made here, however. The bodies start to grow from the point where they left off, providing the "dark records" do not interfere as they do in the following example. Suppose you had a strong and healthy body, but before you died, you committed a very cruel act which caused someone to suffer deeply. It is possible that in one of your future lives you will have a strong, healthy body and then develop a serious illness. Another result might be that you will be born physically defective. The same example may apply to the other vehicles. A wrong done in any vehicle extends simultaneously to the others, and the result may express itself through one or two or all three vehicles simultaneously.

When we use the terms "right" and "wrong," the terms "good" and "bad," they are *not* echoes of the words of religious fanatics or devotees. In every man there is a sense which we will call *conscience*. It is the conscience which a man uses to make judgments, but with this subject we will deal later.

The following example will further illustrate the way in which "dark records" work and affect us.

Suppose:

1. The mental permanent seed is filled with continuous lies.

2. The emotional permanent seed is full of fears and painful emotions.

3. The physical permanent seed is filled with records of pain and unconscious moments.

Suppose the subject dies physically, but the emotional permanent seed influence continues and conditions his life on the emotional plane. His contacts, his life on the subtle levels, his hatreds are all carried with him and become real to him. The cravings that were recorded in the seeds express themselves and take form; the man merges into a real labyrinth of glamors and illusions. Sooner or later the individual dies on the emotional plane and enters into the mental plane, but there he encounters the world of lies which he has previously built. All these thoughtforms of lies are objective things there, and he lives in a world of illusions and delusions. After a short rest, when the time is ripe, he returns again to the physical level life.[1] The physical body is rooted in the physical permanent seed. The switchboard for the blood system, the nervous system, and the glands is in the physical permanent atom. The person has a new physical body, but the latent causes of trouble are in the seeds. Whenever these records are stimulated by various means, the switchboard works automatically and mechanically. It begins to affect the other bodies according to the records there.

On the physical level, the permanent seeds work as follows. An event occurs which has a corresponding similarity in the records of the physical, emotional, and mental permanent atoms. These records vibrate through the Law of Resonance and project an energy which is translated as a mood, as an inner state, or as an attitude. The emotional counterpart and then the mental counterpart of that event tunes in with the physical records. The man is not aware of what is going on in his inner world, but his thinking, feeling, and acting are controlled; he has no power over himself. He has fears, new urges, new drives, the intensity of

---

1 Read *Cosmos in Man* by H. (Torkom) Saraydarian, Ch. XIX.

which is determined by the degree or depth of one body tuning in with another.

In the *New Testament* this information is presented in a symbolic parable concerning a debtor who was put into prison and not allowed to be released until he had paid all his debts. Esoterically, dark records are our debts. A lie is a debt; a theft is a debt; an act of cruelty is a debt. On the other hand, an act of love, service, and compassion is a credit, a seed of light.

The whole mechanism of cause and effect resembles a computer which, by the pressing of a few buttons, adds, subtracts, multiplies, and performs many other mathematical calculations. So it is with the human mechanism. We press a few buttons and the "machine" starts to work. In a short time the physical, emotional, and mental organs, the seeds, and the thoughts begin to work, and eventually the result appears. We do not see the activities of the thousands and thousands of cell-organs in the "machine," but we see the results, the effects.

Fortunately we are not computers, and there is a way to release and annihilate the dark contents of the seeds. All therapists are unconsciously directed to these sources of trouble. They often restimulate the contents of the seeds without being able to erase them, and the condition of the subject becomes worse. They sometimes lock the tiny doors, the channels through which the trouble wave is trying to exhaust itself. Just as our outer nature does not like to keep dead matter in the "bodies," so it is with our inner nature. It pushes such matter out to clear the channels and to purify the system. The energy that controls this eliminating process is symbolically called the *Fire in the Chalice*.

The cause of our psychosomatic illnesses is often found in the three permanent seeds simultaneously. Medical or psychological treatments often fail because they are used to eliminate only one part of the cause. For example, they may eliminate the physical cause, but this is only one part of the total cause in which all three bodies — the physical, emotional, and mental bodies — are involved simultaneously. An effective treatment will be directed to all vehicles or seeds so that the root of the problem is erased forever.

It is important to remember that our physical and emotional permanent seeds register all that happens to us in our "unconscious" moments because most psychosomatic problems have their origin in our emotional permanent seed. A great Master tells us:

> ... [The permanent atom] *serves as a nucleus for the distribution of force, for the conservation of faculty, for the assimilation of experience, and for the preservation of memory.*[1]

Beyond these permanent seeds there is another vessel which is called *The Chalice* or *The Lotus*.[2] This Chalice is formed of twelve different, fiery petals of energy, like the petals of a rose or tulip. Three of these petals form the core of the Chalice. In the average man, this Chalice is practically nonexistent, but as a man progresses on the Path, as he develops his knowledge, love, and sacrificial nature to some degree, a small bud appears, slowly grows, expands, and takes the form of a Chalice. In this Chalice are accumulated the real treasures of man. All achievements of the centuries, the essence of his love, true knowledge, and service are accumulated in the Chalice. A Master Mind says:

> ... *Of course, the treasury of the spirit is the Chalice, and that treasury also guards matter, because the powerful impulse of sacred Fire is laid in it.*[3]

> ... *From the Chalice issue all creative laws and in the Chalice are gathered all cosmic manifestations. Therefore, the enrichment of the Chalice affords realization of all cosmic plans. The foundations are gathered in the Chalice, and each energy can be a creator. Thus, creativeness is molded by the law of containment.*[4]

> *The center of the Chalice gathers all creative threads. Therefore, each cosmic vibration resounds within the Chalice.*[5]

> ... *As a synthesized center, the Chalice preserves the most essential, indescribable accumulations.*[6]

---

[1] Bailey, Alice A., *A Treatise on Cosmic Fire*, pp. 69-70.

[2] Saraydarian, Torkom, *The Hidden Glory of the Inner Man*, Ch. 12.

[3] Agni Yoga Society, *Infinity II*, par. 34.

[4] Ibid., par. 192.

[5] Ibid., par. 152.

[6] Agni Yoga Society, *Brotherhood*, par. 463.

... The Chalice is the repository of everything loved and precious. Sometimes, much that has been gathered into the Chalice remains concealed for entire lives, but if the concept of Brotherhood has been impressed upon the Chalice, it will resound in both joy and yearning in all lives.[1]

... Untold treasures are accumulated in the Chalice. The Chalice is one for all incarnations. The properties of the brain are subject to physical inheritance, but the properties of the Chalice will be determined by self-exertion.

In the Chalice lies the winged child....[2]

Jesus refers to this same fact when He says:

Make for yourselves purses which do not wear out and a treasure in heaven that does not run short, where the thief does not come near and moth does not destroy, for where your treasure is, there also will be your heart.[3]

Nicholas Roerich wrote:

In the cults of Zoroaster there is represented the Chalice with a flame. The same flaming Chalice is engraved upon the ancient Hebrew silver shekels of the time of Solomon and of an even remoter antiquity. In the Hindu excavations of the periods from Chandragupta Mourya, we observe the same powerfully stylized image. Sergius of Rodonega, laboring over the enlightenment of Russia, administered from the flaming Chalice. Upon Tibetan images, the Bodhisattvas are holding the Chalice blossoming with tongues of flame.

One may also remember the Druid Chalice of life. Aflame, too, was the Holy Grail. Not in imagination: verily by deeds are being interwoven the great teachings of all ages, the language of pure fire![4]

---

[1] Agni Yoga Society, *Brotherhood*, par. 464.

[2] Agni Yoga Society, *Agni Yoga*, par. 627.

[3] Luke 12:33-34

[4] Roerich, Nicholas, *Altai Himalaya*, p. 33.

According to your growth shall you yourself gather
pearls. By your own hands shall you match them. By
your own hands will you develop dynamic power.[1]

In esoteric literature, heaven is the mental plane where the
Chalice is found. The treasure is in the Chalice. It was symbolized
as the Holy Grail sought by the Knights of the Round Table. It is
in the Chalice that our true Guide exists, but He cannot express
Himself until the permanent atoms or seeds are cleansed, purified,
and the Chalice is in full bloom, filled with the elixir of life. The
purifying process is the result of the contemplation of the Solar
Angel within us. The Solar Angel vibrates in higher octaves, and
these notes act as purifying streams of energy which throw out all
that does not fit into the plan of the human soul. The act of meditation is a process of conscious assimilation of these energies.

The Chalice is built primarily of the substance of the Solar
Angel. The human soul makes itself ready to wear it as "the robe
of glory." When this body, the Chalice, or the "robe of glory" is
woven or built, the emotional sea disappears, and the astral body
disintegrates. Thus the man enters into direct communication with
the Intuitional Plane. Here lies the source of true and direct
knowledge. This was hinted at in one of the parables of Christ,
when He spoke about the man who had no proper garment to
attend the wedding feast. One may ask how the man who was re-
fused entered the feast.[2] Some people enter into the higher levels
of consciousness through the means of drugs and by breathing
exercises, but if they are not ready to wear the "robe of glory,"
they suffer in many ways.

In the *Bible* we are told about *grace*. Students of the *Bible* and
religion have had great difficulty in finding the real meaning of
grace, but it is very easy to understand the meaning of grace when
you know about the Chalice. *Grace is the essence, the content of*
the Chalice. It is your savings account, accumulated throughout
centuries, and when you are in dire distress, it meets your needs.
It saves you from great danger. It gives you light, illumination,
beauty, attractiveness, and energy. You wonder where these precious gifts came from. They came "by the grace of God" — from
the treasure of your Chalice. You may feel yourself to be unwor-

---

[1] Roerich, Nicholas, *Altai Himalaya*, p. 43.
[2] Matthew 22:11-14

thy of the great help you receive, but it is yours; it is paid to you from your savings account at the right time and in the right place.

The Chalice is the body of the Solar Angel. *Its voice is our conscience.* Nothing can enter into the Chalice which is against the divine Plan, Purpose, and Will. Everything in the three levels of human endeavor which is in accord and in tune with the essence of the Chalice gives you great inner joy, energy, and inspiration. Anything you do contrary to the essence of the Chalice makes you poor, miserable, and you feel the soft small voice of conscience warning you of your wrong action. The Chalice is the vessel of pure wisdom, of true love and knowledge, of beingness and realization.

The twelve petals are divided into four sections. The outermost three petals are called *petals of knowledge.* They extend their influence upon physical, emotional, and mental planes. The higher impressions of light-knowledge pass through the mental permanent seed to the knowledge petals, to the mental unit, to the generative organs on the mental plane, to the astral throat center, to the astral generative organs, to the etheric throat center, and to the etheric generative organs.

The second three petals are called *love petals*, on physical, emotional, and mental planes. The love energy passes through the intuitional permanent atom to the love petals of the Chalice, to the solar plexus on the mental plane, to the emotional permanent seed, to the heart center of the emotional plane, to the solar plexus on the emotional plane, to the heart center of the etheric body, and to the solar plexus.

The third three petals are called *petals of sacrifice*, each extending to the physical, emotional, and mental planes. The spiritual will passes through the atmic permanent atom to the petals of sacrifice, to the base of the spine on the mental plane, to the head center of the emotional plane, to the base of the spine on the emotional plane, to the physical permanent atom, to the head center of the etheric plane, and to the base of the spine where the Serpent Fire rests.

The three innermost petals are *the synthesis of knowledge, love, and sacrifice.*

The permanent seeds function in the substance aspect of an existence. The petals of the Chalice deal with the consciousness or psychical[1] aspect of the existence, while the innermost petals are expressions of pure Spirit.

The Fire in the Chalice cyclically stimulates the permanent atoms, and gradually the spirillae come into action. Their unfoldment brings new urges, new drives, new understanding, new growth, new creative currents, new motivations, and new impulses. As a result of these incoming energies, the bodies respond, and they become more sensitive to inner and outer impressions. These incoming energies may also create problems in the bodies if obstacles or friction exist.

The currents which come through the physical permanent seed are currents of regeneration, vitality, transmutation, and growth. These currents use the medium of the blood system via the head center and the base of the spine. The currents that come through the emotional permanent seed are currents of love, compassion, peace. These currents mainly reach the glandular system via the heart and solar plexus centers. The currents that come in through the mental permanent seed may be called inspiration, intuition, vision. They come down to the nervous system via the throat and sacral centers.

But very often these incoming streams of energies, these rays of power, inspiration, and love are obscured in the seeds themselves by the past accumulations, which are micro-records of painful experiences, fears, losses, wrong actions, negative emotions, wrong decisions, wrong thoughts, prejudices, superstitions, and so on.

Any time a man acts against the principles of love, freedom, beauty, and goodness, it throws a dark shadow into the seeds. These obstructions, hindrances, and distractions always color the incoming energies and condition them. When these higher energies pass through the moods or states of the mental and emotional atmospheres, they create different reactions.

A negative emotional state can poison the incoming energy, and a corresponding organ or system becomes influenced or affected. Thus many diseases appear on the physical level due to improper or negative reactions to the incoming energies. This fact was hinted at by a scientist, Edward Back, M.D., when he said,

---

[1] For further explanation see Saraydarian, Torkom, *The Science of Meditation*, pp. 220-225.

Bodily health is entirely dependent upon the state of mind.... Disease is a kind of consolidation of a mental attitude and it is only necessary to treat the mood of a patient and the disease will disappear.[1]

These moods or attitudes are the effects of the inner contents of the seeds. Sometimes they are thrown out to the surface by the incoming energies or impressions. People should not approach the inner Light in meditation or worship while negative or harmful thoughts are in their minds or while they are subject to poisonous moods.

In the past only the physical permanent seed was active. The physical permanent seed was responsible for mankind's body and for its reactions and behavior. At the present time in evolution, the emotional permanent seed is active along with the physical permanent seed. In the majority of people these two are conditioning the physical and emotional life expressions and problems of man.

Slowly the mental permanent seed is entering into the field and affecting the threefold vehicles of the human being. That is why gradually our mental problems are increasing, and we are building up a complicated system of response apparatus which is difficult to repair by physical or psychological means alone.

In the majority of cases our conscious mind is not aware of and has no control over the physical, emotional, and mental permanent atoms. We are usually polarized in the conscious mind or in the mental unit, which is a separate unit in the mental plane. Around the lower mental plane are found all our thoughtforms, daily experiences, and the center of our daily activities.

But gradually the unfoldment and the development of the Chalice takes place. The physical permanent atom becomes radioactive. Then the emotional permanent atom becomes radioactive. Then slowly the mental permanent atom is organized, unfolding the seven levels of the mental plane.

This unfoldment builds a bridge between the mental unit and the mental permanent atom, and eventually the physical, emotional, and mental permanent seeds come closer, and their electromagnetic auras fuse with one another. This is called *the stage of the soul-infused personality.* The permanent atoms gather themselves around the cup of the Chalice, and they transmit the

---

[1] Back, Dr. Edward, *The Medical Discoveries*, p. 57.

Goodness, the Righteousness, and the Love of the Chalice to their corresponding bodies.

As a result of this transmission, the bodies pass through some serious crises and then emerge into purity and into golden health. This is the *Transfiguration.* All physical level urges and drives are exhausted; the body is built up with higher physical plane substance. The emotional body is cleansed from all negative emotions and becomes a peaceful source of love and compassion. Then these two bodies come under the control of the mental unit, and the reactive mind is washed away completely. The bridge which unites the mental permanent atom with the mental unit becomes a radiant line of light, brings the treasures of the Chalice down to the human level, and opens an infinite horizon of wisdom to the conscious mind.

Now the human consciousness becomes a unit. It contains not only the consciousness of the seven physical sub-planes but also the consciousness of the emotional sub-planes and of the mental sub-planes. Such a man is called an *awakened man*, a man who does not sleep in any of his twenty-one sub-planes of the personality. He has continuity of consciousness day and night. The glory of the Chalice expresses itself more rhythmically as creative splendor, beauty, inspiration, leadership, invention, holiness, and so on, and the man becomes a shining light for future generations.

The glory of the Chalice becomes more and more radioactive. The Central Fire blazes forth, and one day when it reaches its summit of glory, the Chalice is set aflame and vanishes, and the dweller is released from the control of the wheel of life and death. He is a Master now. He has control over earth, water, fire, and air.

The Tibetan Master gives individual names to the nine petals of the Chalice. He calls the three KNOWLEDGE PETALS

1. Petal of Civilization
2. Petal of Culture
3. Petal of Illumination

When the first of the knowledge petals opened and unfolded on the physical level, "it brought a measure of light to the physical plane consciousness of humanity." This happened in Lemurian times, and a materialistic civilization came into being. In Atlantean times the second knowledge petal was unfolded on the astral plane, an emotional, religious culture was started, and man became creative. In the Aryan times the third petal opened on the mental plane and created mental illumination or knowledge. We are told that the teaching of Buddha helped to accelerate the opening of the knowledge petals.

These knowledge petals are formed by three types of substance:

1. the mental substance levels of 1, 2, 3
2. the mental substance levels of 4, 5, 6, 7
3. the mental substance found in matter itself

The *knowledge petals* correspond to the *Law of Service.*

The second tier of petals, the LOVE PETALS, are called:

1. Petal of Cooperation
2. Petal of Loving Understanding
3. Petal of Group Love

We are told that the teaching of Christ tremendously helped these petals to unfold and flood the heart of man with love energy.

It is evident that when the first petal of love opens on the physical plane, man becomes cooperative. The opening of the second petal on the astral plane makes him a man of loving understanding. In his presence you open your heart and bloom. Such a man becomes a great artist. The opening of the third love petal makes a man group-conscious. He lives and works for the group which we call humanity. Great humanitarians belong to this category.

These *love petals* correspond to the *Law of Magnetic Impulse.* As the six petals unfold and open, they will affect the petals of sacrifice and, with the help of the incoming new energies, these three petals will also be opened.

These three SACRIFICIAL or WILL PETALS are called:

1. Petal of Participation
2. Petal of Purpose
3. Petal of Precipitation

With the first petal unfolded, the individual or the group will actively participate in the Hierarchical Plan. All the members of the group will dedicate themselves to understand and work out the Plan. With the second petal unfolded, the individual or the group becomes united with the will of group disciples and touches the Purpose standing behind the Plan. When the third sacrificial petal is unfolded, the individual becomes one with the group of Initiates who work for the precipitation of the Plan. We are told that the *will* or *sacrifice petals* correspond to the *Law of Sacrifice.*

Again, the great words of Hermes, "As above, so below," apply. A Master of Wisdom explains that our Planetary Logos is a twelve petaled Lotus, a Chalice of energy, which sustains the planet. Our Solar System forms a twelve petaled Lotus on the Cosmic Mental Plane of the Solar Logos. Three of these Logoi represent the three knowledge petals, three others represent the three love petals, the remaining three are the will petals, the petals of sacrifice, and the innermost ones contain the Central Fires and the Jewel which is the Solar Logos Himself.

Om Mani Padme Hum

From this Chalice, the life of the Solar Logos pours down to all that exists in Its ring-pass-not, as the life-giving blood of the Cosmic Christ pours from the great Holy Grail. The petals are transmitters of energy. The Central Jewel in the Lotus is the source of highest energy in man. This energy is the life of the physical, emotional, and mental bodies. The petals open, and more life flows into the bodies. As a prism refracts light, producing a display of rainbow colors, so do the petals act upon this energy, changing it into the energy of knowledge, love, and sacrifice. The petals are not only transmitters and transformers of energy, they are also translators or interpreters of the Solar Angel.

The knowledge petals formulate energies and high impressions into ideas and thoughtforms. These ideas and thoughtforms are gradually absorbed by the higher mental and lower mental levels until the brain is able to register them.

The knowledge petals are connected closely to the physical permanent atom, to the throat center, and also to the generative organs. These petals act as a magnetic center to sublimate and transfer the lower energies into the corresponding higher centers. For example, sex energy is sublimated and transformed into the throat center in the mental body, thus producing a very high level creativity.

If there are aberrative contents in the mental unit, in the mental permanent atom, and in the lower mind in general, a state of turbulence is created in the mental sphere, and the flow of knowledge energy is turned into illusions. That is why in olden days the Masters urged the purification of the mind before transmitting higher ideas to the aspirants or opening the window of the knowledge petals.

Love petals are connected to the emotional permanent atom, heart center, and solar plexus. They transmit the energy of attraction, affinity, understanding, and, above all, intuition. When the energy of the love petals flows through the astral body and there meets negative emotions, it creates glamors. A glamor is a distortion of love energy by negative emotion.

Will petals bring will energy from atmic levels and make it available to the three personality levels as fuel for the activities of the bodies. They strengthen the illusions and glamors in the mental and emotional bodies and create *maya* in the etheric body *if* the etheric body is infected with illusions and glamors. There they create blind and uncontrolled urges and impulses which control etheric centers, creating in man an ever-burning desire for sex and material possessions. His dominating center in this case is the sex center. He is like a man caught in a whirlpool of maya, and all his thoughts, aspirations, and desires are controlled by the forces of that whirlpool. He is identified with his urges and with his mechanism. This identification is the greatest cause of maya.

The petals of will or sacrifice eventually dissipate the maya, creating an ever-progressing indifference and detachment and transmuting desire into aspiration, intention, and pure Will.

In the permanent atoms or seeds are built the patterns of our behavior, habits, and convictions, whether positive or negative; they are there and are inherited. They affect the genes of the cells, and through many lives these behavior patterns continue. When I mention inheritability of these behavior patterns, I do not refer to the traits passed down from generation to generation. Man inherits what he has built within himself at one time or another. This does not mean that there are no side effects and other influences on him through his parents and associates. There are, but the main source of his beingness is himself, as recorded in the seeds and stored in the Chalice.

In cases of hypnotic trance one can see how a subject awakens if a suggestion is against the pattern of principles in his seeds. At that time an electric charge comes out of the entire unit and reestablishes the consciousness, rejecting the suggestion. Most hypnotic healings are very dangerous. They block the drainage of a wound which is in one of the permanent seeds. Medicine often does the same thing. With paper walls it blocks the presence of a fire. It often succeeds in putting out the flames, but the embers are there, and they will flare up at another time, through a different vehicle, in a different form, and perhaps in a future life.

If a healing is temporary and occurs in one vehicle only, it is not true healing. It is not a true healing if the healer cures a patient for a Friday only, or for a week only but forgets the coming years, centuries, and lives through which the individual will pass. If the hidden, true cause of sickness cannot be reached, it is better in the long run to leave the expression of the illness free. Let it exhaust its resources. Let nature clean its own house. Once the seed is truly cleansed, the patient is immune to a recurrence of the ailment.

Is there a way to approach the seeds and purify them, cleanse them from the past accumulations, engrams, and records? Some of the master minds know the technique of how to reach them and exhaust the negative contents. "Your sins are forgiven," said Christ, and the man was cured. This sentence is an outer symbol of a complex inner technique.

All dark records in the seeds are sins, something done against Love, Righteousness, Beauty, and Law in the past, perhaps centuries ago, and the record is still there. As long as that record or debt is not erased, it will express itself eventually.

Besides the dark records in the seeds there is also much static in our minds. This static not only interferes with the inflow of the Light from the Chalice and from the Spark, but sometimes even cuts off the current of energy coming to the vehicles and organs.

What is this static? Static is like dust-devils which are formed by opposing currents of air. They are what in common language is called *sin*. A so-called sin is committed by a particular part of the man, by the power of the resistance of that part. But it does not cause static until the opposing current is there. The opposing current is the moral code of fear that the individual has incorporated from his family, his readings, his church, religion, government, or from his way of thinking. These are all impressed in the seeds, and these impressions resist everything that does not agree with them. The contents of the seeds act here as a judge or as an automatic rejector, refusing everything that is against the implanted conduct.

The conscious mind can play a role in solving these "sins," creating buffers in difficult cases. Some of the so-called sins are the result of superstitions and man-made, obsolete codes of behavior. In this case, the "mind" can solve them and create peace in the inner space of the mental plane and reestablish the outflow and inflow of mental, emotional, or intuitional currents. The conscious mind can do this if it is disciplined enough to detach its thinking process from the common thought or from the common code and think in a wider space and periphery, but always tending to the highest good.

If the thinking of the man is in accord with the Fire of the Chalice, the man is released into freedom more and more. But if his limited thinking is creating veils and buffers, then the lower life will gain control, and the progress of the man will be delayed for centuries. He needs then to unveil himself, step by step, from the nets he has woven and is caught in, creating a real prison for himself. The Tibetan Master says in *A Treatise on Cosmic Fire*:

> ... *When mind becomes unduly developed and ceases to unite the higher and the lower, it forms a sphere of its own. This is the greatest disaster that can overtake the human unit.*[1]

The permanent seeds are not only containers of our activities or impressions on the three planes, but also they are seeds, each of which develops its corresponding vehicle.

Each permanent atom has seven spirillae. It takes centuries to develop these spirillae. When the seventh spirilla is active, it contains only very rough impressions and builds a body corresponding to that level of vibration. When the third (counting from above) spirilla is active, the body is of a higher order, built by finer substances, and correspondingly the content of the seed is more complex, more inclusive, and has higher ranges of impres-

---

[1] Bailey, Alice A., *A Treatise on Cosmic Fire*, p. 261.

sions. Only after building our bodies with the third level substance can there be a true channel of Light, Love, and Power for the Inner Man. When the first spirilla is active, the man is divine and one with the Will of God.

Each spirilla is connected with the corresponding sub-plane of that particular plane. Seven spirillae serve for seven mental sub-planes, seven for the emotional sub-planes, and seven for the physical sub-planes. As was stated, the higher planes of any vehicle become active when the higher spirillae of the seeds are active.

The contents of the Chalice becomes richer and of higher quality to the extent that the spirillae of the seeds become active and the corresponding sub-planes are formed and organized. Even the form, the color, and the radiation of the Chalice become more beautiful and more luminous, and proportionately the horizon of the field of your consciousness becomes larger and larger. When it is fully developed, you can see nine flames as petals of a rose, forming the Chalice. Therein are observed three electric-blue flames which eventually will burn the Chalice and release its fiery *essence*.

If the student followed the Path to the "Blue Peak," he is quite able now to detach himself from his physical body and from its problems, from his emotional body and its problems, and especially from his mental body and its problems. He now has a clear idea that he is *not* the body, the emotions, and the mind, but something beyond these. He is a man now who is climbing toward what is called his *Self*. As he climbs, he sees that in a material sense he diminishes, but in a spiritual sense he increases; he becomes richer and richer, and proportionately his horizon becomes unlimited.

As we go toward matter, we become exclusive; as we go toward the Spirit, we become inclusive. To go toward matter means to go into deeper and deeper sleep. To go toward Spirit means to progressively awaken to one's own Self and to be free. The freedom is attained when the Jewel in the Lotus is released. As the Lotus unfolds, more freedom is attained, until the Jewel is released and total freedom is achieved.

Uneven unfoldment of the Lotus may occur. This causes temporary revolts and license. But as the unfoldment proceeds, man balances himself and enters into the real Path of spiritualization, of freedom.

The same thing happens to humanity itself. True freedom for humanity will be achieved as the great Lotus unfolds itself, and the Jewel starts to radiate.

Chapter XIII

THE CONSCIENCE

There are two kinds of inner suggestions which can be confused with the power we call *conscience*.

1. We have inherited patterns of thinking, patterns of urges or drives, which were built throughout our past lives.

2. We have the contents of the Chalice, which is pure wisdom collected through the experiences of our past lives.

True conscience is the voice of the Soul, the "Voice of the Silence," which is the standard vibration of the Solar Angel within us. *This is the true conscience.* The others are inner suggestions, conditioned by time and space and by past lives and experiences. They may fall short of meeting the need in any given situation. But the voice of the Solar Angel is unconditioned and all-wise. It is unconditioned by the past, by the present, and even by our future expectations and man-made dreams. It is the pure, clear-cut Voice of Truth, a voice which is in accord with the fundamental laws of our universe.

When a man has no conscience, it means that the wall between the lower and the higher man is growing thicker and thicker. This wall can be an etheric, emotional, or mental wall in the form of glamor, maya, or illusion. When this is true, the Solar Angel cannot communicate with the unit of consciousness or with the human soul. The man may become a victim of his animal urges, his selfishness and hatred, or even of his accumulated hypnotic suggestions. In extreme cases his behavior may become so bestial that the Solar Angel leaves him. There is no hope for such a man for long cycles. This is the greatest tragedy that can overtake a human being.[1]

---

[1] Saraydarian, Torkom, *The Hidden Glory of the Inner Man*, Chs. 3 and 6.

Conscience can be developed by using its "still small voice" in our everyday affairs. It can be a light on our path and, eventually, the golden thread leading us to our Home.

Chapter XIV

THE SEVEN AND
THE SEVENS

PART I. THE PHYSICAL, EMOTIONAL, AND MENTAL PLANES

We are actually the "I"s, living within the bodies, like a sun at the center of the universe; we are the inner Sparks. We become conscious of ourselves on the planes through which we try to express ourselves. Like a beam of light, we feel ourselves to be in the object or in the substance we strike or pass through. Whatever plane we strike, there our consciousness of *being* is. The Light of the Spark increases toward the center and decreases toward the periphery. Development of consciousness means the enlargement of the field of light in the mental substance where the beam of the light of intellect of the soul hits.

Our consciousness develops from the physical plane world, through the emotional and mental worlds, passing to the plane of Intuition, to the plane of peace, and on to the plane of freedom. The Intuitional Plane is called the *plane of bliss*. In the Ageless Wisdom the plane of peace is known as the plane of Nirvana, the Nirvanic or Atmic Plane. It is the plane of Spirit, the plane of peace. The plane of freedom is the Monadic Plane. It is the plane where Self-cognition is a fact.

- On the physical plane we cannot see ourselves except as bodies.
- On the emotional plane we see distorted pictures of ourselves.
- On the mental plane we catch glimpses of ourselves.
- On the Intuitional Plane we see clearly, but we are not yet ourselves. There is still the mirror.
- On the Atmic Plane, the plane of Spirit or peace, we begin to be ourselves.

- On the Monadic Plane, the plane of freedom, we become Ourselves — a Spark, a glorious Spark in the fiery space of existence.

This achievement of being Oneself is often called *The Blue Peak* amid the high mountains. In ancient literature it is called *The Father Experience* or the experience of talking with God. Moses climbed the mountain and, passing the limit of human experience behind the clouds, came in contact with the Divine and brought back the Laws to the valley. The mountain he climbed was the Path leading to his Real Self. The Presence with which he spoke was his Real Self, the Father.

When asked about the Father, Christ answered,

The Father and I are one.

He was continuously Himself.

The Path is also known as *Jacob's Ladder* on which the materialized spirit is climbing and raising himself toward his spiritualization, toward his essence of Fatherhood. It is interesting that the top of the ladder is "reaching into heaven," to the infinite, or to the level of absolute freedom. On it the "Angels of God" ascend and descend.[1]

On the following page is an illustration of the ladder of involution and evolution, the arc of descent and the arc of ascent. The successive levels represent the rates of vibration or the states of consciousness, the states of being.

A few words of explanation:

a) On each plane the number 1 is the logoic or divine note of that plane; number 5 is the mental substance, the mental note, and so on.

b) You will note that the physical plane mind does not have the same quality of light as the fifth sub-plane of the Intuitional Plane, though they have the same key and the same notes in different octaves.

c) On the evolutionary arc, the Divine Spark first expresses Itself through the physical level. This expression is physical level consciousness. Gradually It develops emotional level consciousness and so on up the ladder.

---

[1] Genesis 28:12

COSMIC PHYSICAL PLANE

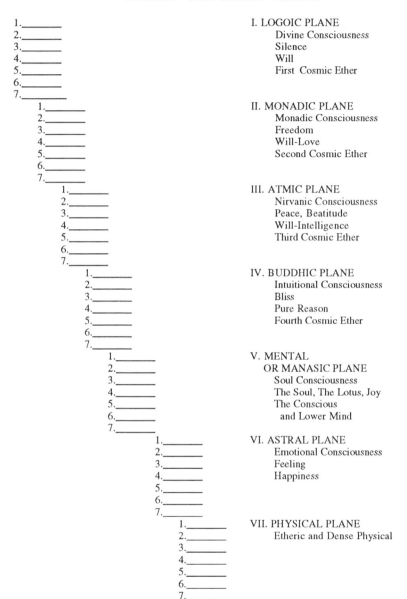

1._____
2._____
3._____
4._____
5._____
6._____
7._____

I. LOGOIC PLANE
Divine Consciousness
Silence
Will
First Cosmic Ether

1._____
2._____
3._____
4._____
5._____
6._____
7._____

II. MONADIC PLANE
Monadic Consciousness
Freedom
Will-Love
Second Cosmic Ether

1._____
2._____
3._____
4._____
5._____
6._____
7._____

III. ATMIC PLANE
Nirvanic Consciousness
Peace, Beatitude
Will-Intelligence
Third Cosmic Ether

1._____
2._____
3._____
4._____
5._____
6._____
7._____

IV. BUDDHIC PLANE
Intuitional Consciousness
Bliss
Pure Reason
Fourth Cosmic Ether

1._____
2._____
3._____
4._____
5._____
6._____
7._____

V. MENTAL
OR MANASIC PLANE
Soul Consciousness
The Soul, The Lotus, Joy
The Conscious
and Lower Mind

1._____
2._____
3._____
4._____
5._____
6._____
7._____

VI. ASTRAL PLANE
Emotional Consciousness
Feeling
Happiness

1._____
2._____
3._____
4._____
5._____
6._____
7._____

VII. PHYSICAL PLANE
Etheric and Dense Physical

"Jacob is sleeping here on the rock."

d) When It reaches the level of monadic awareness, It sees Itself *as It is;* beyond that line, the Spark steps into Its Divinity.

e) On Its journey the Inner Spark, the Monad, comes in contact with the Life or with existence through all Its vehicles of expression. It recognizes the physical plane through Its body and senses. It recognizes the subtle world (the astral or emotional world) through Its emotional or subtle body. It recognizes the mental world through Its mental plane or mental mechanism. It does the same with the higher planes. All planes are like bridges between the individual and the universal. Thus It builds channels between the individualized one and the ocean of Divinity.

f) Each plane has four functions:

Reception

Assimilation

Transmutation

Expression

Reception means to take in "food" — the impressions, ideas, light, and cosmic waves.

Assimilation means to make these impressions, ideas, and the light ready to serve the goal of the unit of consciousness at a given level.

Transmutation is the elevation of this assimilated energy to a higher plane for use in building the mechanism of contact upon that plane.

Expression means to live, to radiate out, to work according to the Plan upon the given level and in the given cycle. Expression is service.

Here we must remember that this ladder of achievement is not yet complete. We have at this stage of human development only the three lower planes: the physical, emotional, and mental planes. The other planes or steps are not organized yet. Some people are not even really conscious on the emotional and mental planes. They think they are. They call their feelings or emotions their emotional world. They call their thoughts their own mental world.

But these feelings, emotions, and thoughts are nothing but physical plane reactions and responses.

To be active and awake in the subtle world, as we are in the physical world, requires long range discipline and education. The same is true for the mental world, because as life on the sea is different from life on land and in the air, so life varies in the physical, emotional, and mental worlds as well as in higher worlds. These higher worlds should be built by our own "hands and feet," by our true and sincere labor.

As we have a digestive system for the purpose of building our physical body, our higher bodies have a similar system which builds the corresponding bodies. Our real food is of seven kinds. We have physical, emotional, mental, buddhic, atmic, monadic, and divine foods. We cannot receive atmic food with our physical digestive system. To receive atmic food we must build the corresponding digestive system and the needed mechanisms of transmutation and expression.

The Monad, in Its descent to physical existence, envelops Itself in the substance of each successive plane. But this does not mean that these substances are fully developed mechanisms of communication between the Monad and the vast sea of existence on the various planes. The different substances which the Monad has around him — such as the atmic, buddhic, mental, and emotional substances — are like raw materials with which the unfolding consciousness will gradually build the mechanism of communication. For example, an engineer builds a radio set with the materials he has within his reach.

The process of building starts with the seventh sub-plane of the seventh plane, the lowest. Suppose we have a body built up to the fifth sub-plane, but gradually, through the right diet, discipline, and fresh air, we bring in a quantity of fourth sub-plane substance, then third sub-plane substance. Eventually we will have a body which is built of the highest sub-plane substance of the physical plane. Whenever you strike a note on a sub-plane, the corresponding notes on the higher sub-planes receive a mild touch. The next succeeding plane begins to come under the control of a conscious man when the lower plane reaches its fourth sub-plane substance, as shown in the following diagram:

V.	1	2	3	4	5	6	7				*Mental*
VI.		1	2	3	4	5	6	7			*Emotional*
VII.			1	2	3	4	5	(6	7)[1]		*Physical*

When the lowest plane (VII) is active with its fourth sub-plane substance, the Inner Lord begins to control the seventh sub-plane of the next higher plane (VI). When the first sub-plane of the lowest plane (VII) is reached, the Inner Lord begins to have conscious control over the fourth sub-plane of the emotional plane (VI), and over the seventh sub-plane of the mental plane (V), and so on. The key to the initiations is hidden in this process. For example, at the Third Initiation, when man has developed the highest substance of the astral plane, the Buddhic Plane starts to penetrate the astral plane with its light; then gradually buddhic light replaces the astral plane and becomes "the main instrument of sentience."

When the mind has developed the substance of the first sub-plane, the Will of the Monad which is expressing itself through the Atmic Plane begins to flood the mental plane with its power, impressing the mind with cosmic Laws of Sacrifice and Synthesis. Here we have a twofold process:

1. The lower opens to the higher.

2. The higher, becoming active, brings in more energy from the center of Light, Love, and Power to the lowest planes. The resonance between the corresponding sub-planes forms the future bridge, which in the Ageless Wisdom is called the *Antahkarana* or the *Rainbow Bridge*. When your bodies are built with the first sub-plane substance of all seven planes, the Inner Lord shines forth and expresses Itself as living Light and Fire, as a great Beauty.

Above the fourth sub-plane the person has more energy under his command, but he cannot use this energy constructively unless he has developed a *sense of responsibility*, which is the result of the energy of the Soul's love acting upon his mental plane. One who builds a wall between the higher mind (sub-planes 1, 2, 3) and the lower mind (sub-planes 4, 5, 6, 7) gradually enters into the left-hand path and cannot receive the Love and Light of higher

---

[1] No human being uses these lower kinds of substances as his body.

planes. A brother of darkness stops his progress on the ladder of evolution for a while and imprisons himself on the lower mental planes, where he finds many kinds of illusions and delusions. It is good to know that nature has its own safeguards, and that a dark brother cannot directly bridge the gap between the higher and lower minds.

The ancients speak of the *gunas*. Guna means a quality or a characteristic. There are three gunas:

a) "The quality of purity, truth, goodness, or substantial reality is *sattva*."

b) "The quality of activity, passion or desire is *rajas*."

c) "The quality of quiescence, darkness, ignorance, inertia, or immobility is *tamas*."[1]

When our bodies or planes are built with the seventh and sixth sub-plane substances, they are considered tamasic or *slow* and filled with inertia on their own plane and in regard to their range of relationships. When bodies are built with the fifth and fourth sub-plane substances, they become rajasic, full of activity, passion, desire, and so on. When bodies are built with third, second, and first sub-plane substances, they become sattvic; they are pure, rhythmic, and radioactive. Tamas means one thing on the physical plane and something quite different on the Atmic Plane. Plane VII, the lowest, is rhythmic if it is built of third, second, or first sub-plane substances.[2]

The highest substance in the body is of the first sub-plane, but in relation to the plane above, the first sub-plane substance corresponds to the fourth sub-plane substance. In its relationship to the fifth plane (V), it corresponds to the seventh sub-plane of plane V. Seen from plane V, the seventh sub-plane of the fifth plane (V), the fourth sub-plane of the sixth plane (VI) and the first sub-plane of the seventh plane (VII) are on the same line. Thus it is clear that the consciousness extends from one plane to another, but when it passes to a higher plane, it comes from sattva and enters into tamas; then it passes into the higher rajas, sattva, and so on to succeeding levels.

---

[1] See the *Bhagavad Gita*, translated by H. (Torkom) Saraydarian, Ch. 14.

[2] Please refer to *The Science of Meditation*, Ch. XIV for more information about the gunas and sub-planes.

The first sub-plane of each plane is the key of that plane. All vibrations of the sub-planes must be tuned to that keynote. The note of the first sub-plane must dominate the rest. Gradually one distinct note will radiate out of the whole plane, and we will have seven clear notes on seven planes. Again, at that time, plane VII and plane VI will be spiritually tamasic; planes V and IV will be rajasic; planes III, II, and I will be sattvic. In a similar way our consciousness will be tamasic if only planes VII and VI are developed. It becomes rajasic if plane V is developed; starting from plane IV and moving to planes III, II, and I, it becomes sattvic, in harmony with the Heart of the Universe.

What are the proper foods for the bodies or planes?

To develop our *physical* body or plane, we need etheric and physical foods which are pure food, clean air, and discipline.

To develop and transmute the *emotional* body or plane, we must try to assimilate beauty in music, in word, in color, in motion, and we must express positive instead of negative emotions.

To develop our *mental* body or plane, we must try to assimilate knowledge, think clearly, face problems as they are, and allow special times for reflection and meditation.

The *Intuitional Plane* is developed through being nourished by love and compassion and by thinking in unity and synthesis. Each time you perform an act of love, you provide nourishment for the intuitional body. The Intuitional Plane develops mainly through meditation on symbols or in symbolic thinking.[1] The highest joy on this plane can be experienced only through love. Only people on this plane can understand the true meaning of brotherhood.

The *Atmic* or Nirvanic Plane is built with will energy and nourished by true acts of will.

We enter into the *Monadic Plane* through acts of freedom, through acts of pure detachment and sacrifice. After the consciousness enters into this plane of freedom, the horizon of the omniscient, omnipotent, and omnipresent ocean of reality dawns upon our being and silence reigns.

Man is the microcosm and the Great Existence is the macrocosm. The Great Existence has corresponding planes called

---

[1] Saraydarian, Torkom, *Cosmos in Man*, pp. 101-104, 263-264; *The Science of Meditation*, pp. 167-185.

Cosmic Planes; for example, Cosmic Physical Plane, Cosmic Astral Plane, and so on. Our forty-nine sub-planes are taken as a whole from the Cosmic Physical Plane of the seven Cosmic Planes. In developing our sub-planes, we touch, slightly, the corresponding Cosmic Planes.

Up to this point we have gained some knowledge of the physical, emotional, and mental planes. Our next concern is the Intuitional or Buddhic Plane.

PART II. THE BUDDHIC PLANE

On the Buddhic Plane we have mindlessness. There is no reasoning, but there is greater light of intelligence. As the pilgrim enters into this zone of beingness, he gradually leaves behind the familiar pictures, concepts, or images of himself. He also leaves behind his modes of reasoning, deduction, or induction. He begins to *know* through direct knowledge because he sees the causal world with its effects.

Sometimes, in rare moments, we live upon that level called *intuition*, sensing things obscure and remote. The next moment our "intuition" falls to the mental level, into the river of rationalization, and we resume our picture-making process. On the intuitional level our consciousness, which is much greater than on the mental plane, has now become *awareness*[1], because the Real Self, which is the light of consciousness, is expressing Itself through a finer atmosphere in which there are fewer particles of "dust, moisture, or smoke." Here the man acts chiefly with great, universal ideas. The world, the Universe, and Cosmos are not separated units for him but parts of a great whole in which there are very close relationships. Here he sees for the first time the unity of all things, and the sense of separateness vanishes. On this level he begins to sense the true needs of other people and the ways to meet those needs. It is from the Intuitional Plane that ideas stream forth. Ideas are strongly charged blueprints, which carry with them great energy.

The Solar Angel, Whose nature is Light, illumines both the Intuitional Plane and the mental plane so that man, focussed in the mental plane, has the opportunity to grasp ideas, bring them down, assimilate them, and bring them into expression. The ideas

---

[1] Read Saraydarian, Torkom, *Cosmos in Man*, Ch. X.

gradually come down from the higher mental to the lower mental plane. There they are organized and materialized according to the need of the time, the capacity of the man, and his radius of influence.

The lower sub-planes of the Intuitional Plane are the sources of divine archetypes or divine symbols (divine algebra) through which the Lord of the Plane contacts the lower world. The Lord of the mental plane enters into the intuitional world by contacting and meditating upon the symbols, the great archetypes, coming from the intuitional level. As we advance to the higher levels, even the symbolism, the divine algebra, ceases and a higher form of contact which has no limitation for the buddhic consciousness begins.

When we speak of the "heart" and the "direct knowledge of the heart," we are speaking of the intuitional awareness, which is the dispeller of all illusion.

> *What is the treasure of the heart?... consonance with the Cosmic Consciousness when the heart, besides its own rhythm, even partakes in the cosmic rhythm.*[1]

The Intuitional Plane is the door to cosmic consciousness. We are told that the Masters act and live on that plane. It is the plane of true love, which we call compassion. The man who functions within this plane cannot criticize or hurt any being.

In Oriental psychology the mind is called the "Slayer of the Real." The *Real* comes from the Intuitional Plane, but as soon as it reaches the mental plane, it is changed through rationalization if the mind is of low order. The story is told of Mulla Nasreddeen who, upon observing a stork, exclaimed, "This does not look like a bird. Let me make it a bird." He shortened the beak and the legs of the stork; then said, "Now you are a real bird. Fly!" — but the bird was dead!

So many wonderful ideas spring from the Intuitional Plane, but they are distorted on the mental plane because of deep-seated fears, prejudices, illusions, and separative thinking. For this reason a man cannot use the Intuitional Plane until he purifies the mental plane, builds it with the highest substances, develops it in the right direction, and uses it to further the Divine Plan. He must then detach himself from all that he knows and all that he has.

---

[1] Agni Yoga Society, *Hierarchy*, par. 106.

This was explained in the *New Testament* with the parable of the rich man:

> *A man drew near and said, "O Good Teacher, what is the best thing I should do to have life eternal?"*
>
> *Jesus said to him, "Why do you call me good? There is no one who is good except the one God, but if you want to enter into life, obey the commandments."*
>
> *The young man said, "I have obeyed all these from my boyhood. What do I lack?"*
>
> *Jesus said, "if you want to be perfect, go and sell your possessions and give them to the poor, and you will have a treasure in heaven; then follow me."*
>
> *When the young man heard these words he went away, sad for he had great possessions.*
>
> *And Jesus said to his disciples: '"It is easier for a rope to go through the eye of a needle, than for a rich man to enter into the Kingdom of God."*[1]

Here Jesus was showing the real Path into the first great expansion of consciousness. The richness of the mental plane must be left behind to enter into the Kingdom of God, into the Intuitional Plane. We are told that the Buddhic Plane is Christ consciousness, through which man passes to the Father, God consciousness. Before a man can pass to the next plane, the Atmic Plane, he must first organize his intuitional body.

We are told that every cell, every atom in the human mechanism has a nucleus of light. This light increases and becomes more radioactive as man goes deeper into the intuitional world. This is the basic cause of the phenomenon we call Transfiguration. For a longer or shorter period of time the nuclei of light of the three bodies radiate under the impact of the Soul and the intuitional light. This phenomenon is partially recorded in mystic literature, and we find in the life of Moses that the people veiled his face because of the strong radiance coming from him.

The man climbing "the Blue Peak" does not remain on the Intuitional Plane. He passes to the next plane, the Atmic Plane.

---

[1] Matthew 19:16, 17, 20, 21, 22, 24

PART III. THE NIRVANIC OR ATMIC PLANE

> *... the will is that divine aspect in man that puts him en rapport with and then controlled by divine purpose, intelligently understood in time and space and implemented by the soul as the expression of loving application.*[1]

Great Sons of Light are consciously active on the Atmic Plane. It is the source from which they shed the true light all over the world. It is called the *plane of pure intelligence*, or the plane of gold-light, of pure reason. It is the plane where the Self reveals Itself.

The Buddhic Plane is the fourth cosmic ether. The Atmic Plane is the third cosmic ether, known in esoteric literature as the *spiritual plane*. We are told that it is on this plane that a man hears the note of the Logos via his head center. According to a Master of Wisdom, Christ now works on the Atmic Plane. From there He pours out the atmic light upon the glamors of the emotional plane, bringing about some purification of that plane. On the Atmic Plane the individual becomes fully group conscious, while at the same time keeping his own separate identity. True will energy begins to express itself when man functions upon this plane. The agent of expression of this true, spiritual, Atmic Will is the head center which must be developed and used.

When the inner Spark expresses Itself through the Atmic Plane, the energy thus produced is called *will energy*. This energy expresses and unfolds the purpose of inner Divinity. As the sun radiates its light, heat, and life, so does the true will energy radiate and unveil the hidden Divinity in man, as intention, purpose, will-to-good, and as guidance toward perfection.

Will is the current of life itself. It is the expression of man's essential Divinity, of his inner Real Self. When this Real Self begins to express Itself and to work out Its purpose, we say that a man has willpower. He is truly spiritual when his consciousness functions on the Atmic Plane. This starts after the Third Initiation. The first sign of a man who is beginning to unveil his own face, to meet himself, is a growing willpower. It is the most solid, most

---

[1] Bailey, Alice A., *Discipleship in the New Age*, Vol. II, p. 298.

dependable bridge upon which he can walk toward the source of energy.

Willpower is the motivating agent, or dynamo, behind all our *conscious* activities. It increases its influence as the vehicles are purified and false "leaders" or "commands" are annihilated. It increases in proportion to our consciousness or awareness, but later on we find that willpower goes even beyond consciousness. It is closest to our essence. One of the Masters tells us,

Will, in reality, is life itself.

When we are free from our glamors and illusions or our hundreds of mechanical influences and impressions, we discover that it is the will that uses all our physical, emotional, and mental mechanisms. On lower levels it often happens that our illusions and glamors are strengthened by the power of the will, thereby increasing the suffering of the world. Willpower is always present, but it needs mechanisms through which to express itself. The best mechanisms are our higher vehicles which are built and organized with their own centers and networks of energies.

To distinguish the real will from the false will, man must be able to observe the forces or energies behind all his physical, emotional, and mental activities. This observation will reveal to him whether he is using the will energy consciously or whether it is being controlled by inner urges, drives, or commands. If a man has willpower, he is a man of self-determination, a man who is his Real Self, who acts through the physical, emotional, and mental bodies, expressing the part of the Plan he has to work out. This plan is a small part or portion of the purpose toward which all creation is striving. Willpower is always there as an electrical power in the body, and man does all that he does with willpower. But this is not the will of the Self. It is important to understand this fact. Here the will of the Self is used by the responses of the personality to outer stimuli; its reaction is mostly automatic.

The central Will, the Self, has seven stations on which to use the will. On each plane the first sub-plane is the reservoir of the will for the lower sub-planes. Any activity of any sub-plane draws its fuel from the first sub-plane. This energy is colored with the color or tone of the given plane. If the substances of the sub-planes are highly developed, they can draw more energy from the first sub-plane; if there are defects in the sub-planes, the energy from the first sub-plane creates psychological or physical "ulcers." Clean and refined sub-planes act more goal-fittingly and more in harmony with the central energy; this condition means that a man is living closer to the Central Fire.

The will energy has yet another quality. In the process of its unfoldment, it expresses itself as strength in the body and as strong urges, desires, aspirations, attention, concentration, intention, dedication, synthesis, and sacrifice. Later it ceases to be the expression of an individual and becomes the expression of a family, a nation, humanity. It becomes more mysterious; it becomes the expression of the Plan behind the Universe and then the expression of the Purpose of the Creative Power. Thus we come to the conclusion that the will has a very close relationship with the Creator and with the essence of creation. Detachment, renunciation, selflessness, purity, freedom, and discipline are all expressions and activities of the will. It is the sword of the Inner Lord, Who has carried on the age-long battle to purify His vehicles of expression, until He has become able to work out the Purpose placed in His heart by the Creator. A Master of Wisdom says:

> ... When the blazing light of the Monad is focussed directly upon the personality, via the antahkarana ... it produces a blazing fire which burns up all hindrances in a steady, sequential process.[1]

Freedom is another goal of the will. All the steps to the Self are steps toward the essential freedom of the will. To develop the will, we must gradually reject all false wills of our personality vehicles and all influences that come through them from different sources, higher or lower. Thus when our mechanism is free from the false masters that often use it, and when the Inner Lord completely controls the mechanism, the personality, the man transforms and becomes Himself. As the apostle says:

> Now we see through a mirror, darkly, but then face to face. Now I know in part, but then shall I know even as also I am known.[2]

The mirror is the personality; we are looking into the world of matter, emotions, and thoughts, forming an image of ourselves through our reactions and responses. This image and the mirror

---

[1] Bailey, Alice A., *The Rays and the Initiations*, p. 30.
[2] I Corinthians 13:12

must be left behind, and we must come face to face with our True Self. We are the sons of God, but we are going to be something else in the future. This will happen when our Inner Self unveils Itself. At that time we will become our Self because we will see our Self as we were and as we are. The shadow will disappear into Reality. To reach this point, we have a long, long way to walk, a way that continues through the days and nights of our lives and passes through hills, high mountains, and deep valleys.[1]

The purpose of all previous exercises given in the earlier chapters was to try to awaken our will and use it. Detachment, demobilization, harmlessness — all are techniques to use will energy. We cannot progress toward ourselves very much by learning, accumulating knowledge, or even by observation until we develop our will. This means that to use our will is to change more and more into our Real Selves, to find our pure Being and to unveil, express, and radiate it, extinguishing the dim candles of our personality in the light of the Real Self.

There is an old saying: "The best rulers are those who know how to obey." What connection has obedience to the will? If we obey a very advanced man, consciously following his instructions and orders, it will develop our will, just as a battery is charged by a new or stronger battery. Those people who became famous rulers of great countries, having lived very difficult lives, were equipped with real discipline — physically, emotionally, and mentally. This discipline was a process of obedience to the need, to the cycle and time, to responsibility, to the inner call, and to their leaders and teachers. Their hardships developed willpower because the hardships called forth the best within them to overcome obstacles on the path of their development.

In the old schools, convents, or monasteries people lived very hard lives under strict rules. The purpose of such discipline was to cultivate or to evoke the willpower of man. For the same purpose man submitted himself to conscious suffering, renunciation, fasting, and abstinence. Under all these conditions people were trying to develop their willpower to control their physical, emotional, and mental natures. Later, however, people adopted these disciplines as their goals rather than as a means to develop willpower consciously.

---

[1] See Saraydarian, Torkom, *Cosmos in Man*, Ch. III.

Through sublimation and purification of the physical, emotional, and mental vehicles we enter into buddhic light and beyond. Proportionally we increase the flow of will energy into our vehicles, until our awareness functions entirely on the Atmic Plane. At this stage our emotional glamors and astral fog completely disappear because essentially our emotional plane is a distorted expression of the Atmic Plane. Hence our emotions — negative or positive — control our life more than our thoughts for a long period of time.

Total cleaning or purification of the astral plane is achieved through the "advancing light" of the Atmic Plane. When the Atmic Plane is fully developed, the will energy expresses itself in seven colors, rays, or qualities:

> ... *The will to initiate.*
> ... *The will to unify.*
> ... *The will to evolve.*
> ... *The will to harmonise or relate.*
> ... *The will to act.*
> ... *The will to cause.*
> ... *The will to express.*[1]

We must remember that above the Atmic Will we have still higher expressions of will: Monadic, Divine, and Cosmic. These seven aspects of the will awaken similar vibrations on the lower corresponding sub-planes. Thus the whole man can align himself with the will of the Spark, Who is the Eye of God in man.

PART IV. HOW THE WILL CAN BE DEVELOPED

> ... *the aspirant's emotional body becomes responsive to the principle of buddhi, reaching him via the love petals of the egoic lotus ... the disciple becomes aware (for that is all it is) of the* possibility *of an impression reaching him from the cosmic astral plane, via monadic levels of awareness.*[2]

---

[1] Bailey, Alice A., *Esoteric Astrology*, p. 605.
[2] Bailey, Alice A., *The Rays and the Initiations,* p. 362.

The will can be developed on each plane by special exercises or disciplines designed only for that particular plane. Let us repeat: the first sub-plane of each plane is the depository of will energy.

On the *physical* plane a man can develop through his will by ascetic living and disciplining the body with various exercises:

1. He can decide to stand erect for five minutes each day over a period of one year or more, putting away all thoughts or drives that he wishes to check. Physical discipline is an excellent means to develop will on the physical plane.

2. He can try to stop all involuntary movements of his hands, feet, limbs, and face.

3. He can try to relax his body every day at a regular time.

4. He can fast often, rhythmically. He can fast for a day or three days every month.

5. He can consciously or voluntarily reject some great pleasure, especially at those times when it is within his reach. He can reject enjoyable food and drink. He can even reject sex for a while until he gains control over it.

6. He can create hard work for himself and do it perfectly and honestly.

7. He can control his sleep, occasionally keeping himself awake for perhaps two days or more, doing his work in the meantime.

8. He can sleep in an uncomfortable place until he does not care for a better place.

On the *emotional* plane he can develop the will:

1. By controlling negative emotions, negative talking, and useless talking in general.

2. By trying to keep calm under exciting conditions.

3. By being indifferent when others are roaring with laughter.

4. By controlling anger; by speaking softly while others are shouting.

5. By smiling as people knowingly or unknowingly humiliate him in some way.

6. By listening to great music by great composers.

7. By studying, observing, or listening to great art, drama, dance, or opera.

8. By keeping his emotional balance and serenity in fearful situations and under nauseating conditions.

On the *mental* plane he can develop the will:

1. By keeping the mind steady and persistent on a chosen course of study or goal. It is good to have a real teacher whose instructions he is determined to obey.

2. By employing all activities of his mind in pursuit of a high goal or aim in his life. For example, the choosing of a subject and writing on it as deeply as he can.

3. By trying at regular intervals to stop his mental activities or to stop thinking about a particular subject that interests him very much.

4. By studying subjects that he has rejected before or studying new subjects in which he has not had previous interest.

5. By making decisions increasingly more difficult to carry out and fulfilling each one on any level or on three levels simultaneously.

6. By performing many acts at the same time; for example, listening to music, talking with someone, and writing a letter.

7. By rejecting mental, emotional, and physical "wills" and contemplating upon the finer, higher will. For example, trying to discover the source of or reason for his many drives and urges; trying to find how such urges and drives express themselves through his personality, and how on various occasions they "pretend" to be his true will.

8. By carrying out his activities of the day consciously and with attention.

In the beginning these exercises should be done for only ten minutes. Later the time period can gradually be lengthened, always observing attentively whatever you do.

A. Van der Naillen, in his book, *In the Sanctuary*, says:

The power of will approaching almost the divine, and vouch-safed only to him who has achieved successive victories over the obstacles that stand in the path of spiritual growth....[1]

We must remember that these "obstacles" that stand in our way are not only individual but are also to be found within family, group, national, and international situations.

The Master Djwhal Khul states:

> *... The mode par excellence by which the will can be developed is the cultivation of the recognition of the divine Plan down the ages. This produces a sense of synthesis and this sense of synthesis ties the man into the plan....*[2]

The exercises and disciplines previously mentioned destroy former habits and crystallizations on any plane. They completely dissolve by wisdom, patience, and tactful actions. Until they are destroyed, a man will not be able to use the will energy properly on any given plane. In spite of all obstacles, the will energy must be awakened.

When man uses the first sub-plane of the physical, emotional, and mental planes, the will of intuition begins to control him, and here the picture changes completely. After the intuitional level is touched upon, the Solar Angel takes charge of all physical, astral, and mental activities. All these planes are flooded with the Will of the Solar Angel in conformity to the Plan. We know that the Solar Angel is the custodian of the Plan, and that It tries to work it out by inspiring man in the three worlds.

Ideas are pieces or drops of the Plan; they are fiery in nature and awaken intuitional responses in men. These responses can create upheavals, conflicts, revolutions, and wars. Ideas come from the Intuitional Plane, but the Hierarchical Plan is "constructed" of Atmic Plane substance. Consequently the ideas are charged with will electricity, and when released at the right time under the right conditions, they cannot be checked or prevented from coming into manifestation and expression.

Very often "strong will energy" is used to achieve our physical, emotional, and mental ends, and we call this energy *the will*. It could be an etheric force, an emotional or mental force, mis-

---

1 Van der Naillen, A., *In the Sanctuary*, p. 57.

2 Bailey, Alice, A., *Discipleship in the New Age*, Vol. II, pp. 298-299.

channeled by a glamor, a complex, a command, or an engram, but it is not true will energy in action. True will energy can be experienced only when a man touches the Buddhic Plane and receives new ideas or has a vision of the Plan. These ideas gradually lead him to the realm of the Plan and eventually to the realm of the Purpose of God. The Purpose is the expression of the Will of God.

Whenever people contact the Purpose or the Plan through ideas, they become stimulated and energized. The Plan is the technique through which the Purpose of God is fulfilled. The Purpose of God is His focussed Will for a great cycle. It is Will which can express itself through us when we begin to act consciously on the Atmic Plane. We say,

Thy Will be done.

When for the first time we repeat these words of power in all sincerity and dedication, we will feel that our whole duty is to express His Will or to consciously be one with His Will.

People sometimes think that "every movement is an act of will." This is not true. It would be better to say that every movement is an act of conscious or unconscious thought. Physical movements can be activated by any emotion or thought. Action can be motivated hypnotically by posthypnotic suggestions, influences, comments, and impressions coming from our environment, from people, and even from space. One can observe that most of our movements are mechanical and automatic. There is no *willingness* behind them. Willing is always conscious. The more highly developed the will, the more light and wisdom it carries with it. Sometimes the will is purposely used for destruction. If it is the *true will*, cleansed of illusions, glamors, and so on, it is used for the destruction of obstacles, clearing the way for higher manifestations.

Essentially the will in its highest expression is *one* in every man. The creation of world understanding will be impossible until man cultivates the higher Will in himself. Each true Will is a Ray of the Sun, and it never conflicts with the true Wills of others. In developing our essential Will, we are constructing a way of approach for our vehicles, making it possible for them to progress toward higher levels. We are creating a path through which the Will of the Highest is reaching down to the lowest. The functions of all vehicles are then synchronized, creating a marvelous symphony of expression — expression of the Purpose of the highest level in man, the highest Beauty and Righteousness. Man is preparing his vehicles for expression on a higher level: the Will of the Planetary Logos. The Will of the Planetary Logos can be used when a man's consciousness has been raised at least to the level of the *Spiritual Triad* and he is able to function on that high level.[1]

If the initiate is using the energy of the higher will through the higher mind, the will energy will be used for the good of civilization. If the will is used through the buddhic aspect, it will be used for religion or education, and if it is expressed through the atmic level, it will be used "in relation to races, nations, and kingdoms in nature," revealing itself as basic laws, leadership, and statesmanship.

Below the Spiritual Triad, will expresses itself as desire on the emotional plane, as aspiration on the lower mental plane, and as determination on the higher mental planes. It is the same energy on all three planes, but its nature changes according to the different levels as it expresses itself in subtle or concrete form.

We have spoken about the permanent atoms or seeds. These seeds can produce better results in our future lives if man uses his unfolding spiritual will and tries to live under consciously created hardships, physically, emotionally, and mentally; under continuous discipline on all three levels; in perpetual endeavor to put his vehicles through a process of transmutation. In so doing the contents of the seeds changes, the will energy increases in them, and when man comes back again to physical existence, he can have a physical, emotional, and mental body which can endure under any strain or pressure. He can survive in any life condition and be an example of heroic action and creative works.

Thus the life of the disciple is a life of hardship and labor. Self-imposed, consciously created hardship is the result of the use of the will upon the lower vehicles. Our life is filled with hardships, but they are forced upon us, and we have a natural resistance to them. Conscious hardship and discipline do not create this reaction and resistance. To those hardships not consciously created and self-imposed, man reacts with rejection and develops negative emotions — the seeds of his future prob-

---

[1] The Spiritual Triad is formed by the manasic, buddhic, and atmic permanent atoms. Each of them is found on the first sub-plane of each of these planes.

lems and troubles. When he creates conscious hardships, all negative emotions are discharged, and positive emotions are developed. Conscious hardship is the shortest way to develop higher will.

PART V. MEDITATION ON THE WILL

This meditation may be used daily for one year. Then, if you choose, it may be used once each week while continuing with other meditations or exercises on the remaining six days. The time limit is thirty minutes or less. This meditation on the will should be used only by people who:

1. are harmless, even in their thoughts
2. are filled with love for all creatures
3. are altruistic
4. have a pure heart, free from negative emotions
5. can think clearly
6. are non-separative

Willpower is a very strong energy and, if it is invoked before careful preparation and purification, it can destroy the subject, creating unimaginable troubles in his physical, emotional, and mental worlds, in his family and social world. The one who meditates on the will must have the purest motive in his heart: *to serve humanity.*

In the process of meditating on the will, if at any time you see evidence of negative thoughts, emotions, actions, selfishness, or aggressive moods, discontinue the meditation until you are sure that you are in such condition that it is safe for you to begin again. To help in bringing about this condition, it will be necessary to form a group of people who, being on your level of development, can meditate with you at least once each week. In this way the danger of the will energy can be minimized or nullified. Please remember:

When, therefore, your life is fundamentally invocative, then there will come the evocation of the will. It is only truly invocative when personality and soul are fused and functioning as a consciously blended and focussed unit.[1]

Also, we must remember that will energy is "... a propelling, expulsive force ... a clarifying, purifying agent."[2] In *A Treatise on Cosmic Fire* the Master Djwhal Khul mentions the fact that a man at the Fifth Initiation ascends to the Atmic Plane and at the Sixth Initiation passes into the Monadic Plane. There he achieves monadic awareness, and there he functions.

> *... At the seventh Initiation he dominates the entire sphere of matter contained in the lowest cosmic plane, escapes from all etheric contact, and functions on the cosmic astral plane.*[3]

The Master Djwhal Khul also states:

> *... The expression of this higher aspect of the will ... is likewise threefold:*

> 1. *There is the* dynamic will, *as it is expressed by first ray egos.*
> 2. *There is the* inclusive radiatory will *of second ray souls....*
> 3. *There is the* magnetic will *of the third ray ego which draws, attracts, manipulates and arranges in accordance with divine purpose. This is not the same kind of magnetism as that of love.*[4]

> *... The will is not ... a forceful expression of intention; it is not a fixed determination to do thus and so or to make certain things to be. It is fundamentally an expression of the law of Sacrifice; under this law, the unit recognises responsibility, identifies itself with the whole, and learns the esoteric significance of the words: "Having nothing (sacrifice) and yet possessing all things (universality)."*[5]

People think that the deeper a man goes into himself, the more he loses his sense of taste, of pleasure, of joy which he receives

---

[1] Bailey, Alice A., *The Rays and the Initiations*, p. 35.

[2] Bailey, Alice A., *Esoteric Astrology*, p. 582.

[3] Bailey, Alice A., *A Treatise on Cosmic Fire*, p. 121.

[4] Bailey, Alice A., *Discipleship in the New Age*, Vol. II, p. 445.

[5] Ibid., pp. 269-270.

in contacting the physical world. As we have said before, this is not true. When a man controls only his physical body, he tastes only through his physical body by having physical sensations. When he passes to the emotional world and controls his emotional body, he tastes the same object in two dimensions; he tastes the physical and emotional parts of the object. If the man is able to control his mental, intuitional, and atmic vehicles as well as the physical and emotional vehicles, his sensation of the object becomes five dimensional. We can imagine the difference found between the object sensed on the physical plane and the same object communicated or sensed with the physical, emotional, mental, intuitional, and atmic senses. In the Ageless Wisdom we are told that eventually man will be able to use his five senses on the five planes: physical, emotional, mental, Intuitional, and Atmic. Master Djwhal Khul says:

> *By the time the fifth round is reached, three-fifths of the human family will have attained this point and will have their five senses fully functioning on the three planes in the three worlds, leaving the two other planes to be subjugated during the remaining two rounds.*[1]

We have seven senses. The first five are hearing, touch, sight, taste, and smell. The sixth sense is the intellect, the mental unit, mind, or common sense. The seventh is the intuition or synthetic sense. We are using our five senses on the physical plane and trying to use the other two higher senses on the physical plane in the same manner. The day will come when we will use our seven senses on the astral, mental, Buddhic, and Atmic Planes. For example, we will taste intuitionally or on the Intuitional Plane. We will smell atmically, see mentally, and so on.

We are told that on the physical plane the first sense that functions is hearing. We must cultivate this sense on the physical level and bring it to its perfection. We must perfect it still further and become able to hear physically, emotionally, mentally, intuitionally, atmically and to register the sound in our brain. Our hearing will open on the five planes first. Later the same will be true of the other senses, and eventually we will be able to hear, touch, see, taste, and smell (even atmically), and it will be registered in our brain mechanism.

---

[1] Bailey, Alice A., *A Treatise on Cosmic Fire*, p. 164.

H.P. Blavatsky says, "Every sense pervades every other sense."[1] "All senses are on all planes."[2] We hear on the astral plane throughout the entire astral body. We see with our whole mental body. We taste with the whole buddhic body. We smell with our whole atmic body.

One of the Masters explains how the senses work on different planes in different forms. He tells us that physical hearing becomes clairaudience on the astral plane, higher clairaudience on the mental plane, comprehension of four sounds (his own, his brother's, his group's, and the Heavenly Man's sound) on the Buddhic Plane. It changes and becomes beatitude on the Atmic Plane. Sight becomes clairvoyance on the astral plane, higher clairvoyance on the mental plane, divine vision on the Buddhic Plane, and realization on the Atmic Plane.[3]

To learn and know the true value of things, a man must reach them through all his senses on every plane, otherwise the evaluation and enjoyment are partial and illusionary. The rich, the more abundant life is a life lived and appreciated through all the bodies, senses, or states of consciousness.

MEDITATION ON THE WILL[4]

1. Choose a quiet place in your home, where you can sit for a half hour without being disturbed. If you are not with group members, visualize them as they meditate simultaneously with you.

2. Take a few deep breaths and relax.

3. Say *The Great Invocation.*[5]

4. Ponder for ten minutes on the will as presented in this chapter. Begin with the first paragraph and use a new paragraph (in sequence) for each successive meditation.

5. Visualize a torch and imagine that you are climbing a steep mountain to light your torch from the fire on the summit.

---

[1] Blavatsky, H.P., *The Secret Doctrine*, Vol. III, p. 569.

[2] Ibid., p. 550.

[3] See Bailey, Alice A., *A Treatise on Cosmic Fire*, p. 189.

[4] This meditation must be carried out in a group.

[5] See p. 304.

With the "flaming torch" in your hand, descend from the mountain to the valley and put it on a high place to illuminate the surrounding area. Observe the "flaming torch" steadily for two or three minutes.

6. Decide upon some action which you will take during the month on the physical, emotional, or mental plane. For example, you will write an article; you will not speak about a certain problem; you will not talk or gossip about another person; you will not smoke or drink; you will exercise physical control. Decide upon some action in your meditation and then *do* it!

7. After you have made the decision, imagine a drop of blue light above your head. Look at the light and let it change into a "flaming diamond." From the center of the "flaming diamond" a stream of will energy is flowing into your vehicles, making them radioactive and magnetic.

8. Try to stand in the center of the "flaming diamond" and invoke "the center where the Will of God is known." See that center as a point in the Sun. Pause for a moment and spiritually inhale the Will.

9. Charged with this energy, return to the world of man and bless all who are filled with goodwill.

10. Say:

In the center of the Will of God I stand.

Naught shall deflect my will from His.

I implement that Will by love.

I turn to the field of service.

I, the triangle divine, work out that Will

Within the square and serve my fellow man.

11. Sound the OM three times, visualizing the point in the Sun and the Jewel within which you stand as a pure Spark.

12. Recall where you are. Relax for a few minutes and open your eyes.

Chapter XV

THE ETHERIC BODY AND THE CENTERS

Not only the physical body but all living forms in nature have an electromagnetic field. This field is a subtle pattern around which the physical body is built. In ancient times people knew about this body and called it the *etheric* or *subtle body*. Not long ago scientists in America discovered that all living organisms are embedded in an electromagnetic field, the patterns upon which and by which the physical body is built. "In the growing embryo, the electrical pattern develops hand in hand with the development of the whole mechanism."[1]

This electromagnetic pattern has two types of energy: dynamic and magnetic. As these two energies act and react upon each other, they create whirlpools of force which manipulate etheric, emotional, and mental substances, establishing a communication line between the physical-emotional-mental level and higher planes.[2]

The etheric body of an Initiate is built of the four higher ethers, which in esoteric terminology are buddhic, atmic, monadic, and divine substances. It is a network of energies. We are told that in and through this web circulates a golden fire. In ancient times the etheric body was called *the golden bowl*. In esoteric literature the whirlpools of energies are called *centers* or *lotuses*. The immediate materialized projections of these centers are the glands, especially the ductless glands through which the centers control the blood and nervous systems.[3]

The etheric body, through its centers, vitalizes and energizes the physical body and puts it in contact with the higher planes,

---

1 *Manas*, Dec. 29, 1948

2 Saraydarian, H., (Torkom), *Cosmos in Man*, Ch. IV.

3 Saraydarian, Torkom, *Thought and the Glory of Thinking,* Ch. 10.

with the energy body of the planet, and with the solar system. At first these centers are not fully active. They come into activity gradually as the consciousness of man unfolds and as the subtle vehicles pass through a process of transformation and sublimation. As these centers open and become fully active, man becomes able to communicate with the intuitive, atmic, monadic, and divine worlds and to register these contacts in his brain consciousness. The seven main centers are:

1. the head center
2. the center between the eyebrows
3. the throat center
4. the heart center
5. the solar plexus
6. the sacral center
7. the base of spine

These centers open and become radioactive as the result of a life of harmlessness, service, and esoteric meditation.

Each of our bodies is composed of trillions of progressing lives. These lives are distributed on the seven levels of each plane, the more advanced lives being on the higher levels. In the center of these advancing, progressing lives there is the greater Life, that super-center we call the Soul.

On each plane the more advanced lives form the centers or agents of communication between the higher and lower planes. Through the centers passes the energy of more life to the lower planes or kingdoms, which are in turn attracted to a higher level through the magnetic force of the centers. *As man is, so is the Planetary Logos.* He also has His etheric and other bodies. They are formed of billions and billions of lives. The most advanced lives of that plane form a communication center. For example:

- The whole of humanity is a center, the bridge between superhuman and subhuman kingdoms.
- The next higher center is the Hierarchy, which is formed of the most advanced lives from the center which we call humanity.
- The next higher center is Shamballa, which mostly is formed of the most advanced lives of the Hierarchy.

A human being is a cell in the body of humanity. Humanity as a whole is the throat center of the Planetary Logos. The Hierarchy is the heart center and Shamballa is the head center.

As these centers, which are composed of many lives, progress, the greater Life also progresses and vice versa. As the human soul progresses, the lives which compose the bodies of man gradually pass into higher sub-planes and form part of the centers. These centers — planetary or human — unfold, bloom, and radiate more energy and light as the indwelling one passes from stage to stage and from one initiation to another. If the Planetary Logos takes an initiation, Its centers are affected, and more Light, Love, and Power flow through them with the inevitable frictions and their consequences.

The planet with its Planetary Logos is a life which forms part of the center of a Greater Life. Our Solar Logos with the solar system forms a center by Itself but is also one of the lives which compose a center for a still greater Life. Each center has several magnetic rings, which are composed of lives in gradient scale. As you move toward the center, the Power and Light increase, consciousness expands, and at the center you find the *Jewel*. Each center has its own jewel. All centers together have a jewel.

- Individual man has a Jewel, the Monad.
- Humanity has a Jewel, the Christ.
- Hierarchy has a Jewel, Sanat Kumara.
- Shamballa has its own Jewel, the Great Sacrifice, the Silent Watcher.

All jewels on the same plane of the planets form corresponding centers in the Solar Logos. For example,

- The Silent Watcher with all other Silent Watchers form the head center of the Solar Logos, the *sacrifice petals* of the Solar Chalice or Lotus.
- All Sanat Kumaras of all planets in our solar system form the heart center of the Solar Logos, the *love petals* of the Solar Chalice.
- All Christs on all planets of our solar system form the throat center of the Solar Logos, the *knowledge petals* of the Solar Chalice.

Thus the reader may perceive the progressive path, beginning with the atom and merging into the ocean of Cosmos.

In esoteric literature it has been suggested that there exists the blueprint of a giant Lotus in Space, constructed by cosmic energies. This Lotus is the electromagnetic body of the Cosmos or of all Creation in Mother Space. It extends not only to the Cosmic Physical Plane but also reaches upward to the Cosmic Mental level where it forms a cosmic Chalice, a cosmic Magnet.

Upon this Magnet the whole Creation takes form. It is the causal body of the Cosmos, in which the *Great Soul* of Cosmos dwells. Each and every atom, every Spark in every form is attracted to that Central Magnet. It is the plan for which each "atom" and each "cell" appropriates itself to build the Chalice of life. We can visualize the great Lotus with its color, energy, symphony, magnetic power, consciousness, and intelligence. From this great Lotus the life of the Cosmic Christ reaches down to the lowliest atom of Creation and becomes a path of return to the Father's House, to Home.

> *... The Cosmic Magnet provides direction as well as destination. In the entire evolutionary process one must seek this destination, and the central point of evolution must be ascertained.*[1]

---

[1] Agni Yoga Society, *Infinity I*, par. 230.

Chapter XVI

DO DRUGS EXPAND THE CONSCIOUSNESS?

Each entity must have won for itself the right to become divine, through self-experience.

H.P. Blavatsky

Throughout centuries people have sensed something greater and deeper within man and nature than our normal waking consciousness can grasp. They have known intuitively that there was something more that they could somehow contact, and from which they could derive more light, more joy, and more serenity. Thus for centuries human beings have aspired to find that deeper Being. In ancient religions this inner or deeper Being was called the Soul, the Spirit, the Buddha, the inner Christ, the Hope of Glory. It was also called the Center of Freedom, the Silent Watcher, the Presence, the Real Self, or the Father.

In order to find that inner Center, sincere people have created various aids such as ceremonies, rituals, yogas; they have gone into seclusion; they have fasted; they have developed special meditations, prayers, contemplations, and samadhi. These various aids, together with a desire to deal justly, to love, to extend mercy, and to walk humbly have enabled men to transcend themselves.

Out of this different religions have come into existence. Essentially religion is but a guide-path toward that inner meaning, that inner source in man and in nature. When the outer incidentals and man-made forms are removed from the life of a dedicated person, a bridge remains which unites the unreal with the Real Man, the helpless man with his inner source of Power.

True psychology, which is the science of the soul, is a study of the search for this inner world. It is a study of the laws of the above mentioned bridge-building process. True education is likewise a search for the Real Man and for the means of developing a technique to bring the Real Man to his fullest expression. Real art, in all its aspects, is an expression of the deeper man. The talented man, the genius, lies hidden in the deeper man and has learned to express himself through words, colors, sounds, movements, and forms.

The purpose of all life is to expand the consciousness to higher and higher levels of thinking, feeling, and acting so that we might have "life more abundant." In the East the approach to the deeper man is through meditation and yoga. In the West it is through philosophic contemplation, psychoanalysis, and the arts.

Another technique, as old as religion itself, has been used to "expand" the consciousness of man. Many people have used special herbs, flowers, or seeds. This has been and still is being practiced by some religious groups in Asia, Europe, and America. The use of drugs was popular in Asia, Egypt, and South America. Listed in their records we find a kind of mushroom, peyote, mescalin, fermented tea, alcohol, opium, special incenses, perfumes, unguents, hashish, and other less well known agents.

It is interesting to note that since 1900 both techniques have come to the attention of the public. On the one hand we have the long and strenuous path of discipline, meditation, contemplation, and a real achievement of higher states of consciousness. On the other hand we have drugs in various forms to "expand" the consciousness mechanically in order to achieve "higher" experiences.

Jesus told a parable which relates to this subject. He said, "Some people enter into the house through windows, and they are thieves." A thief does not dwell in the house, but enters it, robs it, and in the end receives punishment.

Drugs, at best, open a window to the astral plane. They break the etheric wall and force consciousness through this opening into the astral world — a fantastic world full of glamorous, illusive colors and forms. *No drug can elevate consciousness higher than the astral world.* We know that the astral plane is the plane of delusions. Whoever is caught there cannot easily return into the light of reality.

Some people say that they have become creative after they have used drugs. They claim that they receive new inspiration and courage to express it. This may be true, but they do not know from what plane and from what sources that inspiration comes. It may come from the reactive mind where it was recorded. What we read and what we listen to is often registered mechanically in our reactive mind and is later expressed in new forms and colors. We are "drugged" through mental tape recordings.

A man may become possessed by some thoughts floating in space, and he may express them as a medium does. He may become sensitive to the ideas of some astral world inhabitants who want to communicate with our sense world through him. Drugs give an opportunity for them to do this, and the deluded person thinks that he has become creative because of the drugs he used.

Some drug users say that they see such beauties of form and color as cannot be expressed in words. This is true; they see "inexplicable" forms and colors because their consciousness is not yet ready to function on the plane which they have penetrated. Let us examine the following diagram:

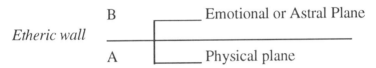

A man is equal to his consciousness. Where his consciousness is, there he is. Suppose A is his level of consciousness. This is his yardstick, his measure which he has in his hand. He can explain things and approach them only through the five senses. But if he takes drugs, a window may open on level B where a different world of mirages exists. A man who has only physical level A consciousness will have a most difficult time interpreting anything on level B. It is true that he will come in contact with a different dimension, a different world, but this does not, *per se*, give him the needed tools to translate and interpret his experiences there. Suppose he has a 200 degree physical level consciousness and is entering a world which needs a 20,000 degree consciousness. Will he not be confused? The poor man looks through a forced crack into the astral world. When he "comes back," his natural measure is partly distorted.

Here we are discussing two different things: *consciousness* and the *mechanism*. The drug is not developing the consciousness, but it is affecting the mechanism (the mind and the brain) and opening a crack between the astral plane and the brain.

Through this crack the dimmed consciousness is looking into an entirely new world.

When a drunken man sees a mathematical equation, of course his consciousness is impressed to some degree, but it is not *expanded* by the new experience because expansion of consciousness takes place when its ability to understand increases. To understand means conscious at-one-ment with the form, quality, purpose, and cause of a given subject.

We know that on the first levels of the astral plane we find our wish-life. There we may have whatever we may desire. Most drug users are caught in such a pleasure world. They "enjoy" it day and night or as long as the effects of the drug continue. When they awaken, they have difficulty in fitting into the physical life again. Continuous users are lost for this lifetime. When the influence of the drug wears off, life seems crude, criminal, and difficult. They escape back to their dream world, where they satisfy every desire without labor or responsibility. Such people lose their spiritual growth and are a complete loss to society.

On the second and third levels of the astral plane we have finer elements and glamors. There we find pride, hatred, and jealousy enacted and satisfied.

On a higher level still we have our devotional life fulfilled. Our objects of devotion are there, as we have colored and vested them, and they bestow upon us the "paradise" to which we are aspiring. On this level we also meet our left-hand brothers, those wolves in sheep's clothing who try to lead us into the ranks of their brotherhood and to influence us to walk the dark path. They mainly overstimulate our sexual desires, our materialistic tendencies, our pride, and our will to dominate.

On a still higher level we come in contact with some artistic forms, musical colors, and fantastic types of art. It is like looking into a kaleidoscope and seeing ever-changing forms. Modern art is a distorted reflection of this level.

On still higher levels of the astral plane we may touch some of the moral codes and archetypes, but all these seem to be mixed together in a phantasmagoric sea of misleading glamors and forces. Drugs lead us into a world where, for a short time, we may fly and become either a monster or a four-winged angel.

When a man enters another dimension — as for example, the astral plane — by the use of drugs or other unlawful means, he finds himself in a state of timelessness. There the past, the present, and the future shift continuously, and most of his sense of proportion and measure are affected and changed. After the influence of the drug has worn off, he has a strong urge to speak or write about his experiences, but he finds that he cannot do this factually because he does not have the needed vocabulary. His brain cannot formulate and translate the impressions coming from the astral plane.

This creates deep confusion in his mind. There arises a real conflict between his deep-seated urge to express himself and the obstacles he has encountered. The man loses his sanity and suffers physically. This does not always come about immediately, but come it will when the world of illusion presses down and mingles with reality.

Before a man can enter subjective levels, he must be prepared; he must build a mechanism which will play the role of a translator and transformer from timelessness to time, from the abstract to the concrete. Higher dimensions add nothing new to a man because he cannot receive a new idea, vision, or knowledge until he has built this new mechanism. *He attracts to himself whatever he is.*

By penetrating into higher planes through the use of drugs, a man is not changed or elevated. For example, he does not change his consciousness if he is suddenly transported from sea level to a 2,000 foot elevation. All a man experiences on the astral plane is the mechanical response to his known or unknown dreams, wishes, desires, aspirations, devotions, feelings, and emotions. In the emotional world all these are released, and they find their total fulfillment.

The spiritual progress of man is achieved by a slow transformation or transmutation of the substance of his mechanism. Suppose a child buys an advanced mathematics book and brings it home. The mere fact of possession does not teach him how to solve complicated mathematical problems. Only after he has had years of education in mathematics will he be ready for that book. This means that he must expand his consciousness, learn many rules and formulas, and use them to penetrate further into the chosen subject. We cannot fly safely in the air without first knowing what kinds of rules, laws, forces, or other conditions must be observed. After we know these, we must have the needed mechanism built according to the requirements.

The same situation applies to the inner space. The astral plane is part of space. When people enter it, they accept everything there as real. They think they are the true witnesses to these things. The fact is that what they see is not real but only a reflection of their own imaginative creations. All that they dream of is actualized there. It is surprising that they do not have the slightest idea that they are dreaming. After the person returns to consciousness, he often speaks about orders or messages he has received from that world, without knowing that all he has received was given to himself by himself.

Some of the "pseudo-prophets," "teachers of wisdom," and "leaders" are inspired on the astral plane through self-hypnotism. They assume that they are important personalities. They are possessed by the idea, the order, the light, or the revelation which they have supposedly received from higher sources. They make every kind of sacrifice to prove to the world that they were "sent" to convey a divine message. Such is the delusion which man enters through drugs or meditations and exercises on the left-hand path.

There are many aberrant people in the world who, in one way or another, have entered the world of delusion and have been caught there. Some of them think that they have achieved Selfhood, that they represent God in the world, or that they are true messengers of God. They are lost in the illusions of the astral plane. It is very difficult to heal them. The best thing for them to do is to try to patch the crack in the etheric body between the physical and the astral planes. Medicine cannot help them; it merely cuts down the sensitivity of the organism which registers the impressions coming from the astral planes. Influences from the astral planes continue to come through and affect the mental and physical life, but the subject is completely unaware of this fact.

Those who enter the higher levels through right meditation and service are known by their actual accomplishments. They become more creative, more tolerant, express a greater sense of unity, a deeper love, devotion, harmlessness, a greater sense of responsibility, the ability to organize, stronger leadership, greater service, conscious suffering for others, will, freedom, selflessness, peace, courage, persistence, loyalty, sincerity, faithfulness, gratefulness. These are the measures by which those following the right-hand path may be recognized.

In most cases, those who use drugs are accompanied by "spirit guides" (discarnate beings), who are the creators of post-hypnotic suggestions. Those who are under the effect of drugs and under the influence of suggestion are trapped in an even deeper glamor. Every suggestion that touches them becomes an active drama or comedy in the astral plane. Then when they are back in their normal consciousness, it becomes a command. It will be difficult to get them out of the net in which they are caught.

A drug user may speak of having a better relationship with other people and added qualities of speech or expression. This is possible, but the Real Man — the consciousness — is not being further developed; it is merely being hypnotized to act mechanically. Once this hypnotic state wears off, the Real Man is weaker than before because a command was activated through him; he was not himself.

There is indeed a similarity between the descriptions of certain states of ecstasy resulting from meditation and those resulting from psychedelic drugs. Our western world is confused about the goal of meditation. We think that the goal of meditation is ecstasy. If this were true, the advocates of the use of psychedelic drugs to create feelings of ecstasy would have more authority. However, for the mature meditator ecstasy is to be transcended, and a higher state of poised mental clarity must be achieved. In this state of poised mental clarity one can perceive great inspirations of deeper meaning and synthesis, and one can anchor them in practical form, which can be used for the service and advancement of mankind.

It is good to know that ecstasy involves varying degrees of experience. We have physical ecstasy and emotional ecstasy. In both states the mind is shut off and suspended for a short time. These states of ecstasy may be realized through sexual relations, alcohol, or drugs. When we experience mental ecstasy, a great joy floods the field of the mind. But these are not true spiritual ecstasies. True ecstasy *starts* when man enters the domain of intuition through esoteric meditation and contemplation. There the little self with its problems disappears, and man sees the true beauty of creation and the glorious future of human beings. The latter state of ecstasy is truly creative and a true peak experience. It is creative because man is conscious during the experience, using a bridge built between the mind and the higher planes. This bridge between the mind and the higher worlds is used to transmit higher experiences to the lower world in scientific revelation and creative forms.

Drugs work upon the mechanism instead of upon the consciousness. This reversing of the process leads only to trouble. Esoterically it is the consciousness which creates the mechanism and which changes it. In developing consciousness, the physical side of man is developed too. His etheric body, mental body, and higher bodies develop as he unfolds his consciousness. True meditation and education are directed toward the unfoldment of the consciousness. As the consciousness becomes higher and deeper, the substance of man's planes becomes more and more organized and refined in order to better express the new light that is striking the substance. Thus the nervous system, glandular system, and the centers are developed for the use of higher dimensional activities. This is the normal and natural process for the development of man's consciousness and its mechanism.

On the path of unfoldment from plane to plane, the bridge must be built before man can be active on higher levels. A university lecture cannot be given to a child who does not yet know how to read. It is true that he can pretend that he is ready, but nature has its own ways, and the child needs to grow and learn on a gradual scale until he is ready to pass from grade to grade with full understanding. Sooner or later man must enter the astral world but with perfect awareness and knowledge of that plane and as an observer, not an actor. Here is self-determination, an approach to the Central-Self and to becoming that Self. In a hypnotized or drugged state a man is getting farther and farther away from his Real Self.

In meditation we are refining the bodies, raising their vibrations, connecting them with higher levels, and unfolding new consciousness. We are approaching the Central Life. By using drugs we are inducing artificial communication with the higher planes, for which our consciousness is not yet ready. It is as though one suddenly put a child on a wild horse and let them both run wild. Meditation is analogous to the process by which the child should be trained and made ready to ride the horse, giving him perfect control of himself and the horse.

Meditation releases the inner beauties and transfigures man through an outpouring of light. It cleanses the glamors of the astral plane as much as possible and destroys the illusions of the mental plane. In short, it gives free play to the consciousness of man.

Drugs increase the glamors and illusions and push the user into a state in which he loses control of his analytical, reasoning, and synthesizing instrument. His compass is lost. A man may enter an astronomy class and see all the symbols, forms, and equations but have no understanding of them. There is need for understanding before entering a foreign land. A mathematical formula that is not understood has no real existence for a person; only as he understands it does it come to have meaning for him. This applies to all the higher levels or planes of existence. On these higher planes are to be found deeper realities and greater beauties than can ever be found on the lower rounds of life.

People often enter these higher realms through merit or grace. As an example, Saint Paul, speaking of himself, says,

> *I knew a man in Christ more than fourteen years ago, but whether I knew him in the body or out of the body, I do not know, God knows: This very one was caught up to the third heaven.... And I still know this man ... that he was caught up to paradise, and heard unspeakable words, for which it is not lawful for man to utter.*[1]

If our consciousness is prepared, we are given a chance to enter such planes, even to dwell there for as long a time as we are able — but then we must return to the world of men as leaders, inspirers, prophets. We have touched the realities. Nothing can change our understanding of them or our dedication to them.

If through some forbidden exercises men enter into the higher worlds, they see and hear a few things, but they interpret these experiences through their understanding of the lower planes and thus create crystallized illusions. In most cases these people lose their balance in the physical world because their measure of judgment is distorted. They live an uncertain and unreal life. Sometimes they destroy all moral codes and live a wild life. They often lose their sense of loyalty and have no respect for rules and laws. This is a sign that they have made an unlawful entry into the higher planes and have lost their compass for the physical side of life. They cannot live on each plane according to the requirements of that plane because their transformers are not ready.

---

[1] II Corinthians 12:2-4

Consequently they are lost for all planes and must start again from the lowest.

H.P. Blavatsky, in a very beautiful way, says,

> *Each entity must have won for itself the right to become divine, through self experience.*[1]

Intensive spiritual efforts made by the aspirant and disciple through meditation and right living allow him to achieve inner peace and other virtues and to enter deeper levels of being, all of which are interconnected by many psychological and spiritual bridges. Across these bridges man goes a little beyond himself, and gradually he transfers his consciousness onto higher levels where he can understand, analyze, and express the Divine Plan.

A man who uses drugs to expand his consciousness loses his part in the Plan. This means that he loses his high calling and cannot take a conscious part in working out the great Plan for humanity. His part of the Plan is there, in the innermost center of his being, but he cannot approach it. Even if he tries to go toward it, he sinks into the sea of glamor, and there he sees a distorted picture of the Plan. Eventually this distorted picture controls his life, and he becomes a degenerated man.

In natural development a man keeps all his attainments with him whenever he passes the threshold to the higher world and returns. When a man comes back by artificial breakthroughs, he has lost whatever was stamped on his consciousness previously and keeps only the wounds on his bodies.

The aspirant on the right-hand path can be compared to the man who makes money in honest ways and enjoys it in long years to come. The aspirant on the left-hand path is like a teller in a bank. He handles vast sums of money during the day, but when evening comes, he must leave the money in the bank for it does not belong to him.

Man must learn to reach the higher levels consciously, step by step. He must control each move and pay the price for each advance. In this way he will have a bridge under his feet all the way, and he may go forward or return according to his needs. As he travels toward the Real Self, he builds the bridges and integrates his seven-fold mechanism, building it by his own effort and la-

---

[1] Blavatsky, H.P., *The Secret Doctrine*, Vol. 1, p. 107.

bor. When the bridge is built between all his vehicles, he can then invoke the Inner Light by saying:

O, Thou Self-Revealing One, reveal Thyself in me.

When the revelation of the Self starts, man slowly removes the scaffold that he has built throughout the ages through his reading and learning. Slowly the sun's light radiates and annihilates all the means that were used to reach the goal, and the True Self is realized.

QUESTIONS AND ANSWERS ON DRUGS[1]

Let reality govern my every thought, and truth be the master of my life.[2]

Q. Do drugs make us more sensitive to the pleasure of sex?

A. Some drug users think so. They think that they become more adequate in love-making and that they enjoy it more intensely. It is true that at first the drug excites the nerves and centers. For a while, those using drugs experience feelings of exuberance, well-being, and satisfaction. Gradually however, they find that the mechanism which was registering the excitement and pleasure of sex is becoming dull and insensitive. In an attempt to regain their former level of enjoyment, they increase the dosage of the drug. As the drug intake is increased, the dullness increases, and their sensitivity becomes less and less. A day comes when their expression of love is completely mechanical. This condition is followed by varying degrees of impotency.

Drug users will never experience a real and deep enjoyment of love because higher love starts on the intuitional level. They are caught as a fly in a web, in astral chaos, and they cannot fly higher to enter the domain of real love.

Q. Does the use of drugs affect coming generations?

---

[1] The material in this section is taken from an actual recorded question and answer period, following a lecture given by the author.

[2] Bailey, Alice A., *A Treatise on White Magic*, p. 239.

A. Yes. The harm done through the use of drugs does not end with our own life but goes on to affect generations to come — our children and grandchildren. They will be affected not only physically but psychologically as well. The children of drug users will not have sound bodies or healthy emotional and mental equipment. Indeed, the relatively wide use of drugs will leave its mark on our whole civilization and culture.

Just as psychosomatic conditions descend and express themselves as sickness and disease on the physical plane, physical illnesses caused by germs go deep and affect the subtle vehicles. When a physical illness is blocked by medication and "cured," the sickness remains in the subtle bodies, possibly expressing itself later in another kind of disorder or deviation from the normal.

Drug users damage their present and future mechanisms from both ends for many generations. When they reincarnate, they will naturally have low level psychism. They will "see," "hear," and "sense." This condition will create serious problems and much suffering for them, as it does for some people at the present time who become victims of lower psychism. Hospitals and asylums are filled with such people, and the best our doctors can do is to listen to them, give them various shock treatments, and try to calm them with medication.

The use of drugs in this life will open some centers in the etheric body, over-stimulate them, and produce an overflow of energy into the corresponding physical organs. In the next life this overflow will continue and will have devastating physical psychic effects. In the present reincarnation the drug user will destroy his brain cells and increase the thickness of the veil between himself and his Soul.

It is true that drugs produce energy through overstimulation of lower centers, especially the lower part of the solar plexus center and the sacral center. The excessive stimulation will draw more and more energy from the higher centers, leaving them in a weakened condition. This will create a slowing down of the higher centers and a burning of the lower centers, thereby causing complete imbalance in the energy system of the man.

Q. If a student of esoteric science through the use of drugs can attain the level of the astral plane, what can he accomplish?

A. I do not think he would try it, but if he should, he would be like the astronomer who, after consuming too much alcohol, climbed up to the observatory telescope to study the stars and record data. He worked very hard for a while, but because of his intoxicated condition he soon became exhausted, gave up, and fell asleep. The next morning other astronomers began to study his calculations only to find them completely meaningless. Investigation showed that he had not used the proper levers and had forcefully moved them the wrong way; he had neglected to turn off the lights, and he had failed to close the telescope. By not following standard procedures, he had caused much damage to the equipment.

If an esoteric student uses drugs, he will touch some realities but will not be able to interpret them accurately. If he continues using the drug, he will damage his brain cells, bringing to an end his progress on the Path.

Q. Is drug usage detrimental to esoteric studies?

A. Yes. Drug users can be possessed very easily by the dark forces and often become channels for them. They are not able to register high level energies and impressions coming from great entities and the Divine Plan. They will be unable to cultivate their centers or use energies intelligently. They will lose the vision in the mud of their low level experiences and fantasies. A reincarnated drug user will have an unbalanced mechanism or vehicle. For example, if you awaken in the morning and start to drive your car but see that one of its wheels has changed to a square, another to a triangle, and another is flat, how will you be able to drive such a vehicle?

We have many unfortunate people in hospitals who have unbalanced natures, but who also have a drive to live and express themselves. There is a greater danger. If the mechanism, especially the mind (not the brain) is badly damaged, the Solar Angel leaves the person for a long period of time. The result may be mongoloid children, retarded children, and deformed births.

Q. What is the difference between meditation and drug experience?

A. The difference is like the difference between a mirage and reality. Meditation is a process of:

    a) alignment

    b) touching the power house of energy

    c) expansion of consciousness

d) correct registration of the ideas precipitated from the higher mind or even from intuitional levels

e) conscious creativity

In the case of drugs, the etheric body has been rent suddenly and the world of illusion and glamor is entered. The human soul is trapped. There is no correct registration, and the self-determination level is at zero. The etheric counterpart of the brain is largely withdrawn. There is no true creativity.

Q. Is narcotic or drug use the worst enemy we have on our path of progress at this time?

A. There is a wonderful passage in the *Fiery World* which will answer your question. It reads:

> *Malice, doubt, unbelief, impatience, laziness, and the other inspirations of darkness separate the earthly world from the Higher Spheres. Instead of following the path of good, people attempt to replace ecstasy of the spirit with various narcotics, which give the illusion of the other world existence. Observe that in many religions there were introduced, as later adjuncts, very clever compounds of narcotics for the purpose of artificially advancing the consciousness beyond the earthly state. Indeed the fallibility of such forcible measures is great; they not only do not bring the Worlds closer, they on the contrary estrange and coarsen the consciousness. Likewise, earthly life is filled with continuous poisonings with which people very affably regale each other. Teachers of all times have taught humanity the pure paths of spirit that lead into communion with Higher Worlds, but only a few have chosen the path revealed by the heart. A special attention must be given to deliverance from poisonings. A considerable part of the Earth's soil is already infected, as is its surface. Besides narcotics, people have invented many obviously frightful substances which instead of being health-giving bring on spiritual death. Masses of poisonous vapors are choking the cities. People devote much thought to the production of many substances which should be considered far more deadly than narcotics. Narcotics bring harm to the addicts themselves, but deadly gases torment everything that lives. One cannot condemn narcotics enough, but also one cannot suf-*

ficiently condemn such murderous inventions. People formerly, at times, fell into error for the sake of illusionary ecstasy, but nowadays they are completely unashamed to kill the intellect and spirit of their near ones, calling this killing an attainment of science.[1]

Q. Do you think drugs can actually expand the consciousness?

A. Drugs do not expand the consciousness. On the contrary, they limit the consciousness, diffuse it, take it out of focus, and dim it to a considerable degree.

This happens because drugs harm the mechanism of consciousness which is the mind, the brain, and the three ductless glands within the head; they impair the health of the human body as a whole; they crystallize a portion of the mind, creating habit patterns and thus distort the rationality of man. In drug use, people see what they like or dislike seeing. They do not see things as they really exist, as they really are. It is a self-deceiving mechanism.

Man may obtain "insight" into his own problems, but he is not seeing his real problems — only those that he thinks he has. Even though, in some instances, there comes a moment in which he is truly aware of his problems, he lacks the initiative and drive to solve and overcome them. He is like a child who takes a watch apart and then is unable to put the parts back in their proper places. He forces the tiny wheels of the intricate mechanism into place and makes the watch completely useless.

Seeing the problem does not mean that you understand it or that you are able to handle it and solve it. Suppose you need a car. This is your problem; you see it, but you have neither the money to pay for it nor the ability to learn how to drive it.

A man under the influence of drugs is highly sensitive to hypnotic suggestions, not only verbal ones but, more often, telepathic suggestions. When a drug is taken by a group of people, they literally pollute each other's minds with hypnotic suggestions through their verbal and telepathic messages. Following a situation such as this, the users of drugs feel confused and lack direction because of the many commands implanted in their minds. They have many contradictory urges and drives, fears and loves, positive and negative emotions. When a man wants to be totally

---

1 Agni Yoga Society, *Fiery World II*, par. 351.

positive, the negative creeps in, and he cannot decide between the two because of many other interventions. The result is that he falls into apathy, confusion, and sleep.

Such a state creates dependence upon others. A man often obeys any command in order to save himself, but inwardly he rejects the command. He falls apart and cannot pull himself together. Such men are sometimes used as unconscious slaves by other people to satisfy their physical urges or their criminal intentions. These circumstances eventually create deep hatred and distrust of all people. They lead a man to many kinds of crimes and eventually to suicide.

Consciousness is a field of light within our mind which we use to handle our life constructively: to secure our own and other's survival and to create communication and beauties toward greater goals — goals which bring greater joy and greater understanding and which enable us to handle others' problems as well as our own in creative ways.

Drugs impede such a possibility. I know of a famous author who, after producing some well-written books, began taking drugs. His later books show a tremendous decline in goal, construction, and depth. He distorted the flow of his inspirations, damaged his mechanism of creativity, and brought upon himself a great sense of failure.

A group of actors found themselves in a similar situation. Eventually they gave up and became "swimmers in muddy waters."

Q. Sometimes we hear that drugs help the users to have better communication. Is this true?

A. It seems so, but in reality drugs distort true communication. A man can communicate with others if the communication system within himself is up-to-date and in good order.

People think that their drug experience is spiritual. Spiritual does not mean hallucination, daydreaming, illusion, and emotional or astral turbulances. Spiritual means steady progress in awareness of facts, using them for the greater good for the greatest number of people.

The spiritual path is a progressive experience of enlightenment in responsibility and of growth in creative ability. Hallucinatory drugs lead only to confusion, in which you cannot trust your own experiences as being real. This creates an increasing and destructive doubt about yourself and the world. How can a man communicate with his friends through his telephone if his line is out of order?

The *assumed* communication of drug users can be analyzed as follows. The drug user loses his likes and dislikes, he loses his discrimination concerning things harmful or dangerous, and he accepts any activity and anything as joyous or pleasure-giving — but he cannot use his ability to respond to dangers and the true needs of his fellow beings.

Under the influence of drugs, a man or woman can go to bed with any man or woman, regardless of whether the person is healthy or sick. Users obey any command and thus avoid friction because they feel weak. Eventually they become puppets of their habits or of the wills of other people.

In true communication there is a high level of understanding between two parties. The differences are seen, the similarities observed, and through a higher vision or idea they cooperate and try to bring that vision or idea into fulfillment. True communication is possible only when the communicants are striving toward the same goal and are laboring in the same field of service, though in different ways and on different levels.

I have witnessed many happenings in groups where drugs were being used. Once, for example, a young man named George was sitting on the floor, eating from a plate in his lap. John entered the room, jerked the plate away from him, and began eating the food. He stood in front of George, calling him ugly names and using vulgar and profane language as he emptied the plate. John's actions and words did not bother George in the least. He sat meekly in the corner and continued smiling up at John.

In the same group, Jim was sitting on the grass in the yard when Tom came by, stopped in front of him, and urinated on his head. Most men would have been outraged, but Jim just sat there and laughed loudly along with Tom.

In another group one of the girls was sick with a high fever. The boys stripped her and painted her whole naked body. They then used her for their satisfaction without getting the least resistance from her.

I listened to many conversations in these groups and found that these people cannot follow any direct line of communication.

They jump from one subject to another and most of their talk is limited to their physical urges and criminal drives. These incidents are defined as "good communication" according to their dictionary.

In communication we have a response that carries with it a high voltage sense of responsibility and clear knowledge of the motives and goals of the communicants. Drugs hinder this process, though they give glimpses of reality in distorted forms. These glimpses are always lost because of the lack of power to grasp them, to see through them. Suicide and crime, which are common among drug users, are clear evidence of distorted communication within themselves and with others.

Q. Some drug users see colors and many unusual forms. How, in your opinion, do these things happen?

A. When you are loaded with certain drugs, for example LSD, your brain cells are highly stimulated. This stimulation increases the sensitivity of the cells, and they begin to record vibrations or impressions coming from the emotional planes, from lower mental planes, and even from space. These are translated into colors or sound sensations according to their range of vibration. Impressions are distorted at the time of reception because the extreme stimulation of the brain cells disturbs the incoming vibrations. The impressions are then transferred to the etheric brain for translation. The etheric brain translates them according to the contents of the mind, the emotions, and suggestions coming from people and the surrounding environment. The result is again reflected to the brain, which mixes the result with the new distorted impression, and so on, ending in a total confusion of colors, forms, and wishful experiences.

Sometimes the drug rends the etheric protective web, and direct impressions pour down to the brain from the astral world. Eventually the brain fails more and more in its function, and the man becomes an irrational being as he loses his sense of timing, the sense of space, and the sense of relativity.

Q. What about transpersonal experiences as, for example, being out of the body or floating in the air?

A. LSD users have that illusion, but I do not call it an experience. A young girl whom I knew, feeling out of the body, wanted to test her new achievement so she jumped out of a window. She died immediately. Maybe that was an experience!

I do not deny that there is a genuine experience of being consciously out of the body and doing things with directed will, but such an achievement is the result of long years of meditation, aspiration, and of a life of service.

To be spiritual does not mean to hear and see things that you cannot understand. To be out of the body and to feel oneness with all the universe does not mean spirituality. Many devils and witches are out of the body. Feeling one with the universe under the influence of drugs deprives you of your sense of individuality and your sense of duty and responsibility.

Let us say that you have had spiritual experiences. This does not mean progress if these experiences occurred while you were under the influence of drugs. They may even mean retrogression.

Many people are not yet ready for high psychic experiences. If, by chance, they have such experiences, they do more harm to them than good. Such experiences often delay their progress on the path for hundreds of years. We must not strive for psychic experiences until we have developed our physical, emotional, and mental natures, and until we have proved that we can use them as tools of service, as a healthy mechanism for experiences.

We may say that a man enjoys having sexual experiences, but suppose he is a nine-year-old boy, and someone imposes his will upon him and causes that little one to have a sexual experience. It is probable that the child will hate the thought of sex after this experience and will suffer for many years, if not for his whole life. He may totally reject sex or continue to hold the painful memory of such an experience.

Q. What about that feeling that they are one with the universe?

A. I think that this is another symptom of a deranged nervous system caused by drugs. I once asked a man who had this universal feeling, "How do you explain your so-called experience?"

He said, "Just a great feeling that I was one with everything."

"If you were one with everything then you were a flower, a fish, a bird, an animal, a tree. Can you tell me how a fish feels, how a tree or a bird feels? Can you respond or react as a fish, as a bird, or as an animal?"

The man hesitated to give an answer because he now felt that it was an illusion, not an experience.

Experience is gained when the consciousness is in the process of elevation and is gaining control of its mechanism. Experience is lost when the consciousness is becoming lower and growing dimmer. True experience increases your sanity, reveals new horizons, and strengthens your power to expand and control. Experience makes you know yourself better and gives you a stronger urge to improve yourself.

Most of the experiences that man undergoes are nothing but pain and suffering, registered by him when his consciousness is not in focus. Such experiences are registered as post-hypnotic suggestions in our minds.

Q. Is such an experience of unity recorded in any book?

A. You have it in the *New Testament* where Christ told one of His disciples to go to the sea, catch a fish which had a coin in its mouth, and pay the tax "... for me and for you."[1]

This shows that one who has mastered the unity of consciousness with the universe knows whatever is going on within the parts and within the whole as clearly as he sees his face in a mirror.

Q. What about past reincarnation experiences?

A. Even the memories of past reincarnations of average, sound minded people are not valid. What about the experiences of those who hallucinate under the influence of a drug? A man claimed that under a drug he was able to know his past reincarnation of which he was very proud. I asked him to prove it, but he was unable to present any proof. On the contrary, after using drugs in trying again to see his past reincarnation, he lost his present one in the hospital.

I do not deny that man has been born before, but to know your past lives, you must be able to bridge the gap between the lower and the higher mind and between the personality and the higher Self, through occult meditation.

Drugs cultivate a spirit of dependence. When you try to depend on drugs and on the people around you, you cannot cultivate independence. No one can enter the path of conscious evolution if he becomes dependent physically, emotionally, or mentally. The goal of the human being, for a long time, should be the achieve-

---

[1] Matthew 17:27

ment of independence. To depend means to be controlled by outer conditions, to become the effect, not the cause. As long as a man is living an effect-life, he cannot develop himself and unfold his latent powers and achieve mastery. To master means to be a cause; to be a slave means to be an effect. Drugs make us slaves. Those who are praising drug usage in youth are slaves of their own greed and ignorance. Man is here on this planet to bloom and unfold his latent seeds of beauty through all his expressions. All his talents are the result of labor, striving, and self-mastery.

Once a man depends upon mechanical means to reach unknown goals, he fails to improve his own inner powers and falls into the pattern of habit. Habits make you lose control of your mechanism. I have observed that a person who loses control of his physical, emotional, and mental mechanism is like a boat on a river which becomes a waterfall. If the boat is far away from the waterfall, it is possible to save it; if it is at the midway point in the current, it is difficult to save it; if it is caught in the current and is moving rapidly toward the fall, it will be almost impossible to save it. Such is the story of those who are caught in the current of their habits.

Q. Do you not think that marijuana relaxes some people?

A. It does for a while, but then it creates such a great strain upon the body system that it forces the man to use more and more to relax. Thus he loses the opportunity to depend upon his own mental ability to overcome his difficulties through his own power and to achieve a degree of self-mastery. A man will become able to master his problems by mastering them, not by ignoring them. Marijuana makes you ignore the dangers and the difficulties but does not eliminate them or help you to master them. Thus, instead of being your own master, you become the slave of the drug.

Q. Do you think that the experiences they are having are valid?

A. I wish I knew what experiences you are talking about.

Q. For example, many drug users have had the experience of seeing colors; they have experienced carelessness, rest, and peace. Are these experiences valid?

A. It depends upon what effect they will have on their mechanisms as a whole and what results they will bring in their life. But in general I would say that these are artificial experiences you are talking about. Experiences can be real only when there is someone who experiences them in full consciousness. Experiences that are imposed upon our organism without our full consciousness are purely post-hypnotic suggestions.

Many, many apples have fallen upon your head in the past, but only Newton was able to discover the Law of Universal Gravitation. This is a valid experience because the consciousness was awake enough to reach conclusions through a deep thinking process.

One word that you used caught my attention. You said, "They had experiences of carelessness." Carelessness is not putting your problems into writing and then burning the paper to rid yourself of them; it is a state of consciousness in which your troubles cannot bother you because you can handle them and stand above them.

The world will never advance through escapism or "carelessness" but through facing our responsibilities and duties. True serenity is reached not through drugs but through overcoming our mechanical responses and handling the impressions with wisdom and insight. A true careless state of mind is achieved through the practice of detachment, by non-identification with changing world conditions and situations, and by firmly stabilizing oneself in one's highest core of wisdom.

Spiritual experiences urge us to sacrifice ourselves for the service to humanity, to minimize humanity's suffering, and to bring greater wisdom and joy to all.

It is true that they are, so to say, "seeing" colors, "hearing" notes, and "traveling to the stars." But when they awaken, they are weak, lost to themselves and to society. They are chiefly responsive to negative emotions and to the collective emotional reactions of humanity.

The expansion of consciousness expresses itself as a greater sense of responsibility, a greater urge to labor, a greater clarity in seeing problems, and greater talents to meet the problems.

I had two friends who were studying mathematics and physics. They were very interested in the idea of creating some kind of smog device to save people from that poison. By chance they started using marijuana and proceeded to LSD and heroin. They left the university and now live in a commune infected with venereal diseases. Drugs "expanded" their consciousness to such a degree that they did not even think about their own health and well-being, and they were forced to satisfy their cravings.

*Q. How can people who use drugs for the purpose of conscious-
ness expansion, as they were led to believe, tell the difference
between a distortion in consciousness and a genuine expansion?*

A. If their consciousness is truly expanded, they will exercise a
tremendous control over their physical, emotional, and mental reactions and be *themselves* instead of becoming the plaything of
outer influences and drives.

*Q. What are the signs that one's consciousness is truly expand-
ing?*

A. We have already mentioned some of them, but we can add
more:

1. A true urge to know more and to be more.
2. A steady watchfulness and observation of one's own life
   and relationships.
3. An increasing urge to serve and to uplift other people.
4. An increasing control over one's own actions, feelings,
   thoughts, and words.
5. Clear thinking and seeing things as they really are.
6. An increasing enthusiasm for the welfare of humanity.
7. Better relationships with others.
8. Greater ability to understand the problems of others and to
   meet their needs.
9. An increasing sense of harmlessness.
10. An increasing power of creativity.
11. An increasing insight into the Plan for humanity and the
    planet within the solar system.
12. An increasing sensitivity to impressions coming from
    great planetary, solar, and cosmic Lives, which results in
    creative action and scientific discovery, and which may
    reveal to us the answers to most of our misery and isola-
    tion.

These are a few of the results of an expanding consciousness.

A man is his sanity. If his sanity is fifty percent, he is a fifty
percent man; if he has no sanity, he is lost to himself and to humanity. *Sanity is the percentage of a person's willpower, love,
and intelligence.* As these three factors increase, his sanity

increases. As the three factors decrease, his sanity becomes doubtful and eventually vanishes altogether.

Drugs work against sanity because they weaken the will, make a man harmful to himself and others, and obscure the intelligence. Drugs are an endeavor to escape from the realities of life. A man does not realize that this escape does nothing to help eliminate the realities but rather makes him unable to handle them. When he realizes this, he feels extreme pain, which leads to self-destructive actions.

Q. What can a person do to expand his consciousness in a natural and healthy way?

A. I would say that a person must study and learn in school or out of school. He must choose a course of interest to him and pursue it to the end, having in mind the service to humanity. He must associate as much as possible with talented individuals in many fields of endeavor. He must visit many countries and come in contact with various religious philosophies and traditions. When he is ready, he must start building the bridge of continuity of consciousness between his practical mind and his Inner Core.

Another excellent way to expand the consciousness is to create a field of service and dedicate oneself to it. Service will show the need. In trying to meet the need, the consciousness will expand.

I also recommend study and regular periods of clear thinking upon chosen subjects. This is the scientific meditation to which I am referring.[1]

Q. In your opinion, what is the reason that people are using drugs?

A. I am going to give you what I believe to be some of the reasons:

1. People are influenced by fantastic promises that they will break through and touch higher dimensions of consciousness or life. They are told that they will be able to face and solve their own problems easily and joyfully; that they will feel greater pleasure in their many relationships; that they will not be bothered by adverse conditions and will live life as it is — in great contentment.

---

[1] The fundamentals of meditation are given in *The Science of Meditation* by H. (Torkom) Saraydarian.

Making such promises is misusing the inner urges of people to reach a state of invulnerability, a stage of enlightenment and power to enjoy life more abundantly. Behind these promises is greed for money.

2. There is also a political aspect. In many countries the temptations and weaknesses of youth are used. Many kinds of drugs are spread among young people to prevent them from bringing decisive changes in the social and political life of the country — changes which would be disadvantageous to the ruling interests. For this reason it seems to be very difficult to prevent or stop drug traffic within a country or from country to country. My mother used to say that it is most difficult to find the thief who is a member of the family.

3. Our educational system may be partly responsible for the growing use of drugs. I know many high school teachers and college professors who smoke marijuana and perhaps use other drugs, too. Could it be that they also sell them?

   In better educational systems not only must the teacher's knowledge and background be approved, but his self-control and purity of motive must seriously be considered before he is given a position in any school.

4. I also think that our television programs are a great factor in inducing a mechanical way of thinking in our children through well-prepared hypnotic suggestions, advertisements, and criminal films. Mechanical thinking makes a man susceptible to forceful suggestions and weakens the power of the will to resist the pleasures that are eventually harmful. A man who cannot use his judgment can easily be led to criminal action.

5. Family conditions are also a contributing factor in the wide use of drugs. A happy family life is becoming less and less common. Children are left without guidance and love, without the image of an honest, working, loving father and loving mother who care. Sometimes the home conditions weigh so heavily upon the hearts of the little ones that they want to escape from these situations through self-destructive actions.

6. Incorrect information concerning drugs is being presented in the teaching of history. Drug advocates say that some ancient civilizations and religious sects used and are still using herbs, flowers, seeds, and other drug-producing plants. It is true that they were used in ancient times, but history lessons fail to in-

dicate that the use of drugs was one of the main factors in the decline of these ancient civilizations and religious sects. Its use made people unable to face increasing problems of life and to solve them for their own betterment.

7. We must consider, too, the tremendous energies coming from powerful minds and from Great Ones. New energies are precipitated from space through the signs and heavenly bodies due to their new relationships with our solar system and earth. These energies exercise a great influence upon our etheric centers, especially upon those centers that are already active, and we are "carried away" in all our activities. If the energies are not assimilated and directed into creative channels, they will produce insanity, emotional imbalance, and manifold physical problems. The handling of these energies will not be by escaping through the use of drugs but by conscious striving toward a more creative and beautiful life — through meditation and sacrificial service.

Q. It occurred to me that many drug users are intelligent and promising young people. How can you explain this?

A. Your statement is true. They are tempted more because of their intelligence, sensitivity, and ambitions.

To retard the progress of a group or a nation, you must eliminate those who have good intentions and well-developed minds to put their intentions into practice. The agents of materialism and dark forces are not dull people. They look for advanced people to be used to their own advantage, and they use those methods which appeal to above average persons as they try to lead them into self-destruction or slavery.

They do not always succeed, however. Here and there, young and dynamic ones break the chains of their habits and come into the light. They are the ones who know how to fight against such destructive forces and how to live life more seriously. Their past suffering, the misery they have seen, the destruction that drugs have brought to their friends and to their own minds are recognized and rejected. Their greatest ambition now is to live more consciously and more creatively.

When you really know that you can lose something of great value, you appreciate it more.

Q. What is the astral plane?

A. It is a kind of cloud formation upon a sentient energy around our bodies and around the planet. This cloud formation has a certain range of vibration, which attracts and retains the waves of desire, glamor, and figments of our imagination, based upon our cravings and negative emotional reactions to people.

Each desire, each negative emotion has its own wave length and its own frequency. A certain number of these wave lengths and frequencies accumulate and form an overcast of an illusionary world. Those who tune in with this world through drugs or sickness bring in many glamors from that plane because of their associations and their particular rate of vibration. They may even tune in with entities that are living in those spheres and become a channel for their folly.

The term *astral world* or *desire world* is a classical expression in esoteric science. I am sure that in the future advanced psychologists will give it a different name-symbol, closer to its true meaning. The main thing is to free ourselves from the glamor of that sphere. We are told that those who follow the Teaching of the Christ are eventually released from that sphere of influence.

Q. If on the astral plane people can have whatever they want to have as real, why then do they try to possess people in order to satisfy their desires?

A. As astral entities pass from the astral plane to the mental plane, they leave their astral bodies in the astral sphere. There they float about as a piece of wood upon the ocean, and because of their finer material they last for many years.

They are charged with all the desire qualities that the entity living in them accumulated or used. They are extremely magnetic and can easily be tuned in with those astral vibrations that have any similarity to them. When they are tuned in with a person's vibrations, they possess him through a remote-control mechanism, and they transfer into him urges and tremendous cravings for drugs, alcohol, meat, crime, and suicide. The influence is so potent that the man is divided between his own emotional urges and the urges coming from astral possessions. A drug user is an open channel for such influences for a long time after he stops using drugs.

On the astral plane are agents of the dark forces whose duty it is to create separations and to cause criminal actions, inertia, tyranny, and materialism. They are very careful not to lose an opportunity to enter into an astral body and energize it. When a person or a group is tuned in with such an astral vehicle, which is saturated with various desires and vices, the dark forces pour their destructive influences into the person or the group, causing much suffering to their victims.

We also have those earth-bound human beings who have passed on, but who, because of their very material and emotional ties, cannot progress, and they awaken on the astral plane. They are mechanically attracted to those vibrations that are produced in whorehouses, in slaughterhouses, through crime, through hatred, and in negative emotional atmospheres. They float unconsciously into such locations and, when tuned in, possess people and use their mechanisms for their own satisfaction. There are many instances in the *New Testament* where Christ cast out such entities from the sphere of the man and healed him.

Q. How do you help drug users?

A. There are many ways of helping them. I usually try to make them see and realize the damage that they are doing to their bodies, to other people, to their future well-being, and to their expected achievement in many fields. I try to help them create a progressive goal, a vision, and encourage them to strive toward it. I try to make them realize that they are not acting of their own free will but are subject to many outer or imposed influences which create in them blind urges and forceful drives.

I suggest that they write articles and improve upon them periodically. I do not suggest that they write poems because they feel that they are doing well when they are constructing only unrelated sentences, just as some users think they are painting when they are simply throwing paint on a canvas and calling it "modern art."

I give them heavy labor which includes climbing mountains, digging ditches, cleaning, gardening, running, and swimming. Swimming is very beneficial; group dancing is good. All these activities must be carried on and on until they are exhausted.

The main thing I try to do is to awaken their willpower and continually strengthen it through physical, emotional, and mental discipline and exercise.

All our help will be superficial unless we develop in them the will to control and guide their mechanisms according to the highest goal they have created for themselves so that they can use that will in a field of service that will evoke the best within them.

There are many other means, but I shall add only one more. I try to make them realize that I truly love them, and I endeavor with them to achieve a state of freedom in which all their talents will spring forth and flourish. "Thus one can avoid the chief enemy of mankind — all narcotics."[1]

---

[1] Agni Yoga Society, *Heart*, par. 123.

Chapter XVII

TIME AND OUR LIFE

... If people but knew that they live for only an insignificant number of years in comparison to Eternity, and if they would stop thinking that this stage is limited by cosmic ordainment, then the beauty of cosmic evolution would unfold before them.[1]

We are taught that time is separated into three dimensions: the past, the present, and the future. What is the past? The past is the seed, the point from which we started. In that seed were placed all our future possibilities, the model, the "likeness of His picture" toward which we are traveling age after age. Thus the entire life of man is the process of achieving and fulfilling that "high calling," of producing the "picture." The present is nothing but the steps taken toward that goal. What is the future? The future is the fulfillment of the purpose of the seed. The seed is the past, the beginning. The tree coming out of the seed is the future. The present is the process through which the seed becomes the tree, the steps toward fulfillment. It is the moment of transformation from seed to tree.

People believe that we have the opportunity to alter or to change, to build or to destroy our future at any moment of our choosing. This is true if we look at life as a short period. It is not true if we view life from the standpoint of eternity. Eternity is the time period from the seed to the tree, from beginning to fulfillment, *the only real time*; it is unbroken and without division.

Man is composed of two elements. One is the substance of eternity which we call *Spirit*, *Essence*, or *Inner Man*. The other one is the substance with which the body and personality, the outer man, is built. For the inner man, there is no time; there is only eternity, one unbroken line. But for the outer man, time is divided into days, weeks, months, and years. The problem is that

---

1 Agni Yoga Society, *Infinity I*, par. 110.

each one of us identifies himself with the outer man and loses himself in it. We no longer exist except as an automaton; we are born, live, work, suffer, die, and disappear. All that we do is done in response to outer influences. Our whole life is a series of reactions and reflexes, while the Inner Man sleeps deeply. Most of humanity is living as bodies in deep sleep.

For such people time is divided into periods of varying lengths, and each period has a new message or warning for them. Each period is either a victory or a defeat. To those with this attitude, the events of time exert extreme tensions. When they succeed in a current undertaking, they are extremely happy, acting as though they had reached their ultimate goal, as though their life's purpose had been fulfilled. On the other hand, if failure, sickness, loss, or other misfortunes occur, they quickly lose themselves, thinking that all is lost. Their mind cannot see beyond the moment. They have no hope.

Hope is a look into eternity. It is an inner conviction that everything has not ended, but that there are coming possibilities, opportunities which can change the situation completely. Hope is a moment of detachment from the "present," from the events that cause depression, confusion, and complications which force a person to believe that everything has come to an end. Hope opens new doors toward eternity. Hope is that moment in which we become conscious of the transitory nature of everything, aware that there is eternity with its numberless possibilities. At the moment that hope enters our hearts, the pressure of time becomes weaker and weaker, and new energy begins to flow within us. The past is not fearful. The present with its difficulties challenges us. The future becomes brighter and brighter. Here our viewpoint changes. We do not stand in the ever-flowing present with our regrets, disappointments, remorse for our past, and fears for the future. We stand now in the light of eternity, in which the Spark gradually becomes a Sun. In the vision of this gradual and eventual achievement, time with its sorrows, sufferings, happinesses, losses, and gains disappears, and peace descends upon our hearts.

Whenever I hurt myself in my childhood, my mother would say to me, "My son, when you grow up, you will forget. You will forget your pain and fear." These words gave me real comfort because my mind immediately began to detach itself from the painful present and concentrated upon the future, in which I could see myself without pain and fear. I saw myself as I wished to be, happy and without pain.

We can use the same technique for all our difficulties, sorrows, failures, and adversities when they are pressing heavily upon the heart, paralyzing our whole being, darkening our life path, and imprisoning our soul in immediate events, in immediate moments. It is at such moments that the mind ceases to act. The mind is obscured, and man is forced to find a way to handle the situation. He may commit a crime or suicide, he may destroy many objects around him, or he may sink into deep apathy. When his time concept is extended, however, he understands that there is a tomorrow, a time when many things can be changed, many possibilities born. Immediately a beam of light will enter his dark room and gradually illuminate his inner world.

To uplift man is to open a door to his future, to open for him the vision of eternity — the endless way which starts as a point and disappears into the Source of life through endless spirals and cycles. What does one loss mean after three hundred years? What does failure mean after four hundred years, two thousand years, if you have done your best? Again and again, life will give you opportunities to grow, to cultivate, until your inner seed has flourished perfectly, completely, and fully, until you have reached the destination toward which you were traveling from the beginning of time. In eternity your failures and losses will help you to rise higher and higher. All your sufferings will be roses on your path.

All holy books and deep literature of the world deal with timelessness. They are not the literature of the past, of the present, or even of the future. They are of eternity and for eternity. The *Bhagavad Gita* is timeless. In each line of this ancient writing, the consummation of the man of eternity can be seen. The picture of the God-man who belongs to all eternity is there.

The same is true of the *Gospels*. There is Christ and the way leading to Christ, the way of transmutation into the eternal. All true arts of the world belong to eternity. If you look at them through your inner eyes, the eternal awakens in you. For a moment time vanishes, your being goes beyond time and space. It enters eternity. *Every real victory is a victory over time and space.*

In the *Bible* we find the story about the wife of Lot. When God was destroying Sodom and Gomorrah, He ordered Lot to flee from the city and not to look back. Lot's wife did not listen.

She looked back, "... and she became a pillar of salt."[1] She was attached to the past and was unable to look to the future, to eternity; she limited herself to the past and became crystallized, a pillar of salt.

If we delve deeper into our studies and observations, we will see that all human ills are the result of a mind which is attached to the past, to the present only, or to the future. Eternity is like a river. The waves and the shadows upon it represent the hours, the months, the years, the ages. On the surface it is divided into fragments, but in its depths it is one — one stream of timelessness. People attach themselves to a wave, and after a while they are enveloped within the wave itself. This wave may be a memory, a possession, a dream, or an expectation. Because these things are identified with the passing minutes, days, or years, they produce a vacuum in the heart of man. In attempting to fill this vacuum, to quench this thirst, the man pursues the pleasures of his lower nature: material objects, dreams, jealousies, and hatreds. But the vacuum of his heart cannot be filled with the material or pleasures of the body. He is greedy, and because of his greed he attaches himself firmly to worldly things. He identifies with every pleasure to the degree that he loses himself in the objects of his pleasure.

Here his problem begins. When the objects of his pleasure cease to bring him enjoyment, he falls into the tide of depression, hopelessness, nervousness, and tensions with eventual complications. Detach this man from the passing waves, make him look at his life from the standpoint of eternity, and you will release him; you will establish peace, joy, and health in his mind, heart, and body, and the vacuum will be filled.

The progress of man can be seen in the following diagram. His progress is numbered from 7 to 1. At number 7, man is undeveloped, and at number 2 the man is fully developed.

7. Sleep
6. Present
5. Present — Past
4. Present — Past — Future
3. Future

---

[1] Genesis 19:26

2. Eternity

1. Duration

People on level 7 are those for whom life is an extended sleep. They have no concept of time. They live in a dreamy state of consciousness or in consciousness similar to that of a person in a drunken stupor. The lives of people on level 6 are directed or controlled by the present only. They are slightly more evolved than animals. People on level 5 are those whose lives are chiefly controlled by the past. They live and plan in reference to their past. People on number 4 live a balanced life between the past, present, and future. They are practical, advanced historians and politicians. Some outstanding lawyers belong in this category. The lives of people on level 3 are conditioned mainly by the future. They are the great visionaries of the world. Master Morya says:

> ... *You know that Agni lives in the hearts of those who love the future.*[1]

The term "future" has two meanings. The first concept concerns time. For example, next month is the future. The second meaning is that the future is a vision. When Christ said, "Be perfect," He was speaking about the future. If you are able to see through your imperfections to a state of being in which you are relatively perfect, you are seeing the future. If you love that future, the fire of aspiration is active within you and will push you forward toward your future. The visionaries of the world create great beauties, setting aflame the hearts of millions, thus conditioning the formation of the future. These holy dreamers or contemplatives are often responsible for the bringing about of great utopias.

Eternity belongs to the domain of time but a time which is not divided into past, present, and future. It forms one straight line or one unbroken circle. Only great Initiates are able to live in such a state of awareness.

Duration is out of the domain of time. In the *Stanzas of Dzyan* we read:

---

[1] Agni Yoga Society, *Fiery World II*, par. 26.

> *Time was not, for it lay asleep in the Infinite Bosom of Duration.*[1]

Where there is no manifestation, there is no time. There is no past, present, or future. Duration is a synonym for Space, in which all phenomenal existence disappears during the night of creation.

The greatest works of art have three elements: past, present, and future. As a whole they stand for eternity. Any artwork or action that is limited to one fraction of time is weak and transient. A work that belongs only to the past is a dead body. A work that belongs only to the future is attractive but too abstract. Those artworks that belong to eternity are the real creations of the indwelling soul.

Evil is that which is from the past but persists, forcing its continuance in the present. The continuation of that which is obsolete prevents progress in any field. Something may be very good for the present, but after ten years, if one is still attached to it, uses it, or teaches it, it becomes dangerous; it becomes an obstacle upon the way. Here we have conflict among conservative, opportunist, and progressive minds. The first is attached to the past, the second to the present, and the third to ideas, doctrines, or dreams of the future. Thus we have the agitations of the world, the revolutions, and the wars.

The same happens in the human psyche. There the past, present, and future are in conflict with one another, and a person is continually drawn to one or another of these aspects, tasting their bitterness. His state of mind is constantly changing because he has not yet arrived at the rock of eternity within himself. He has identified himself with his body, the past, and its associations. He has identified with his emotional nature, the present, and its associations. He has identified with the mental nature and its associations. These three natures are like ever-changing clouds, and a man has no peace, no assurance, no joy until he finds the eternal within himself.

Time is the path upon which the eternal pilgrim is walking to find Himself, the eternity within man. The eternity within man is the Real Man Himself. When he has found his Home within him-

---

[1] Blavatsky, H. P., *The Secret Doctrine*, Vol. I, p. 551.

self, the rights, values, and forms will be in proper proportion, and he will direct his life from the seat of eternity. Remember:

> ... *You know that Agni lives in the hearts of those who love the future.*[1]

---

[1] Agni Yoga Society, *Fiery World II*, par. 26.

Chapter XVIII

THE RAINBOW

*I set my bow in the clouds and it shall be for a sign
of a covenant between me and the earth.*[1]

Ancients spoke about a communication line between the Real and
the unreal, between the objective and subjective, between the true
man and the vehicles of expression. They symbolized this line of
communication with a rainbow, a bridge, a rope with seven
knots, a ladder, a pathway to point out an esoteric fact in the inner
world of man.

The verse from the *Bible*, given above, symbolizes a way of
communication between God and man, and we are told that it
marked the end of the flood. This is important to note, because
when the inner psychological bridge is built, it ends the flood of
glamors of the emotional world. The rainbow is mentioned also in
Revelations, wherein an angel appears having "the Rainbow of
the cloud upon his head."

There is an interesting fable from India about the goddess
Kundalini, who saw a rope hanging from Heaven. She wished to
climb it, but instead of going up, she went down. The rope ended
on an island, which was in the midst of a great ocean of darkness.
As she was descending, the rope was cut, and Kundalini fell
down, down into the deep, dark sea. Tradition says that this rope
has seven knots which symbolize the seven etheric centers. These
centers flourish in extreme beauty when man is able to climb the
rope or to build the bridge.

In Sanskrit language this bridge is called the *Antahkarana*. It
means the inner organ, the inner instrument through which the
Real Man receives experience. The Master Djwhal Khul says, "It

---

[1] Genesis 9:16

is the science of Antahkarana which lies behind all conscious awakening of the centers and their relations."

In the ancient mysteries of Eleusis there was an order of Bridge-Priestesses whose duty was to prepare people to build their inner bridge for their passing "from death to immortality." The name of their goddess was "The Lady of the Bridge." In Rome the priest was "The Bridge Builder Pontifex." In Norse mythology the rainbow is again mentioned. We are told that this bridge is built of light substance and that only the sons of God can travel upon it.

In Zoroastrian literature also we find reference to the bridge:

> *For all of them a path will be opened across the Kinvad Bridge. Moreover, the bridge becometh a broad bridge for the righteous, as much as the height of nine spears and length of those whom they carry is each separately three reeds; and it becometh a narrow bridge for the wicked, even unto the resemblance to the edge of a razor. And he who is of righteous passeth over the bridge... he who is of wicked, as he placed his feet upon the bridge, on account of affliction and its sharpness, falleth from the middle of the bridge and rolleth over head-foremost.*[1]

The Mohammedans speak of the bridge as being "thinner than a hair and sharper than a sword." According to the Moslem tradition, "the good man will be able to pass over the bridge, but the wicked will soon miss the footing and fall into hell."

The Great Pyramid symbolizes the bridge or the path of approach into the mysteries. The main passages lead from the outer door to the pit, from the pit to the Queen's Chamber, to the King's Chamber, and to "the secret places of the Most High." There are four air passages in addition, making seven passages in all. The disciple first descends to the pit, then rises slowly to the Queen's Chamber, next to the King's Chamber, then to be resurrected to "the secret place of the Most High." Psychologically he is building similar passages in his own inner pyramid.

Long ago in India, an initiation ceremony was held for those who were entering into the service of God. One of the interesting things they did was to invest the candidate with a sacred *thread.*

---

[1] Dawson, Meander Miles, *The Ethical Religion of Zoroaster*, pp. 239-240.

This thread consisted of three strands of yarn twisted into one thread and three of such threads braided and knotted into one circle. The yarn signifies the great principle of three in one and one in three. The one who was thus invested was called *Upanitor*, one who was brought close to his teacher. This thread was called *Yajnasutra*, which means a thread that ties a man to his Spirit or God. Another name for the thread was *Tridandi*; *tri* meaning three, *dandi* meaning to control, to conquer, or to correct. The disciple must make three great conquests: control over his speech, his thought, and his action. Three threads interwoven also signify three triads of the Universe which must be linked: Spirit, Soul, and Personality; Will, Love, and Light; Shamballa, Hierarchy, and Humanity.

In Christian literature the bridge is symbolized by the cross upon which the Christ (the Path) was crucified. The resurrection of the Lord symbolized the fact that the Path was no longer nailed, blocked, or cut but was set free, joining humanity with God. This is a wonderful symbol of the Antahkarana or the Golden Bridge, which must be built before a man can enter into the mysteries of his inner world.

PART II. THE RAINBOW BRIDGE

Step by step and stage by stage we construct that path, just as the spider spins its thread. It is that way back which we evolve out of ourselves.[1]

... A bridge must be found to prevent the loss of consciousness and to become enriched by the Higher World.[2]

... There appears a triangle on the mental plane, produced by manasic activity, and this triangle of fire begins slowly to circulate between the manasic permanent atom, and a point at the centre of the egoic lotus, and thence to the mental unit.... This triangle of fire, which is formed of pure electrical manasic force, waxes ever brighter until it produces an answering vibration from both the lower

---

[1] Master Djwhal Khul.

[2] Agni Yoga Society, *Hierarchy*, par. 397.

and the higher. This triangle is the nucleus of the antaskarana.[1]

 Before a man can tread the Path, he must become the Path itself.[2]

The field of our experience is not limited to our waking state or to our brain consciousness. We have contacts with higher levels. At times the contacts are with the emotional world, with the higher mental planes, or even with the buddhic world. However, these contacts are not fully registered because there is no transmitting agent, no direct line of communication. Our experiences resemble the sun's rays which sometimes pass through small openings between the clouds, falling upon our head for a moment and then disappearing again. In like manner, higher energies may touch our subtle bodies, and because of the lack of a transmitting agent, fail to be registered, assimilated, and used on lower planes.

Since ancient times we have been told that man is like a house with many stories and many rooms, but the lines of communication within the house are poor and inadequate. Some of the doors are locked and cannot be opened; others are too narrow, and those which can be opened allow for only very narrow passage. The stairs leading to the upper rooms are only partially constructed or are blocked by furnishings. Under such conditions a man lives in the lower part of the house and has little opportunity to use the other rooms. A man who lives in one room is not interested in the other rooms, and he is completely unaware that there are higher stories in his house. His house has no running water, although there is a water main close by. It has no electricity, although there is a fuse box on the wall. He has no inter-communication, although there are facilities for communication available. The man is using only two percent of his house, living a limited life, and not fulfilling the destiny of his soul.

If he awakens and recognizes the possibilities of his house, if he decides to live a full life, he must engage in a threefold activity. He must lay a network of electrical lines in every part of his house — a network that will bring life, energy, heat, and light to the whole house, integrating and aligning every part of the building. He must build a system of water pipes in all rooms and on all

---

[1] Bailey, Alice A., *A Treatise on Cosmic Fire*, p. 709.

[2] Blavatsky, H. P., *The Voice of the Silence*, p. 14.

levels of his house. He must install a system of communication, connecting all levels and all rooms so that he may live in any room, on any level, and be aware of all other levels or stories of the building. When he has carried out these projects, his dwelling will be an organized house. The people living there will be very close to each other, and the owner of the house will be aware of all that happens in any part of his home.

This is the picture of our psychological world, our inner world. We are using only a small part of our mechanism. At times we live only on the physical plane, briefly on the emotional level, and on rare occasions we are forced to use our mental rooms. People who are more advanced are using higher levels with more facilities, and those who are initiated into higher mysteries are using their Intuitional, Atmic, Monadic, and even Divine Planes. To pass into higher levels and to act there consciously, we must build a network of inner communication lines, lines of consciousness, lines of livingness, lines of creativity.

To build bridges means to establish communication between the Self and the not-self. These are the two poles between which man must build the sevenfold Rainbow Bridge. In esoteric literature hints have been given about the process of building the bridge. In the past thirty-five years, however, this literature has increased.[1] The Masters gave bits of information on this subject through Helena Petrovna Blavatsky, and the Master Djwhal Khul gave more instructions about the bridge through Alice A. Bailey. In esoteric terminology this bridge, the Antahkarana, means the eternal organ, the eternal instrument, the Path, the Rainbow Bridge.

Throughout our journey to the Blue Peak, to the Jewel, we are forced to pass through deep abysses, and across these chasms we build many bridges. We build bridges in that region of the mountain which we call the etheric-physical plane. We build bridges between the emotional and mental planes. All our bridges are built in substance and consciousness. We build hundreds of such bridges in our mental world, extending our interest from one object to another, gradually eliminating the limiting walls of our prejudices, and opening our hearts to all Creation, to the flowers, the trees, the animals, and to humanity.

---

[1] Written in 1969.

In our psychological world, to build bridges means to make an idea complete; to connect it with another idea, forming a new synthesized idea for a special purpose; again, to connect this synthesized idea with a higher and larger idea, with the energies on higher planes, and so on and on until we touch the Divine Plan, the Purpose and the Will of God.

The building of psychological bridges takes place in two directions: first toward the lower planes and secondly toward the higher planes. Toward the lower, the unit of consciousness, wherever it is focussed, tries to gain conscious control over the action, emotions, and thinking processes of these lower bodies, building them into goal-fitting mechanisms. This endeavor continues until the world of personality is integrated with "power lines" and presents a unique whole, sensitive in all its parts and acting as one organism. Man must try to connect the integrated personality with the Soul or with the Chalice and bring about a Soul-infused personality. Then comes the striving to connect the Soul-infused personality with the Spiritual Triad, the glory of which will shine through the Soul-infused personality as great creative glory and beauty.

On this path of ascent, men build bridges between the Self and the not-self. The bridge is the consciousness between the two. The not-self is the previous self, left behind, to be used as an instrument of expression and contact on its plane. If man's consciousness is identified with one sub-plane, he is not able to observe that plane or its activities because his self *is* that sub-plane. His unfoldment is a process of detachment from his identified level and the establishing of identification with the next higher sub-plane.

Our earth consciousness starts with the not-self. We see the existing universe, but we have no ability to detach ourselves from that universe. We completely identify with the universe; our universe is that portion of the existence with which we come in contact.

The diagram on page 203 will offer further clarification. At 10 degrees we are slightly awakened, and we begin to sense that the universe has its own individual existence. We start to sail away from the shore of our mother as a newborn baby.

At 25 degrees we begin to doubt that our physical body is our Self. In this way, the universe becomes the not-self, the body becomes the not-self, but the rest still persists as Self.

At 50 degrees we separate ourselves from the emotional world, its responses and reactions so that eventually the emotional world also ceases to be a part of our Self and becomes a part of the not-self.

At 75 degrees our mental body detaches and becomes a part of the not-self with all its modifications.

This pole is called the "Pole of Self and not-self."

SELF

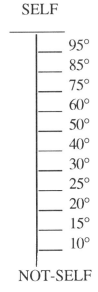

	95°
	85°
	75°
	60°
	50°
	40°
	30°
	25°
	20°
	15°
	10°

NOT-SELF

Up to 95 degrees and beyond, the not-self is mixed with the Self. At 10° and below, the Self is present within the not-self.

At 85 degrees we pass into the intuitional world.

At 90 degrees the atmic body separates.

At 95 degrees we enter the Monadic Plane.

At 100 degrees we become our True Self, one with the "Father." At this stage we realize that we are one with the Self in the Universe.

This is an approximate picture of the bridge building process by which the Real Man reaches out to his Home — the Blue Peak.

To explain this process further: Spirit and matter crossing each other produce the selves in us or the centers of consciousness, the "I's" in us. This is illustrated in the next diagram, "The Pole of Spirit."

The point where Spirit and matter meet forms the "I" of the man or the controlling center. If the proportion is equal, let us say 15 and 15, we have a balanced man on low levels.

A Soul-infused personality has a 50/50 balance, when man radiates the glory of the Spirit through the lower man as much as possible. After the fiftieth degree, the Spirit gains momentum, and the man becomes spiritually radioactive. He undertakes great services on higher levels, in larger areas.

THE POLE OF SPIRIT

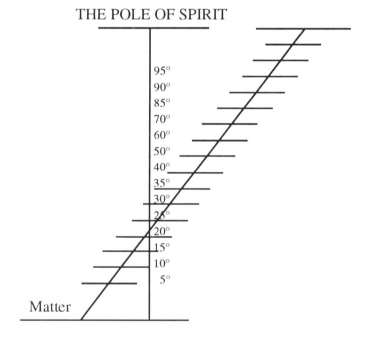

Actually these two poles are one pole: "The Pole of Spirit."

They are shown as two poles to indicate the percentage of Spirit and matter in any given condition of achievement.

To make the picture even clearer, the following diagrams are given.

SPIRIT

MATTER

This diagram indicates the two poles of the one existence. The vertical line is the Spirit aspect; the horizontal line is the matter aspect.

SPIRIT SIDE

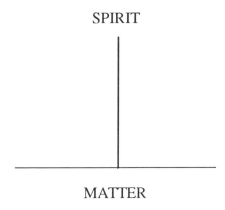

MATTER SIDE

This diagram indicates the proportions of Spirit and matter.

At its lowest degree or at the lowest crystallization of Spirit, number 1, Spirit striking matter, an atom is created.[1] This is the mineral kingdom.

Number 2 is the vegetable kingdom.

Number 3 is the animal kingdom.

Number 4 is the human kingdom — the average man.

Number 5 represents the aspirant.

Number 6 is the disciple.

Number 7 represents the Master.

Number 8 is the Christ.

Number 9 symbolizes Divinity.

In all these diagrams the following points are emphasized:

- Matter in its highest form is Spirit.
- Spirit in its lowest aspect is matter, as is taught in *The Secret Doctrine.*
- Going toward Spirit, matter (or limitation) decreases, and a time comes when matter is spiritualized.
- The spiritualization of matter produces the unfoldment of consciousness and the blooming of hidden treasures of the Spirit.
- At the point where Spirit and matter cross each other, consciousness begins to unfold. As the crossing point rises, you are acquiring more consciousness; with more consciousness, you live a more abundant life.

To increase your consciousness means to build bridges until you are fully awake on all levels and in all states of being. On the scale of Spirit and matter we find explanation of all love and hatred, bliss and misery, power and weakness, light and darkness, creativity and inertia, health and sickness. As Spirit dominates, virtues increase; the Inner Man proportionally gains more control over his mechanism or the not-self. Because of his newly built bridges and extensions, the Real Man begins to control his home.

---

[1] Please refer to the second diagram on page 205.

PART III. THE BRIDGE

The bridge has three main parts or threads:

- The first one is called the *Sutratma* or *life thread.*
- The second is called the *Antahkarana* or the *consciousness thread.*
- The third is called the *creative thread.*

The *first thread*, the Sutratma is anchored in the heart, and it brings life to the body. It is the bridge between the Spirit and the heart or the blood stream. Sometimes it is called the *life cord.* It comes directly from the Monad.

The *second thread* comes from the Soul and anchors itself in the brain. This is the part of the Antahkarana which gives man consciousness. This cord is called the consciousness thread and is the lower part of the main Antahkarana which bridges the gap between the mental unit and mental permanent atom. The Antahkarana thus links the personality with the Monad because it bridges the highest aspect of personality, the mental unit, and the lowest aspect of the Spiritual Triad, the higher mind, via the manasic permanent atom found on the first sub-plane of the mental plane.

Once a relationship is established between the personality and the Spiritual Triad, the will energy starts to flow into the personality. We are told that this is very dangerous in the early stages if it is not balanced by the love energy of the Soul. Will energy can be very destructive if there are negative and separative thoughtforms in the mental plane and heavy glamors in the emotional plane. The will energy can be used extensively by these negative forces to increase the suffering of the world of men.

The *third thread*, the creative thread, is constructed by man himself. It is an extension of the life thread and is triple.

The first strand of this triple thread starts from the heart and reaches the spleen, uniting the physical body with the vital body, passing through the etheric permanent atom to the force-field of the will petals of the Chalice. The second thread passes from the solar plexus to the heart, to the astral permanent atom, and then to the force-field of the love petals of the Chalice. On its way it picks up the energy of the first thread. By this process the astral and etheric bodies are bridged. The third thread starts from the ajna center and goes to the head center and reaches to the force-field of the knowledge petals of the Chalice, on its way entwining the two other threads. In this way the astral body and the mental body are bridged and connected with the Chalice.

We are told that when this creative thread — which is an extension of the two basic threads — is sufficiently constructed, it is anchored in the throat center.

When the third thread is built, man becomes more active in his expression. He can externalize his dreams on canvas, in clay, or in marble. He can create great music. He can be a capable surgeon or a real statesman according to his rays because now his inner beauty has a way to express itself on the physical plane.

To a greater or lesser degree, true artists are bridge builders. They have built bridges within themselves and thus became a channel to give expression to their creative energies, inspirations, and visions. They also create bridges in those people with whom they come in contact, directly or indirectly, through their creative works.

In *A Treatise on Cosmic Fire* we are also told that "lower types of humanity use the Sutratma as it passes through the etheric body." Average man utilizes almost entirely that part of the Sutratma which passes through the astral plane. Intellectual man utilizes the Sutratma as it passes through the lower levels of the mental plane, down through the astral plane to the physical plane in its two sections. Aspirants on the physical plane use the Sutratma as it passes through the lower sub-planes of the abstract levels of the mental plane. They are beginning to build the Antahkarana between the Triad and personality.

> *Applicants for initiation and initiates up to the third initiation use both the sutratma and the antaskarana, employing them as a unit. The power of the Triad begins to pour through, thus energising all human activities upon the physical plane, and vitalising in every increasing degree the man's thought forms.*[1]

Corresponding to these three threads we have in the spinal column another threefold thread. We are told that this threefold thread is the externalization of the former three threads. In the spinal column we have Ida, Pingala, and Shushumna. They

---

[1] Bailey, Alice A., *A Treatise on Cosmic Fire*, pp. 959-960.

correspond to the Antahkarana, to the creative thread, and to the Sutratma. Ida, Pingala, and Shushumna are called "a threefold way of approach and of withdrawal." The Father aspect in man can reach the basic center and raise these three fires when the Antahkarana is built. In this way the channel opens between the base of the spine, the brain, and the head center, making man capable of escaping out of the physical body in order to have continuity of consciousness upon higher planes.

In esoteric literature the *Kundalini Fire* is often mentioned. The Kundalini Fire is nothing else but the union of these three fires. The Tibetan Master says, "These three paths of life are the channels for electric fire, solar fire and fire by friction...."[1]

All these three fires are focussed in the base of the spine. The union of these fires or *Kundalini* may be raised up through the spinal column to unite with the head center at the time the Antahkarana is built and the centers are awakened if the channels are unobstructed. As the building of the Antahkarana continues, correspondingly these three also rise to build new systems of communication within the human frame.

As the Antahkarana is in the process of construction and the three-fold fires are in the process of rising upward, the creative center of the human being shifts from the sacral center to the throat center and then, eventually, the ajna center becomes the creative center of the human being. From this center the true observer watches the drama of life and expresses the Divine Plan to the world of men.

In connection with the Antahkarana we are told that there are three glands which form a triangle in the body. These glands come into activity through the downpouring forces of the higher planes. The *pituitary gland* becomes active when forces flow into it from the lower mental, the astral, and the etheric planes via the Sutratma. The *pineal gland* starts its activity when forces enter from the Soul. The *alta major center* becomes active when the Rainbow Bridge is built. These three then become a fiery triangle when the man enters into the Third Initiation. At the Third Initiation the Antahkarana is completely built.

This bridge building process at present is going on within individuals, and in the near future the individual bridges will be so

---

[1] Bailey, Alice A., *Esoteric Healing*, p. 185.

numerous that we will have a great rainbow: a group Antahkarana connecting humanity with the Hierarchy and Shamballa.

As this bridge becomes stronger, the influence of Love, Wisdom, Light, and Power will increase in the world. We will have more scientific revelations, arts that we never dreamed of, and social orders which will give humanity the real joy of cooperation and brotherhood. Brotherhood will be an established scientific fact. Actually to build the Antahkarana means to open all channels through which the will of the Self will flow and radiate. It means to build a new wiring system through which the life of the Universe can circulate, giving health and happiness and leading humanity to higher dimensions of living.

The Tibetan Master says,

... When the antahkarana of a group is rightly constructed, then the individualised group-will will disappear in the full consciousness of the monadic purpose or clear directed will.[1]

This will also give man a sense of *continuity of consciousness*. This means that he will be aware of whatever is going on upon any plane. In his brain consciousness man will be able to register all that is happening upon the astral, mental, intuitional, and higher abstract planes. He will be able to work and express himself through any plane as consciously as he does now on the physical plane.

At will he will be able to pass into the astral, mental, Intuitional Planes, and up. He will be conscious after he goes to sleep and passes into higher levels. This is what continuity of consciousness means. This will give him the highest advantage to work on the physical plane and bring down into expression all impressions, inspirations, and visions seen and contacted on higher planes, greatly enriching his life. This will help him also to see things in their right proportion and relationship. Little waves of problems and difficulties will not disturb him. Gradually he will serve with higher and higher groups. He will contact one of the Master's Ashrams, he will meet his Master, he will be assigned responsible work in the Ashram, and gradually he will become sensitive to impressions coming from "the Center where the Will of God is known."

---

[1] Bailey, Alice A., *The Rays and the Initiations*, p. 30.

The Antahkarana is the Path. Once man puts his feet on the Path, he starts to enlarge his relationships, communications, and sense of reality. At the end of the Path he has an oceanic consciousness.

PART IV. HUMAN LIVES

Like the pearls on a thread, so is the long series of human lives strung together on Sutratma.[1]

In the process of building the Antahkarana, slowly some of your past lives may appear to you, first in parts, then gradually in wholes. Thus your sense of continuity, the sense of immortality, becomes clearer. You understand the meaning of some of the happenings in your present life, the reasons for many events, and you walk through life with more faith, more vision, and with a better sense of proportion.

After the Antahkarana is built, the two worlds become one world. The inner world and the outer world become one because man is able to work in both consciously. Because of this, a man's life becomes richer and more encompassing. Whatever he does in the physical plane world, he does according to the blueprint and inspiration of his inner world. In this way he acts wisely with grace and proportion.

Most of us are only fish in the "sea," not knowing about life on land or in the air. When the bridge is built, man will consciously act on all levels, or rooms, upon all planes of existence. All his thoughts, emotions, and actions will be goalfitting and in harmony with the Great Plan.

The esoteric wisdom teaches that:

It is we, the living, who are drawn toward the spirits, but that the latter can never, even though they would, descend to us, or rather into our sphere.[2]

In true esoteric work, people do not communicate with the spirits of the dead through mediums, calling them down to earth, but they consciously go from plane to plane and can even meet those with whom they want to communicate. Once the Antahkarana is built, man will be able to come in contact,

---

[1] H.P. Blavatsky.

[2] Blavatsky, H. P., *Collected Writings*, Vol. I, p. 36.

consciously, with the guides of the race, with disembodied human beings, and with very advanced spirits.

Through this communication and through raising his consciousness to high levels, he will touch beauties, colors, music, perfumes, and forms that surpass everything in this world. He will be given keys to enter the locked rooms of the Holy of Holies in his own nature and unveil secrets of the Laws of God and bring them down to ordinary life for the spiritualization of humanity. The further he penetrates into the higher planes, the closer he comes to the real source of Beauty, Goodness, and Righteousness. The further he enters into the higher planes, proportionally the spirit of bliss, the spirit of understanding, and the spirit of power dawn upon his daily life. This makes his relationships magnetic, radioactive, and blossoming.

The connecting wire between the conscious man and his higher possibilities is the Antahkarana. Man gradually becomes the Path himself, not the Path alone but the Truth and the Life too. Through meditation we build the Antahkarana, and after the Antahkarana is built, again through meditation and contemplation, we use the Antahkarana as the strings of the lute of Orpheus.

The experience which we call *illumination* is the result of the use of the Antahkarana, which transmits the light of the Spiritual Triad into the personality. This also causes the experience of *Transfiguration.*

The experience which we call *inspiration* is the result also of the use of the Antahkarana, which transmits to the personality the purpose, the will of the Soul and of the Monad, even the Plan and the Purpose of the Hierarchy and Shamballa. Once this web of light is built, man is in contact with the whole, not only within his own sphere but also within planetary and cosmic spheres.

The experience which we call *Samadhi* or contemplation again is a state of the Antahkarana, where the Real Man retreats, withdrawing into the sphere of the life of the Monad. There he recharges himself with the highest life-energy, coming in contact with the radiation of "the center where the Will of God is known." This is the real mountain from which the man brings the principles of leadership and great beauty to the world once he again comes back to the world of men. This is the true "peak experience."

Only through the Antahkarana does man change into an eternal fountain of Goodness, Beauty, and Righteousness. He can stay forever within the light, continuously transmitting the higher energies to the world as inspiration instead of as momentary flashes of illumination and inspiration. Thus he becomes a source of energy, which radiates through all his expressions and contacts, enlightening, strengthening, and leading man from chaos to beauty.

Once the Antahkarana is nearly built, some more inner cleansing also takes place; some deeper purification processes begin also. Many, many blind commands, complexes, and dark urges accumulated throughout ages in the inner levels slowly come out to burn and disappear, giving man great psychological and spiritual release. Through the use of the Antahkarana man actually renews all his vehicles. The not-self changes completely. A transmutation process starts in all vehicles, and the highest rhythmic substance replaces the lower substances. This is the process of true sublimation. Here man experiences the saying of the Lord, "You are in the world, but not of the world."

PART V. LIFE AND DEATH

We are told that our body is surrounded with a web of light, which gives life to our body. This is called the "etheric body." The etheric body is formed by the substance of the four higher planes, namely Intuitional, Atmic, Monadic, and Divine Planes, also known as *the four ethers*.[1] As the life energy comes down through the planes, it absorbs the substances of the planes and forms a path of life which is called the *Sutratma*, the *life thread*.

At the time the physical body is to be formed, the Solar Angel spins the Sutratma and creates a coil or etheric body in accordance with the records stored in the permanent atoms. This etheric body, or coil, is woven of energy threads as a web. For the average person it is mostly constructed of buddhic substance.

As we know, the Sutratma is anchored in the heart and the Antahkarana in the head. At death the Antahkarana, the consciousness thread, withdraws itself from the head center; the Sutratma, the thread of life, withdraws itself from the heart center, and the physical body starts to disintegrate. If the consciousness thread is still there, man feels the "death chill." The sensitivity of the physical body dies away as the consciousness thread with-

_____

[1] See Chapter XIV, *The Seven and the Sevens.*

draws itself from the head center. The head center is the synthesis of all centers, and as the life thread departs from it, all centers in the etheric body correspondingly are affected and are rendered insensitive to their corresponding organs.

When the life thread is withdrawn from the heart to the Soul via the head center, all centers are left without this integrating life; the body starts to disintegrate, and the man passes into his etheric body for a short while.

There is no death for those who are able to build the Antahkarana because these people go and come back consciously as the path between the seen and unseen is built. This means also that man can free himself from the prison of time — from the past, present, and future — and live in eternity.

The second step of withdrawal of the life thread is from the etheric body. This is easily done if the physical body is cremated. Cremation cuts the attraction or the link between the physical body and the etheric coil and helps the etheric body to be dissolved in a short time.

The next step of withdrawal is from the astral body, then from the mental body. With these four withdrawals, all these bodies are dissolved, and their life is centralized within the three permanent atoms. The true individuality still persists in the sphere of the Chalice. The man, though cut off from his bodies, still can come in contact with the three worlds through his permanent atoms. He is a free man now, free from the chains of matter of the three planes — the physical, emotional, and mental planes.

When man reaches the Fourth Initiation, in the process of building the Antahkarana, the monadic energy starts to flow down the Antahkarana and burns the Chalice, releasing its Central Fire or Jewel. The man is now resurrected, and the Father is seen. From that moment on, the personality is in direct relationship with the Monad.

As the man tries to bridge the gap between the personality and the Spiritual Triad, he is building also a way of approach to the "pairs of opposites" and walks the noble path, the noble middle path, balancing the extremes, and using them as the materials with which to build the New Age.

Actually the Path begins its building process when the disciple starts to balance the pairs of opposites and to use both of them for the Plan. The Path is an indication that the pairs of opposites are no longer conflicting extremes in the consciousness but two faces of the same object. One of the pairs which attracts so much attention from humanity is *life and death.*

For those who have built the Antahkarana, this pair no longer exists in their consciousness because they know that there is one reality which is the existence, the beingness of the essence in man. They know that life and death are two phases of the same existence. The *Bhagavad Gita* gives this very beautifully:

> *The Blessed One said: Arjuna, you grieve for those who should not be grieved for, and yet you speak like those who are learned. The wise man grieves for neither the dead, nor the living.*

> *Verily, there was never a time when I was not, nor you, nor these rulers of men; nor shall come a time when we shall all cease to be.*

> *The Dweller in the body experiences, in this life, childhood, youth and old age, and then acquires another body. In this, a wise man finds no reason to grieve, nor to be confused.*[1]

PART VI. BUILDING THE BRIDGE

> *... the real building of the antahkarana takes place only when the disciple is beginning to be definitely focussed upon mental levels....*[2]

Before we give the technique of the building process, the following points will clarify the subject and the Path. We know that the real builder of the Antahkarana is the soul-infused personality. The energies used are three in number: the forces of the personality — etheric, emotional, and mental — fused and blended; energies radiating from the Chalice; and then the energy pouring down from the Atmic, Buddhic, Manasic Planes via the Spiritual Triad. All these energies are used in building both the lower and the higher part of the Antahkarana. For the first half of the bridge we used mental substance; for the second half we use mostly light or buddhic substance.

---

[1] The *Bhagavad Gita*, translated by H. (Torkom) Saraydarian, 2:11-13

[2] Bailey, Alice A., *The Rays and the Initiations*, p. 446.

PRELIMINARY STEPS FOR BUILDING THE BRIDGE

1. *Start thinking on abstract levels of the mind.* You can use books written on abstract subjects, for example: *The New Testament*, the *Bhagavad Gita*, *The Yoga Sutras of Patanjali*, *The Upanishads*, *A Treatise on Cosmic Fire*, *The Rays and the Initiations*, *In Search of the Miraculous*, *The Secret Doctrine.*

2. *Do some preparatory meditation on symbols.* Try to unveil the ideas behind the symbols, for example: the circle, the cross, the five and six pointed stars, the pyramid, the cube, the rose, the lotus, and so on, using each symbol fifteen to twenty minutes for two weeks. This will help you to create some connection with the intuitional level and to draw some higher energy for the building work. Try also to create some symbols that express a complicated idea you have in your mind; then make it more universal and cosmic.

3. *Establish some periods of solitude.* As the *Bible* says, "Enter into thine inner chamber and, having shut the door," build some communication lines between your present self and the future Self. See yourself on higher levels of being, closer to Light, closer to Love, and closer to Power. Then carry on your daily duties, having this awareness within your heart and mind. These periods could be once a day or once a week, according to your time, aptitude, and aspirations.

4. *In all your daily relations, attitudes, and thinking cultivate a deeper sense of humility and tolerance.* "Let your horizon be wide, my brother, and your humility great,"[1] says the Tibetan Master. Try to be inclusive. See the one meaning behind many forms and expressions and use them for your spiritual project. In its social aspect, to build the Antahkarana means relationship, communication, understanding, friendship, brotherhood, respect, gratitude, sincerity, tolerance, benevolence, and constancy. As we try to express the above mentioned qualities, we build the bridge in our social life.

As the bridge building process continues upon subjective levels, correspondingly the spirit of communication and understanding increases in humanity. The day will come when all men everywhere will act as an organism of a higher being,

---

[1] Bailey, Alice A., *Discipleship in the New Age*, Vol. II, p. 3.

which will be the sum total of those who built the bridge and stand on the *Blue Peak.*

By building the Antahkarana, we will be able to transfigure our individual, family, social, and international life and make it a real unit: one kingdom with one serving body. That is why the Tibetan Master asks us to be interested in the problems of humanity. In this new era, where the building of the Antahkarana is faster than ever, there is no mine and yours; there is no close or distant. Every problem of the world is our problem. Every nation or race is a part of our real family. The lines of separation are found only on the maps and in the minds, not in reality.

5. *Live a life of dedicated service to humanitarian causes*, service rendered without personal expectation or reservation. The Tibetan Master says this very beautifully in the following:

> *I am seeking here to divorce your minds from the* idée fixe *that the initiate works because he knows. I would reverse the statement and say he knows because he works. There is no point of attainment at which the Initiator says to the initiate: Now you know, and therefore you can work. Rather it is: Now you serve and work, and in so doing you are embarked upon a new and difficult voyage of discovery; you will discover reality progressively and arrive at whole areas of expression, because you serve. Resulting from this service, certain powers and energies will manifest, and your ability to use them will indicate to you, to your fellow initiates and to the world that you are a worker, fully conscious upon the inner side of life.*[1]

> *... the construction of the bridge ... is primarily brought about by a definitely directed life-tendency.*[2]

6. Most people function on one of two lines of approach: the buddhic-astral line or the buddhic-lower mental line. If they continue such a line of approach, they cannot succeed in building the bridge properly.

---

[1] Bailey, Alice A., *Discipleship in the New Age*, Vol. II, p. 282.

[2] Bailey, Alice A., *The Rays and the Initiations*, p. 447.

The first group needs mental development in scientific studies to cultivate lower mental sub-planes. The second group must develop the heart center or their feeling nature through compassion, love, and altruism. Master Morya says this very impressively:

> ... *Not words, nor fear, nor habit, but communion of heart is the most immutable and most eternal manifestation. Thus the rainbow bridge will bring that shore closer.... Not the withered leaf of autumn, but the flaming heart shall cross all bridges.*[1]

It often happens that some intuitional light comes down and contacts our astral or mental nature and, if it is not integrated and fused with the rest of the vehicles, the light does not give a constructive or creative result. For example, if the intuitional light reaches the astral substance — assuming that this plane is free from glamors — it creates there a strong fire of aspiration, devotion, dedication, and enthusiasm. These gradually lead the man into fanaticism, attachment, and superstition if the mind is not prepared to use common sense, analysis, and synthesis to appropriate that fire at the right time, in the right proportion, for the needed activity, planned intelligently.

On the other hand, if the intuitional light reaches the mind and does not find any response from the astral substance, that intuitional light may create a strong mental stimulation by which man tries to formulate and plan. This could result in dogmas, doctrines, and mental crystalizations in which the living element is missing. We have brilliant theologians, Sunday school teachers, ministers, and priests but very few living saints or servants in the world. However, if the astral heart line is developed, then the moment the intuitional light contacts the mind — assuming that the mind is cleared of illusion — the mind is impressed and starts to digest it and formulate it. In the meantime the wave passes to the astral substance, is charged with heart energy, and turned into a living experience even on the physical plane.

If the mind is not cleared of illusion and does not have moments of peace and silence, the light of intuition is lost

---

1 Agni Yoga Society, *Heart*, par. 256.

immediately or restimulates the illusions found there. So on the way to building the Golden Bridge, we must try to cultivate our minds and hearts and make them function as one mechanism. This is itself a bridging process once we know where we need to carry on our work of cultivation: in the heart realm or in the mind realm.

It often happens that in a very subtle and quiet way the intuitional light hits our mind or the harp of our emotional body. We do not see the originating source at all, though immediately it creates mental or emotional reactions and responses. We sometimes sense these reactions and responses. They are of two kinds: low-level reactions and high-level responses.

The conditioning factor of the light is the contents of our minds and emotions. If the contents of these vehicles is on low levels, then the intuitional light mixing with low-level thoughtforms or negative emotions creates many illusions and a thick wall between the light and the personality. However, if the contents is of a high level, then each descent or flight strengthens the communication between higher and lower. That is why the purification of the bodies is so imperative, especially when we try to build the Antahkarana.

It is very easy to see these two kinds of reactions and responses once you are able to stand above the emotional and mental levels and observe them as they react. Only in this way can you see how mechanically and automatically these bodies act and react, and how man takes these reactions as the motivating energies of his attitudes, decisions, and activities. The most fundamental way to escape from this danger is the way of purification, integration, and soul-infusion. It is the Soul that can project its light to the Intuitional Plane and to the world of the personality, revealing them to each other. Once the personality is integrated and fused with the Soul, the light of the intuition creates wonderful responses as is the case with great artists, scientists, or leaders.

7. *Create a group of people around you*, who are gathered together to perform a service to enrich each other's lives and to form a channel of Light, Beauty, Righteousness, and Goodness.

This is a dangerous step upon which most of us lose our humility, selflessness, and respect for others. Once we succeed in gathering a group around us, we long to be the center of the group, the authority, the limit, and we want to have the attention of each one. The true disciple must be aware of this and help his fellow travelers to contact their own Souls and the Plan and then to take part in fulfilling a part of the Plan that is the next step in that area, in that exact period of time, for that special location or environment. You must help them to let their own flowers bloom, facing the same sun in their individual ways but in group formation. This will help you to become a better server and a better builder.

8. *Students of the Rainbow Bridge cultivate themselves also to see and feel things as they are* — not only in the world or in an individual life but also in one's own nature, in one's own inner world. This is not an easy task, but the rewards are very gratifying. Perhaps it is not so difficult to see that we are mostly occupied in deceiving ourselves in regard to our friends, to people, to events, to conditions, and to happenings. Once we start to build the Antahkarana, we must be very careful to see things as they really are. This helps us tremendously to clean our mental-emotional nature and build communication lines with higher planes, where there is more light, more reality, and more facts. Now perhaps you understand why so many exercises were given to you on the previous pages.

9. *At this stage there is another quality which must be developed to its highest degree. This quality is fearlessness.* The more fearless you are, the closer you come to your Self. Fearlessness is not foolishness, the absence of a sense of responsibility, or the result of ignorance and carelessness. It is the radiation of your True Self. This radiation dispels all fears, all separativeness, all cravings, all expectations, and gives you the solemn assurance that nothing can move you from the center where you truly live.

Every time any kind of fear enters your mind, just stop and withdraw your consciousness into the central Self and observe the situation or the condition from the viewpoint of eternity, from the viewpoint of the whole.

Some people think that to be fearless means to be forceful, imposing, commanding, and pushy. This is not true. Fearlessness is a state of consciousness which can be understood only if it is experienced. At the time you are truly fearless, you are extremely calm, clear-minded, discriminative, sharp, joyful, and circumspect. You have a wonderful intuitive cognition of how to act or wait. In cultivating fearlessness, you extend another bridge toward the Peak.

These nine steps will help the disciple to go deeper into soul-infusion. At this stage the Light, Love, and Will of the Soul will fuse with the three aspects of personality, and a soul-infused personality will emerge. This is one of the higher peaks which must be conquered.

After a higher peak is reached, the disciple strives to climb the highest, the Blue Peak, to the monadic awareness and realization where the personality and the Spiritual Triad become one, and the Soul stands apart.[1]

PART VII. THE SIGNS

When the higher part of the bridge is under construction, we notice numerous signs which appear through our mental, emotional, and physical expressions in our daily living. It is interesting to know that these signs are observed by others before we do. Briefly, the signs are as follows:

1. *Open-mindedness* — The student is open to any truth from any source, at any time, at any place.

2. *Illumination* — He sees things as they are. He sees the relativity of things and events and their meaning and purpose of existence. No one can deceive him. He has a real sense of value. He sees the motives. He reads your heart. He has deep insight. He senses the Great Plan, and all his activities are motivated by the Plan.

3. *Inspiration* — All his actions have a radiance of grace. He is in the flood of new age ideas. He has new ways of approach. He is full of psychic energy pouring down from inner sources. Through this energy he creates and heals. His presence has a healing influence and creative stimulation.

4. He has a clear sense of *vocation*, of high calling. He knows his aims, his goal. He sees the guiding star. He

---

[1] See Saraydarian, Torkom, *The Hidden Glory of the Inner Man*, Ch. 12.

subordinates everything to that goal. He is persistent and determined.

5. *Faith, acceptance, endurance* — He has continuous relations with the inner core of everything. He knows that everything, everyone, every event is his helper on the Path of Evolution.

6. *Sense of reality* — Life has meaning for him. He is not living in vanity and in illusion but in reality. He is observing the three worlds from the center of reality. He is awake!

7. *Self-determination* — He lives as a cause, not as an effect. You can never push him unless he chooses it. He tries to express the highest in himself through all his expressions.

8. *Compassion*, a deep sense of *responsibility,* and *humility.*

9. *Honesty, generosity, kindness, nobility* — All his speech, manners, and relationships are of high quality.

10. *Harmlessness* — He is harmless as far as your highest good is concerned.

11. He is *happy, joyous,* and *blissful* in any condition of life. He has a deep sense of *humor.* He has a *smile* on his lips, even when in tears.

12. He has a great *sense of unity.* He has *no barriers in his mind.* He *respects* all races, all religions, all philosophies, all arts. He sees the common denominator in everything. He is *universal* and *cosmic.*

13. He is *heroic.* Fearlessly he places himself in danger for a principle, for a high cause. He acts by the will of the Inner Glory. He gives his life for his friends.

14. His *senses are accurate.* He registers everything as it is. He is never hypnotized, but he is always alert.

15. He has a *sense of beauty.* He sees beauty. He enjoys it in great admiration. He knows how to enter into ecstasy.

16. He *never judges.* He *never condemns.* He sees the facts, understands, and keeps silent.

17. He is always *detached, impersonal,* and *indifferent* as far as the world of personality is concerned.

18. He is full of *gratitude*. He never forgets the good done for the Plan or the Cause, and he expresses his gratitude even for "a cup of water."

19. He has mastered the science of *self-observation*. He ceases to identify himself with the man on the physical level or on the emotional and mental worlds. He watches people from his high level, never becoming confused by the glamors and illusions of the lower worlds.

20. He *forgets* and *forgives*. You never see any sign of revenge in his eyes.

21. He lives for the *future*, for *eternity*. All his acts are motivated by the future and eternity.

22. He is very *adaptable*. He fits everywhere without losing his inner *solemnity*.

23. He is balanced in his words, in his acts, in whatever he does. You sense a great *equilibrium* in his manners and expressions.

24. He can *relax*. He can stop his physical, emotional, and mental activities at will and withdraw into the inner chamber of serenity.

25. He *leads* without force and fear but through Light, Love, and spiritual Power through vision.

26. He exercises great *economy* of energy.

27. He *loves*. Gradually his love becomes deeper and unchangeable in any condition, at any time, under any circumstance.

These are the signs that start to appear in those who are building the second half of the Antahkarana. At the beginning the pilgrim can only express these qualities five or ten percent, but as the rainbow approaches completion, they gradually become dominant and shining until that time when the man expresses them in their full beauty and glory, and he himself becomes a shining light.

PART VIII. SIX ASPECTS OF A BASIC BUILDING TECHNIQUE

The builder is the soul-infused personality. The substance that must be used is predominantly the higher mental substance mixed with higher etheric and astral forces and with energies drawn from the Chalice and brought down from the Spiritual Triad.

The technique of course is *occult meditation* by which man tries first to contact the Intuitional Plane, bring down intuitional energies, see the new age ideas, and touch the Plan. Once the man touches the Plan, he changes into a server. The Plan radiates through his physical, emotional, and mental life; he pours light upon the world, guiding, leading, healing, and bridging.

The Tibetan Master gives six aspects of the basic building technique. They are

- Intention
- Visualization
- Projection
- Invocation-Evocation
- Stabilization
- Resurrection

1. INTENTION

We can explain this word more easily if we divide it into two parts and change the second part of the word as follows: *in* and *tension*. The mind is in tension, in extreme tension, charged with a great purpose and gathering within its radius all the energies with which it is going to build the bridge. So the mind is in an intensely electrified condition, in its highest rate of vibration, and aimed toward the Monad. It is like a mobilization process during which the aim is clear, the forces are ready, the technique is known, and the communication is perfect.

2. VISUALIZATION

We can develop and control our mental plane with a technique called *visualization*. This has three stages.

a) First we choose an object, say a triangle, and try to visualize it. Then we try to visualize it in seven colors successively. After this we visualize it in various motions. Then we choose another object such as a circle, then a five-pointed star, a rose, a lotus, a torch, a flaming sword, a tree — each time adding a motion and a color.

After a while we can add to each object a quality of the other senses. For example, a smell, a taste, a note, a sensation. As we do these exercises, we develop substance and bring it under our control.

In visualization the form and the colors are very important. Each color and each form transmits a different kind of energy into the mental plane and thus creates there more awakening in the atoms of the mental substance. It is this awakened and highly charged substance that will be used in building the bridge.

To this end we suggest that you do some exercises on your own until you are able to visualize easily. This must be done with ease and without any physical or mental tension or pressure.

As we do the above exercises, we build a bridge between the astral and mental bodies. If these visualized objects are of high quality and in line with the service of the Plan, the bridge extends toward the higher plane where the Soul is located. Then the Soul uses these mental objects to transmit energies for creative works. Here the true white magic starts. Man learns how to handle and direct energy and how to work out the Hierarchical Plan.

b) In the second stage we have three important factors:

- The pool of energy, in highest tension in the mental plane.

- The impression coming out of the Buddhic Plane and forming special images in the highest astral levels.

- The visualization process, in which these special pictures are lifted up into the mental plane to mold the mental substance, building there the blueprint of the future Rainbow.

Here visualization takes place on the mental plane where images of the highest astral levels (built by *creative imagination*) take form through the mental substance and become visible in the inner sight. Here we can see that it is the Buddhic Plane that affects the higher astral levels through impressions and brings out the activity we call *creative imagination.* Creative imagination is the response of the higher astral levels to the impressions coming from the Buddhic Plane.

c) The third stage of visualization is a little different. On this stage the act of visualization is not the lifting of the creative imagination up to the mental plane, but it is a process of pictorial or symbolic translation or interpretation upon the mental plane of those impressions and energies which are contacted on the intuitional level, come from the Plan, or are contacted through the extension of awareness on higher planes. This is real visualization: the formless energies and impressions take form and become visible on the mental plane with their tremendous push for expression and creativity.[1]

3. PROJECTION

Here starts the true use of the will. With the help of the Solar Angel, the pilgrim uses the will energy with effort and projects a beam of light toward the "Jewel in the Lotus." He cannot do this if previously he has not lived a life of true service, expressing a high degree of Righteousness, Beauty, and Goodwill in all his relationships, thus opening the petals of sacrifice of the Chalice. In this process the disciple uses his will, visualization, and also a *word of power.* The word of power with its special vibration cleanses the space between the two shores. The will pushes up the mental and light substances, and the first lines of the bridge are seen across the gap.

After the projection is complete, man comes under the influence of the Hierarchy and eventually of Shamballa. He becomes a true server of humanity.

4. INVOCATION — EVOCATION

Invocation — The word *invocation* here has a deeper meaning. You can be invocative after a long period of strenuous intention, visualization, and projection. This means that through a life of service, sacrifice, and achievement you create such a high vibration that you impress yourself upon higher planes and create responses from them. You are magnetic and spiritually demanding.

---

[1] Please see Saraydarian, H. (Torkom), *The Science of Meditation,* Ch. XIII.

Evocation — This is the response given from the higher planes to the invoking disciple. The Real Self extends its hand and grasps the hand of the returning disciple. These two extended hands form the bridge and symbolize the ingoing and outgoing energies coursing through the Antahkarana. This is all done in the hours of occult meditation, wherein the realization comes that the man is the Path himself, through which he, as a Self, serves humanity, carrying out the Will of Shamballa.

5. STABILIZATION

This is the condition of the bridge, a bridge that is built strongly and beautifully and across which the consciousness of man can travel back and forth. The network of Light, Love, and Power is complete now, and the Self can come in contact with any plane and consciously express itself fully. Once stabilization is achieved, man possesses continuity of consciousness; he is aware both above and below, of the subjective and objective worlds.

6. RESURRECTION

The prisoner of the body and the world is now free; he is released from all glamors and illusions and from the dominance of the vehicles. He is himself. Now he sees the unlimited horizons of the Spirit. He is now one who can say, "Be courageous. I overcometh the world!"

The more people who can achieve this linking of the higher and the lower aspects of human nature, the more rapidly will the task of world salvage proceed.[1]

PART IX. THE WORDS OF POWER

Words of power — so called because they affect the subtle and fiery bodies — cleanse these bodies and make way for the higher energy to flow down and be used for the upliftment of humanity and for the dissipation of glamors and illusions on the road of life. These words of power also create relationships between man and other energy centers of the Universe.

If they are chanted or sounded with knowledge and concentration, they are very powerful. These words of power are very

---

[1] The Tibetan.

sacred, and they must be used only when the man is ready and prepared to handle the incoming energies for the fulfillment of the Divine Plan.

From time immemorial we were given many words of power. One that is universally used is a Sanskrit word of power and is as follows:

OM MANI PADME HUM

It means, "Salutations to the Jewel in the Lotus" or "Salutations to the God within."

These words of power or mantrams, as they are called in the East, are built in such a way that, when sounded properly, they create the desired vibration in the subtle and fiery bodies of man. Then this vibration extends into space, purifying and electrifying it, and makes man an invocative station of power.

For the bridge building process the Tibetan Master gave us the Seven Words of Power for each ray in the book *The Rays and the Initiations:*

1st Ray	*I assert the fact.*
2nd Ray	*I see the greatest light.*
3rd Ray	*Purpose itself am I.*
4th Ray	*Two merge with One.*
5th Ray	*Three minds unite.*
6th Ray	*The highest light controls.*
7th Ray	*The highest and the lowest meet.*[1]

These are translated from "their ancient Sensa form," and the Master says,

> *... it would not be possible for me to teach ... their ancient and peculiar pronunciation or the note upon which they should be sounded forth.... What does matter is the ability of the disciple to* feel *the meaning of the Word of Power as he silently utters it. It is the quality of his idea which will bring the right effect, and not the way*

---

[1]See Bailey, Alice A., *The Rays and the Initiations,* pp. 515, 516, 517, 518.

in which he makes a sound with the aid of his vocal cords and his mouth.[1]

As we know, the builder is the soul-infused personality; so while he is using the word of power, he must choose his Soul ray word which is dominating his personality ray.

These words of power will be sounded inaudibly by the disciple at the time of projection, while concentrating deeply on the meaning of the words to feel their essence. To do this, we must first of all study and find out our Soul and personality rays, see whether the Soul ray is dominating, and then use the Soul ray words of power.[2]

The Tibetan Master also says,

... When correctly uttered, this Word produces three effects:

a. It keeps the channel for the descending light of the Spiritual Triad clear of all impediments.

b. It reaches (by means of its vibratory activity) the centre of power which we call the Spiritual Triad, focussed temporarily in the manasic permanent atom, and evokes a response in the form of a thread of descending triadal light.

c. It causes a vibration throughout the antahkarana which in its turn evokes response from the "rainbow bridge" as built by all other disciples. Thus the work of constructing the racial *antahkarana is furthered.*[3]

---

1 Bailey, Alice A., *The Rays and the Initiations,* p. 513.

2 The best sources for the study of the rays are the following books by Alice A. Bailey:
   Esoteric Psychology, Vol. I, pp. 201-212, 316-334, 401-403, 411-430.
   Esoteric Psychology, Vol. II, pp. 259-401, 442-443.
   A Treatise on White Magic, pp. 109-121.
   The Rays and the Initiations, pp. 575-589, 643-653.
   Esoteric Astrology, pp. 596-601.

3 Bailey, Alice A., *The Rays and the Initiations,* p. 510.

PART X. MEDITATION ON THE ANTAHKARANA

The meditation in Section One must be done every day for six months. After the six months do the second meditation in Section Two for another six months. Then, for another six months, do the meditation in Section Three. In eighteen months you will complete the meditation. Then you will start studying this book from the beginning. Do not do this meditation if you have not performed the exercises given in previous chapters.

SECTION ONE

> *Straight is the gate and narrow is the way that leadeth unto life and few there be that find it.*[1]

Visualize a high mountain where everything is beautiful and upon which you see a man sitting in deep meditation. See how he is sounding the Sacred Word, the OM, while concentric sky-blue circles of his voice are filling space and reaching out to you.

Visualize first the man starting with the O. His mouth opens as an O, and he directs his voice to the center of his head and upward. The length of time for sounding the O is only ten seconds. Immediately after that, he closes his mouth to sound the M for another ten seconds. All you are doing is listening to him as clearly as possible.

In your imagination sit near that man. Close your eyes, and visualize a blue flame above your head from which is radiating a thread of orange fire. This thread is passing through the Chalice and up to the Eternal Star, the Monad, anchoring itself in the Star. Now stand away from your body and see how some spiritual electricity is passing down the thread and radiating Light, Love, and Power to your personality.

Wait a little and observe it in joy, as this spiritual energy is filling the whole of your being and then radiating out to space.

Do not hurry, take your time. Do not strain yourself. Be relaxed, deeply relaxed. Then visualize how you are going to distribute this incoming energy through your service rendered upon the lower and spiritual planes. Just think, visualize, and create new channels of spiritual expression in your life. This

---

[1] Matthew 7:13

will be done with creative imagination. For example, see yourself lecturing, if you so wish, singing, playing music, writing books or leading a group, organization, or school. Do anything through which you can render a true service to humanity and use the incoming energies. Gradually you will find your exact place in life where you will render maximum service.

This daily meditation will take no more than fifteen minutes.

SECTION TWO

After you have done the above meditation for six months, add the following one to it. Do not exceed twenty minutes in all.

After you visualize your new channel of service in your imagination, open this book and recall the first part of this chapter, then the next day the second part, and so on, repeating this for six months.

Visualize that you are entering a dark cave. Stand in the darkness for a short while and then light a candle. See the beauty of the flame, and observe the big deep cave. Here, in your imagination or visualization, stand away from your body and see seven revolving wheels, one foot from your physical body; one at the base of the spine, another one further up the spine, another on the solar plexus, on the heart, on the throat, one between the eyebrows, and a larger one on the head. Remember, they are at least one foot from the body.

See little sparks in the center of each wheel. Sounding the OM each time, approach the sparks with the candle, starting with the base of the spine and thus up to the head center, connecting them together with a thread of light. Then place the candle in the head center and let it burn brightly and shed its light on the body. See the whole body transfiguring into orange-colored light. When your whole body is shining with the orange light, start to visualize the Buddhic Plane of the planet. Put yourself in contact with the consciousness of that plane and say:

> *Let vision come and insight.*

Ponder upon these words and then say:

> *Salutations to the Christ, the Head of the Hierarchy.*

After a while visualize the Monadic Plane of the planet and the will center of the planet and try to establish a contact with that "center where the Will of God is known." Let the Will of God slowly fill your being, saying:

In the Center of the Will of God I stand.

Ponder upon these words. Sound the Great Invocation. Sound the OM three times. Sit three minutes where you are and then slowly come out of your meditation. Continue sitting there for a while, until you are again back in the world.

SECTION THREE

The meditation in this section must be done for six months, and must not exceed thirty minutes.

Ponder upon the words,

In the Center of the Will of God I stand.

Then follow the following six points, which are the six steps of building the Antahkarana.

Intention

Enter into deep silence. Invoke the Light of the Soul and the Power of the Triad. Affirm that the spiritual energies are gathered in the mental plane to be used for construction of the bridge. Feel the tension.

Visualization

Visualize the bridge extending from point to point. See the golden thread passing from plane to plane. See the seven colors of the rainbow, each sensitive to one of the seven rays upon which you have built in the past.

Projection

Concentrate all your energy. Visualize the points between which the bridge should pass. Then, by an action of will, project the energy like a flying rocket and connect the personality with the Spiritual Triad and then to the Monad. Use the word of power for your ray. Wait there a little and observe the picture of the network of light.

Invocation — Evocation

Feel that you are now an invoking center and see how a beam of Light descends from the Monad in order to meet your projection.

Stabilization

See the bridge built by which the higher meets the lower. You are now able to use it and to reach abstract levels and bring Light, Love, and Power to the world.

Resurrection and Ascension

Raise your consciousness into the consciousness of the Spiritual Triad. Be lifted up, surpass your personality awareness, and stay there for a while, never losing the consciousness of your identity. Put your hand into the Hand of the Unknown and with the other hand bless the world.

Say the following mantram:

> *In the center of the Will of God I stand.*
>
> *Naught shall deflect my will from His.*
>
> *I implement that will by Love.*
>
> *I, the Triangle Divine, express that will within the*
>
> *Square and serve my fellowmen.*

Sound the OM three times, inaudibly.

Relax and stay where you are for a while. Return to your normal consciousness.

It is advisable that after this exercise you keep silent for about fifteen minutes or more if possible.

Chapter XIX

THE MEANING OF SILENCE

Over the door of some schools where advanced studies in the Teaching were offered are these words:

TO KNOW

TO WILL

TO DARE

TO BE SILENT

There are several reasons why silence was so strongly emphasized in ancient mysteries, teachings, brotherhoods, temples, and in earlier, true Christianity.

1. In advanced teachings, students were trained and prepared to know, to dare, to will, and to be silent. Although silence was not needed in the schools where the Teaching was given, it was necessary for students to be silent under other circumstances. Silence was essential when they came in contact with lower level people to prevent incorrect, unclean thoughts from corrupting the purity of the Teaching. The main reason for silence was to protect the Teaching and the students.

   The Teaching should be protected because people live on different levels of development, and each person understands according to his own level.[1] For example, a group of students is studying advanced teaching concerning, perhaps, the Laws of Life or of Cosmos. The Teaching will remain pure and safe providing the students do not speak of it in outer circles. However, if they do speak of it outside, the Teaching becomes degenerated. The listeners do not understand it as it is given from the source. Each one interprets it on his own level and passes his version on to others on another level. This continues until the Teaching eventually emerges as a complete

---

[1] Saraydarian, Torkom, *The Hidden Glory of the Inner Man*, Ch. 17.

distortion. Thus occurs the degeneration of the sublime Truth of the Teaching. Each low level person adds something or changes something according to his background, his development, his degree of understanding, and his level of beingness.

2. The students themselves must be protected. Knowledge is power. Whoever has knowledge has power, and with this power people can be controlled. In olden days this knowledge, the Teaching, was given only to those persons who were pure in heart, filled with love, compassion, and the spirit of service. The wise teachers knew that if the knowledge were passed on to those who were intelligent enough to understand it but were lacking in the quality of holiness, the Teaching then would become a dangerous instrument in their hands because it could be used to enslave people.

The same holds true today. The most important thing in the world is to develop a pure heart, for only through purity of heart can one have right motives. The chief purpose of the Teaching is to develop purity of motive. When purity is acquired and expressed as service to our fellowmen, knowledge can be given. Without purity and service, knowledge cannot be used for creative purposes.[1]

Those who do not have purity or holiness of heart and motive may develop deep pride or selfishness when they acquire knowledge. Then if they try to use or teach this knowledge, their pride increases, and they are led onto the left-hand path, the path of destruction and evil. In the old mystery schools of education, students were instructed to remain silent for years to avoid this from happening.

3. There was, and still is, another reason for keeping silent. Teachings dealing with high levels stimulate lower tendencies and bring out the worst in each of us. A man may possess much knowledge of the Teaching. He may even be able to express it verbally to others. But if he does not live by the standards of his teaching, he distorts and corrupts it, thereby increasing the evil in humanity. Because the Teaching is a highly charged energy, students are forbidden to speak of it. They are instructed to keep strict silence in all areas, to culti-

---

[1] Holiness or purity is attained at the Third Initiation.

vate observation, to learn the importance of silence, and to try their best to live by the Teaching. In some schools, students are trained to keep silent among themselves in their classes for many hours. They are instructed not to speak with one another about the Teaching to avoid exerting any influence on one another and to protect their inner freedom. When a beautiful vision or idea has passed from the teacher to the aspirant or disciple, he should not dwell on it for a while. To maintain its purity, he should not mix it with his low level thoughtforms, ideas, and short range vision.

Outer silence is only a step toward inner silence. By practicing strict discipline, people can learn how to remain silent with their tongues, but most of them continue to speak with their minds. They talk on many subjects with their minds. They praise, criticize, gossip, and so on, but the purpose of outer silence is to cultivate inner silence. Therefore the student must try hard to develop inner silence. We cannot say that the discipline of silence begins from the outside or from the inside. It begins from both sides at the same moment if the student is following the right discipline.

People are sometimes forced by outer controls to keep silence, but they continue to talk with their minds. Very often they actually have nothing to say, nothing to give from their minds, but they continue to talk and talk automatically as outer happenings influence them. There is no connection between their heart and their tongue. They are mechanically expressing their ideas and opinions, but the thoughts they express do not come from the inside; they are mere reflections.

People are sometimes surprised when they are first told about inner silence. They do not understand what it means. If they would observe, they would find that we talk continuously within ourselves. This is strong proof that we are identified with our environment, problems, and questions. We have identified ourselves with our thoughts. However, *we are not our thoughts*. It is possible to stop the mind's automatic agitations, control its movements, express only the ideas we choose, and keep our mind absolutely quiet. When the mind is calm, we can expect higher ideas to be impressed upon it. We will be able to look at the outer world clearly without fog, glamor, or illusion. This is the way in which we collect true knowledge. True knowledge cannot be impressed upon an agitated, talkative mind.

Outer silence gives the opportunity:

a) To observe the inner state of the mind.

b) To decrease the possibility of reactions, talk, and so on.

c) To develop the willpower of man so that his mechanical side comes under his conscious control.

d) To control the speech mechanism as well as the emotional, feeling nature. There is a very close connection between our speech and our emotional nature.

e) To keep oneself away from gossip and the complications which gossip creates. A silent man cannot be confused by the talk of others because he is aware of the fact that many people lie through their speech.

Inner silence:

a) Saves the most precious energy of mind and of vitality, which is wasted through ordinary gossip.

b) Vitalizes our body, heart, and mind.

c) Makes our speech strong and impressive. People who talk too much within and without cannot impress others. Their speech has no power for it does not have the deep note of Beauty, Righteousness, and Power. True energy is lacking in their words, no matter how hard they try to impress others. Only a silent mind can transfer a true idea. A true idea is condensed electricity. It is not words that lead nations but the inner power that comes through words. If the words are not charged with that power, they are only empty shells. A silent mind does not mean a lazy, idle, or sleepy mind. On the contrary, a truly silent mind is like a huge magnetic mirror which takes in and reflects great ideas coming from higher levels.

d) Integrates the different parts of our being. A consciously silent man is an integrated man, if this silence is gained by the most severe discipline. We read in the epistle of James: "If any man offend not in word, the same man is a perfect man, and able also to bridle the whole body."

The same is true of the inner silence, the inner word, because "Out of the abundance of the heart the mouth speaketh," and "He who keeps his mouth, keeps his life, but he who openeth wide his lips shall have destruction."

e) Creates an atmosphere in our psychological world where man is able to carry on high creative activity. In this silence the two poles of man — the divine pole and the human pole — come closer. This meeting results in creativity.

Silence protects man from outer influences. It keeps away the winds of jealousy, hatred, and evil which try to reach him as energy waves through space. A silent man builds "a wall of light" around his existence, around his being. Negative waves cannot enter his mechanism to create reactions. They are automatically rejected. The more of these influences or waves a man rids himself of, the more he radiates, the more he shines, and the closer he comes to releasing his inner essence.

Our speech throws a great responsibility upon us. Our words can lead people into the light or into confusion. Our words can stimulate the best in people or the worst. The reactions range from zero to one hundred, from minus to plus. Therefore, we must learn:

1. how to speak
2. what to speak
3. when to speak
4. where to speak
5. when to keep absolute silence

"There is a time to speak, and a time to be silent," said a wise man of old. Discrimination, discipline, and wisdom must be cultivated thoroughly to realize and express the five points mentioned above in our lives. Man is searching for that point of silence where he can meet Himself. But there is no silence in the world. Wherever one goes there are constant noises from the material universe. It is good that we are not yet able to hear all the noises or sounds around us, coming from every kind of object on earth and even from the planets which form our solar system.

Sometimes we respond to voices or noises which we do not hear. We respond through the many moods, feelings, or thoughts that they evoke from us without our knowledge. Although our physical ear is not able to pick up some notes or tones, our emotional-mental aura picks them up and reacts to them, often mechanically. Our mental atmosphere reacts to mental vibrations or waves; our emotional atmosphere reacts to emotional waves, and if our subtle senses are open, we will hear unexpected sounds from higher worlds.

This means that silence is not conditioned by the outside world but by an inner control. Space is full of numberless currents of vibrations. The secret of silence and peace is the secret of rejecting all vibrations and building a psychic wall around us. The Great Pyramid was a symbol of this achievement. The King's Chamber was the innermost center in man where all physical sounds were unable to penetrate, thus giving to the initiate the opportunity to focus his mind before he experienced the mystery of passing from one level of consciousness to another. During this transition it must be made impossible for physical sounds to disturb the mind by keying in ancient experiences.

The psychic wall is built by the radiation of the Inner Fire, which cleanses the emotional and mental vehicles and extends out of the body to build a fiery sheath around it. At this stage the attention of the person is concentrated on the innermost center of the Self. The Master Djwhal Khul says: "The soul... has withdrawn out of the three worlds, and in the 'secret place of the most high' is at rest and at peace, contemplating the beatific vision."

The King's Chamber in the pyramid was the symbol of the inner chamber within the head, where we must enter to find the real silence and hear the voice of our Inner Lord, the "Voice of Silence." This inner silence is reached when our consciousness is completely focussed within the fiery Chalice. When this is achieved, all outer vibrations can make no impression on our senses or bodies, if we so choose. We can enter our inner chamber, "closing the doors and windows, and speak with our Father in Heaven," the Spark, the Self. A man who is able to raise himself to this level can withdraw himself to the point of silence in the midst of all noise or sound. He literally rejects sound; he does not hear.

There are those who think that our senses are automatic. They think, for example, that a person will smell any odor and hear any sound within range of these senses. This is true to some degree, but it is possible to control your senses completely and reject any sensation, even visual sensation, so that the senses are at rest. Of course this requires long years of development and advancement toward the Self. Many of us have this experience for a short time. We often miss something that we might see, hear, smell, or sense. In our daily life there are seconds or minutes in which we enter into the inner sanctuary, but it is so short a time that we do not recall subjective happenings except to have the feeling that we were absent for a short time from our physical environment. This inner chamber is the healing center of oneself. The supreme quality of silence is to heal, to release, and to relax. In silence the inner radiation penetrates and floods our mechanism.

To reach this inner silence, throughout ages people chose to enter convents, monasteries, wildernesses, mountains, and caves to cut themselves off from the "noises" of the three worlds. It is true that such solitude and seclusion help and even heal many psychosomatic illnesses because of the absence of restimulation or pressure on the nerves and mind. They create a sense of proportion in man and enlarge the inner space.

In solitude, knowledge and many experiences can be digested and assimilated into the treasury of the Soul. Silence must be entered into only after a man is a dweller of the inner silence and is able to remain detached because if he enters before this, it would increase his craving for the world. It would serve to amplify and release suppressed sounds and voices in the emotional and lower mental worlds.

When we are in the wilderness, in forests, and in mountains, our petty troubles seem to become nothing. This is because in such beautiful places of nature, our inner space becomes larger, and we see ourselves in comparison to the majestic mountains, the lakes, the ocean, and the vast deserts. Most of our troubles are the result of our having narrowed the inner space and lost the sense of relativity, the sense of proportion. Solitude often restores that sense. In solitude and silence you extend yourself into the Soul of Nature. When you feel this extension, your vanities begin to disappear, and you become more yourself. These realizations are all steps leading you into the inner silence. After leaving behind all the noises of the world, most people go to the wilderness only to find that they hear even more world noise in the form of desires and numberless attachments within their hearts and minds. They realize that quite often retreats, monasteries, and solitude are not giving them the help they need, and they begin the long and difficult path toward the inner pyramid through the path of concentration, meditation, contemplation, and service.

Chapter XX

SINCERITY

Some people think that sincerity is the act of expressing our feelings and thoughts as they are at a given moment, but we must consider:

1. The one to whom we are expressing ourselves.
2. Our feelings.
3. Our thoughts which include our ideas and plans.
4. The unit of consciousness or the "I" who wills to express.

Under most circumstances, man expresses himself according to what he is at a given moment, and because he is not always the same man, his expressions change, giving the impression that he is not a sincere man. But sincerity has to do with *motive*. It is not easy to differentiate between an act as being sincere or insincere, but when the motive is seen, one is able to discern the reality behind the expression.

None of us can be truly sincere until we enter into the domain of the permanent "I" within us. This requires progress in two ways. On one hand, the body, the emotions, and the mental nature must be so disciplined and purified that they exactly express the Will of the Inner Man. On the other hand, man must progressively become his *True Self.* The highest sincerity in man begins at that moment when he becomes his own Lord and is able to use his vehicles to express himself *as he is.* Sincerity is the exact externalization of the Inner Man through his words, emotions, thoughts, ideas, and gestures. To be sincere is to be what a man essentially is and to express that essence in supreme simplicity.

Hypocrites are people who change their expressions ceaselessly as their motives, their interests, and their focus of consciousness change due to their attachments to their bodies, feelings, and thoughts. They are unstable and mechanical people. A more advanced hypocrite is one who has a doubtful motive on one of his personality levels and hides it in his various expressions, giving the impression that he is an integrated man, a self-actualized man.

Sincerity is the radiation of a man who has achieved oneness with his True Self. That Self is now able to express Itself, unimpeded, through all Its vehicles. Sincerity is a direct touch from that Inner Spark.

Chapter XXI

LOVE

True love is the magnetic energy radiating from the Divine Spark in man. Man is essentially a drop of the supreme energy, which we call "love." The majority of people around us are not human. They are like machines, plants, or mere bodies. The Real Man is a Christ, a person who is able to experience his own essential Divinity. The following diagram will clarify this fact.

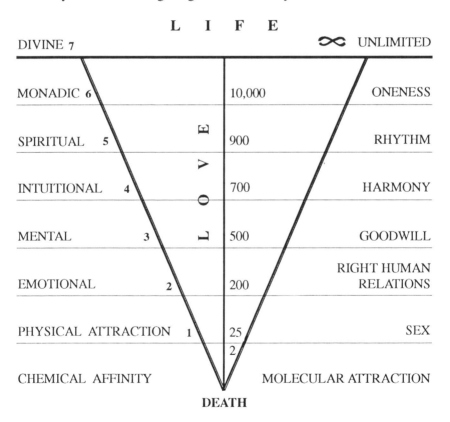

As shown in the diagram, love extends and unfolds as it ascends. The lowest point is death. The highest point is life. Life increases in proportion to the increase in love. When love increases, life increases.

Every union is formed by love energy. If two bodies come together, it is love that brings them together, but it is a love working through the physical body. If the love deepens, it means that the higher level, emotional plane love has begun to express itself, and the two persons come closer to each other. If love begins to express itself through the mental plane of both individuals, the energy of attraction becomes stronger. These two persons practically register one another's thinking and feeling. They begin to live in right relations with humanity, and goodwill dominates their thoughts and activities. When they pass into the intuitional awareness, they begin to sense real love. They feel the love energy in the Universe. They sense it in green pastures, in the music of the trees, in flowers and mountains, in birds and animals, in stars and the waves of the sea, for they live in the ocean of love. Love makes them bloom.

A man once bought some wheat from the marketplace and took it to his village. Upon arriving at the village, he noticed that there were many ants in the wheat. He was distressed, for he thought that the tiny creatures would have a most difficult time away from their home. So he walked the five miles back to the bazaar where he had purchased the wheat and returned the ants to their home. This story depicts a sense of love which reaches down to the little creatures because the man was able to feel his unity with them.

Another story also illustrates this kind of love. A young and beautiful village maiden arose early in the morning and went to the well to draw some water with a bucket that was hanging by a rope. Suddenly she noticed that a climbing vine had entwined itself around the rope, and from the vine blossomed a lovely blue flower. She thought that if she let the bucket down into the well, the tender stem of the blossom would be cut, and the life of the lovely flower would be destroyed. So she went to her neighbor and asked, "My dear neighbor, would you please give me a bucket of water to wash my face? A little flower is holding the rope of our bucket."

On the spiritual level, love expresses itself as revelation. Through unity and identification man becomes aware of the hearts and thoughts of others. He reads their hearts and minds, and nothing is hidden from his eyes. Meanwhile he radiates a healing energy through his thoughts, emotions, and activities. His eyes and words heal, uplift, and lead others into the freedom of life. Under his influence a transmutation process begins in their lives. On the divine level, man touches the essential electrical and magnetic love. He becomes a transmitter of all healing, bridging, purifying, and enlightening energies. He becomes a co-worker of the Divine Plan.

This is the path of love which begins with chemical affinity and carries us into the ocean of unity. This is the path of glory which begins with a Spark and changes into a Sun. The ladder of love is the ladder of glory, of victory, of achievement, of Divinity. It starts at the zero point and ends in Infinity.

Your number on the graph is the measure of your achievement. *The more you love, the more you are; the more you love, the more life you have.* You have more glory, more perfection, more achievement, more joy, and more bliss. The value of a person is determined by the rung upon which he stands on the ladder of love. He is a man of second degree value if he is living on the second step of the ladder. His value is 200 if he is living on step 200. He can move up and up toward Infinity, for the life of immortality passes only through the ladder of love. When you reach oceanic love, you receive oceanic joy through a pure kiss, a smile of love, a handshake, a touch, a word.

Your ascent up the ladder of love does not limit your joy on lower levels. On the contrary, after you have advanced to higher levels of love, any love action on lower levels brings in the bliss of higher planes and leads you into ecstasy. This is the way in which some very advanced saints speak with God — through the smile of a baby, the song of a nightingale, the beauty of a flower. They touch God when they touch their beloved one.

Love is happiness on physical, emotional, and mental planes. It is joy on the soul level. It is bliss on the Spiritual Plane. Whenever you use love energy, you have a sense of expansion, freedom, unfoldment, and creativity. Every man has this magnetic substance of love within, but because of the lack of integration and development he cannot express it as an active unit, as an active whole. He uses it in parts, selectively, and thus limits the joy and usefulness of love energy. Suppose your body loves another body. You enjoy it, but this enjoyment does not last if your heart does not love the heart of the other person. You have pleasure for the moment, but if you are not extending your love into the future as well, your love will not last. Each time you lose the object of your love, you suffer because you are limited. You are descending on the scale, coming closer to inertia, closer to death.

Love is love only when it is used as a whole for infinity. Master Morya says:

> *... It is correctly pointed out that love is a guiding and creative principle. This means that love must be conscious, striving, and self-denying. Creativeness requires these conditions.*[1]

Inspiration for creative works or for heroic and sacrificial actions is but a downpour of love. The depth to which a man expresses the energy of love determines his creativity and radioactivity. To create means to bring out the harmony and the rhythm of love from higher levels or to awaken the love principle in the hearts of men. *All beauties are materialized love.*

Some people think that consciousness and love are separate things. We cannot say "conscious love" for there is no unconscious love. There is limited love, and limited love is self-ishness and darkness. In the *Bible* the beloved disciple tells us, "Those who love live in the Light." Of course he was referring to complete love, to whole, inclusive love — a love that extends to all planes of existence. Only through love do we understand; only through love do we recognize or know each other as well as ourselves because love is light — a light that reveals, unfolds, and penetrates. The knowledge gained by love is true knowledge.

Love energy cannot be developed and become deeper until it creates response. Only through response can it change into creative energy. On whatever level it evokes response, on that level it becomes creative. A rejected or ignored love energy crystallizes and produces a hindering force which spreads into the mechanism of the person, causing psychological disturbance and illness. This condition gradually produces more difficulties between two people until there is a separation. Then a total

---

[1] Agni Yoga Society, *Hierarchy*, par. 280.

indifference toward each other becomes an established fact, or the love may change into a selfish, attacking force which we call *hatred*.

Hatred is a demanding love, a love that wants to possess. If a person cannot possess, he tries to destroy the object of love so that others cannot possess it. This is the way in which love changes into rejection. One who hates never sees the good in another. He sees only the wickedness. As he concentrates his force upon these weaknesses, he increases the wickedness in himself and becomes a destructive force in the world of men.

It is for this reason that the leaders of humanity often advise us to forgive and forget and try to remain indifferent because the worst and strongest attachment is the attachment of hatred. Unconsciously we copy the things we hate. To forgive and forget is a process through which we dissipate the accumulated, rejecting, negative forces which are continuously poisoning our psychological and physical mechanism. Through forgiveness and forgetting, we release these crystallized forces and change them into love energy.

All creation is the effect of love. Man cannot create except through love. If he is using only twenty-five degrees love, his creation will have a corresponding value. If he is creating from a high level of nine hundred degrees, his creation will have a similar value. For example, if in our love action we are tuned only to physical love, our children will be low level human beings. If in our act of love we are tuned to a very high level, we will draw into our sphere of life greater souls, more advanced beings.

In olden days Masters of Wisdom gave special meditations in the *Upanishads* to be performed before the act of love to attract a more advanced being into incarnation. In mystic literature the higher levels of consciousness and realization are explained as a spiritual marriage between bride and groom.

The use of this metaphor is very fitting because in real and highest love, man loses his selfhood, merges into the other, and they become one. If unity is on higher levels, then joy and bliss are real. This joy of higher realizations can be compared only to the bliss that you register with expressed love, a love that comes from higher planes. You feel that you are lost in each other, you find yourselves in each other, you are a complete being. You have lost those negative elements which prevent complete merging, and when these elements are eliminated, the free flow of love makes you one. You feel that the other being is you, your real "body."

The ecstasy does not stop there; it passes upward to the hearts. The two hearts begin to merge with each other. On this level the real joy of unity begins. Two divine streams of music blend into each other, and a symphony begins to flow through the hearts. The hearts become greater and embrace the whole Universe. When their hearts are merging, a couple feels a sense of nobility, sublime feelings of beauty, purity, kindness, forgiveness, forgetting, holiness, and an urge to sacrifice themselves for each other.

The current of love does not stop here; it carries them upward toward the mental plane. Here their minds merge, giving a rare sensation of joy. Out of this unity comes a unified purpose: to lead a life of radiation, service, and dedication. The oneness of these three levels goes deeper and deeper until suddenly the two Sparks within them unite, and complete bliss is radiated throughout their whole being. They are now one body, one heart, one mind, one spirit. Love vibrates throughout their bodies and clears away all mental, emotional, and physical obstacles with its purifying current.

This is the age-long work for which we are called. Life after life we build the steps higher and higher until that day when the ladder of love is finally built, and the souls can meet each other and be one. The eternal pilgrim passes through forests and deserts; he finds and loses his mate many times until one day his long labor is consumated; the two meet each other. Blessed is that moment when they meet!

People often think that as soon as they marry, they will have complete happiness. This is a wishful expectation which usually ends in sorrow and suffering. In true marriage the two approach each other to build the temple of happiness. The temple is not already constructed. They are called into duty to build it — to build it with their best thoughts, best feelings, and best acts in devotion, in culture, in sacrifice, and in respect. Their task now is to cultivate the seeds of beauty in each other until the full flower radiates out through their beings. They are to release the supreme values, the supreme lights in each other, cultivating one another as a gardener cultivates his garden, for only through a progressive development can a couple fulfill its destiny.

To build the temple of joy and bliss, special instruments are needed, and the builders must always be ready with the tools in their hands:

freedom

non-criticism

admiration

sacrifice

education

gratitude

sense of responsibility

Through the use of these seven tools, the temple can be built because they are the seven pillars of wisdom by which the temple is constructed.

1. *Freedom* is the first tool. Our partner must have complete freedom to do, to feel, to think in the way he or she thinks is proper. Only a free mate can be a true mate. The greatest touchstone is freedom. One partner is not the property of the other. They are both free beings. They are there together to build the temple of joy and understanding in the family. The temple can be built in mutual respect for each other's freedom. The will of one should not be forced upon the other. The freedom of the couple must be conditioned by the highest goal of the family.

   In its true meaning, freedom is not the forcing of your ideas or wishes upon another. To be free means to be able to express your Light, Love, and Beauty in your own way. To be free means to be free from those thoughts, feelings, and acts which are selfish, harmful, limiting, dark, separative, and destructive. A man who has achieved soul consciousness is a free man because he is not the slave of his body, his emotions, his thoughts, or his ideas.

2. *Non-criticism* is the second tool. To criticize means to force one's will on another. It is not intended that we make a partner the shadow of ourself. Let us allow our mates to blossom into their own flowers with original colors. Let us try to understand their motives and be ready to help when we are asked. Let each one learn in his own way.

3. *Admiration* is the third tool. By showing our admiration for good deeds, for each spark of Light, Love, and Beauty expressed in our partner, we increase the energy behind the expression. Showing admiration is like watering your garden. Admiration brings out soul energy and, by magnetic rapport, releases the soul energy in your partner. Soul energy creates more love, more joy, more understanding. To admire means to see the highest in your partner.

4. *Sacrifice* is the fourth tool. In its true meaning, sacrifice means to destroy within ourselves those limiting forms, feelings, thoughts, and habits which prevent progress toward deeper joy and understanding. Such limiting forms must be sacrificed because they may also prevent the blooming of our partner. With every act of sacrifice a new power operates within ourselves and within our family. The ladder of progress is built by the steps of our every sacrifice.

5. *Education* is the fifth tool. We are intended to complete, balance, and release each other. We cannot do these things unless we develop our physical, emotional, mental, and spiritual natures. We must have something to give, something to add to the union. We must develop stronger and stronger wings if we wish to soar to the highest altitudes to keep company with the flight of our partner. If one of us is unable to share our higher joys, light, and admiration, equilibrium is lost, the unity becomes weaker and weaker until the one who is left behind is completely lost, feeling lonely, depressed, and miserable.

6. *Gratitude* is the sixth tool. It is the highest form of respect. To be grateful to one another means to appreciate and to give recognition to each other. To be grateful is to have in your consciousness the good deeds, feelings, and thoughts that you enjoy in your partner. It is this and more, for it extends to all Creation. It is feeling and expressing gratitude, in some form, for everything in Creation with which we are blessed.

   • Let us be grateful for our friends, for the smiles of husbands and wives, for the joys of children.
   • Let us be grateful for the birds, the trees, the flowers.
   • Let us appreciate life, for this is also being grateful.
   • Let us feel the Divine Presence in every living creature, in everything, and be grateful.

- Let us appreciate and be grateful for the good in everything, and let us enjoy it with all our being.
- Let us be grateful for the Will of God.

When we are grateful, we release the constructive energies within ourselves, within our family, and within our environment. The face of a grateful person radiates joy, love, and light; he is a powerhouse for others.

7. A *sense of responsibility* is the seventh tool. This is the consciousness of being one with the other. To understand it simply, we can ask ourselves:

- Do my words, acts, feelings, or thoughts increase the happiness, the joy, the light, and the health of my partner?
- Do I know that everything that is good for my partner is also good for me?
- Do I know that I will pay the cost for all those words, deeds, feelings, and thoughts that retard or prevent the progress of my mate?
- Do I know that a small seed of evil can grow throughout centuries and block the door of light for myself and others?

If a person can answer these questions affirmatively, he has in his hand the most important tool: a sense of responsibility. Those who have it are the guardian angels of humanity.

We do not belong to ourselves. We belong to each other, to our family, race, nation, humanity, and even to the Universe. We can promote the well-being of the Universe, or we can be an evil within it. With the sense of responsibility we unite ourselves with the constructive forces, with the forces of light in the Universe, and we are blessed in our individual and family life. When we have acquired a sense of responsibility, it ends our selfish motives and egocentric activities.

By using these seven tools and meditating upon them every day, we can build the temple of happiness, joy, and bliss in our families. If such families increase in the world, humanity will enter into its true heritage of bliss. The energy behind these ideal conditions is the energy of love.

When two advanced people are attracted by true love, the following occurs:

1. They establish magnetic lines of communication between their hearts.

2. Their auras begin to merge.

3. The assimilation process begins after the merging, and each one enriches the other's aura with his colors and vibrations.

4. The centers begin to give corresponding signs of vibration. Thus sublimation starts.

5. New energies awaken, bringing down new inspiration and light.

6. Their physical, emotional, and mental levels are united, and soul infusion becomes a fact in the more advanced degrees of love.

A lasting love between two people is not ready-made. You cannot purchase it or find it by chance. You must plant the seed, tend it, protect it, and give it the needed soil, water, light, and energy. In time it will flourish.

The growth of love between two people resembles climbing a high mountain. The farther they climb, the closer they come to each other, and one day they meet on the peak of the mountain. To climb the mountain means to raise the level of being, to gradually clear the consciousness, to enlarge the horizon of light and service, and to enter into deeper levels of responsibility toward each other. Only through such living is the path of life built.

Thus we may say that those who love each other deeply and sincerely are those people who meet more frequently and walk together more often on the path of love toward the peak. Many people are climbing with us. In every life we meet some of them. The path that takes us up to the peak is in the form of spirals, and on every turn, people's paths cross. These crossroads represent our earthly marriages and lives. On one of the crossroads two people meet, love, and marry. After passing at the crossroad, they gradually become farther and farther apart until again they meet. We cannot say that these same two persons will meet again and again. It depends on how they walk, at what speed, how they live, how they grow, and how they react to one another.

This meeting at the crossroads will continue into eternity, until nearer the peak two persons will meet more frequently, upon every crossroad. They will know each other immediately and will fall in love, true love. They will sacrifice themselves for each other. They will do their utmost to make the life of the other more beautiful, glorious, and supreme. The day will come when they will meet so often that they will never separate, for they will have reached the peak of love.

People speak of soulmates. There is no ready-made soulmate. We can, however, build one with great labor and sacrifice over centuries and throughout eternities. When you meet the one on the top of the mountain, he or she is yours eternally. Together you are one. In this unity of soul and spirit is hidden the glory of love. The higher you climb, the deeper you breathe, and the deeper you radiate love.

Love is life. Love is the song of the Absolute. All manifestation is a harp through which He is playing His music, expressing His love. Therefore the supreme duty of every creature is to love. Each time we truly love, we express that divine current, that divine song. Each time we act against love, we impede the divine circulatory flow; we break the harmony of His music, of His song. We cut ourselves from the energy of life and suffer in innumerable ways.

Saint Francis of Assisi wrote these beautiful lines about love:

Blessed is he who truly loves and seeketh not love in return.

Blessed is he who serves and desires not to be served;

Blessed is he who doeth good unto others and seeketh not that others do good unto him.

Saint Paul summarizes these thoughts and our explanations in a most beautiful expression:

Though I speak with the tongues of men and of angels, and have not love in my heart, I am become as the sounding brass or a tinkling cymbal.... Love is long-suffering and kind; love does not envy; love does not make a vain display of itself, and does not boast ... bears all things, believes all things, hopes all things, endures all

things.... And now abide faith, hope, love, these three,
but the greatest of these is LOVE.[1]

---

[1] I Corinthians 13:1-13

Chapter XXII

THE BLUE PEAK
THE JEWEL IN THE LOTUS

He was the true light which lighted every man who came into the world.[1]

As there is not enough room for all on a summit, whoever ascends it will likewise discover that the ascent cannot take place with a heavy load. Furthermore, there is no place on the peak for anything superfluous. The ascending spirit must constantly bear in mind the necessity to break away from the attachments to everyday life.[2]

In every man there lives an image of what he ought to be; as long as he is not that image, he ne'er at rest will be.[3]

I am of today and heretofore, but something is in me that is of the morrow and of the day following and hereafter.[4]

If you have read carefully and practiced the exercises intelligently, then you have already created a division within you. This division may be only upon the physical level, but you can honestly say that you are not your physical body. The physical body is a mechanism in your hand: you use it, control it, feed it, rest it, leave it at the time of sleep, and gradually transmute it. Of course, to completely dominate the physical body takes centuries and centuries. We see the highest example of control and domination of the body in the *New Testament*.

---

[1] John 1:9

[2] Agni Yoga Society, *Fiery World III*, par. 19.

[3] Friedrich Rueckert.

[4] Nietzsche, *Thus Spake Zarathustra*.

You remember how Jesus fasted for forty days, how His body was transfigured, how He resurrected His body, and how He used it after resurrection. Here one can see that He had complete control over His body, which was made of the finest elements of physical substance.

If you have some control over your body, over your hands, fingers, feet, and so on, and if you know that the body is not the real you, then you are developed pretty well. No one can completely explain to you the sensation of being other than your body. You must feel it for yourself. As you are able to detach yourself from your shoes, it is also possible, on a higher level, to detach yourself from the body and cease all sensation even when you are awake.

It may be possible also that you are able now, due to your studies and exercises, to know yourself as being other than your emotional vehicle or emotions. It is very interesting to note that most of our emotions pretend to be our True Self. We are glamored mostly by our emotions and identify with them. Even other people recognize us mostly through our body and expressed emotions. Thus we live in a thick fog. Neither do we see the things as they truly are, nor do others see us as we are. However, if the *crack* is there, then it is possible to make real progress toward the knowing of the Self which is other than the emotional self.

By now some of you are able to notice that all your mental activities and mental modifications are under your control. You do not yet have the experience of being your Real Self. However, you know that you are not your mind, and that the mind is a machine, though a very complicated machine, which can be used or even stopped at any time you want. If you have reached this level, it means that you have purified and cleared your body of all controlling emotions and thinking and can now use it as a tool to express your purpose in life.

But who is that Self? Who, through years and years, gained control, putting away all pseudo-selves in the field of his existence?

In the beginning your body was your self, the lord. Then your habits, your fears, your pleasures, your different emotions became conflicting selves. Each of your ideas, thoughts, prejudices, superstitions, plans, or intuitions became your self, trying to control your life. Then often other individuals, their orders, and their suggestions became your selves. Also some uninvited guests in your consciousness pretended to be your self. However, now all these selves are nil. The machine is the machine. No "evil spirit" can enter into any wheel of it and cause it to work against your will or decision. Blessed is a man if he is able to detach himself to such a degree and control his vehicles. Such a man is a free man.

Now comes the big question: "Who am I?" Of course, I am not the body; I am not the emotions, the sensations, the feelings that come and pass through my organs. I am not the thoughts that are playing their music through my mind and brain. I am not the unknown "hands" that are directing my life where they want me to go.

People tell me I am a soul, or a spirit, or an angel, or a spark of light. These are very beautiful expressions, but have I a real experience in being myself? How tragic is this? How comic? I "know" I exist, but I do not know what or who I am. I can see my physical expressions on the physical plane as my body. What does my emotional existence look like on the emotional plane? Or how does my existence look upon the mental plane? Do I have the same form, or any form, or no form at all? Can I imagine myself as being in existence without a form or in different forms? Is it possible to leave all the vehicles behind, put them away, and still have a sense of identity, a sense of self?

In my childhood, my mother used to tell me stories, especially at the time of rest. The one story that I liked best and will never forget is as follows.

There was a child who was living near a lake, a beautiful and clear lake. He was a child of nature who used to eat fruits and certain grasses. He did not feel lonely because he had a friend, a beautiful boy who often used to appear in the lake when he went to drink water at the shore. With innocence and inner joy, he would speak with that water-boy, smiling at him, and enjoying his friend's love until the wind and waves would take him away. However, one day an earthquake took away the little clear lake, and only a narrow stream remained. The boy lost his joy because his friend was gone. He was very sorry and depressed. For many, many sunsets he sat under the trees and cried for his friend. At last the sorrow became so heavy that he left that place and went in search of his friend. To this day, he is still searching.

This is the story of the human being. He lost himself as he descended into matter, and through all his endeavors, through all the sciences and the arts, he is searching for *Himself*.

Chapter XXIII

THE NATURE OF SELF

There are three main opinions about the Self.

The first says there is no Self. This is the teaching of Buddhism, exoterically understood.

The second says there is the Self, but it is like a bubble, and it disappears when you pass away. This is the teaching of materialism.

The third one says that there is the Self, and It unfolds forever on higher and higher dimensions. This is the teaching of the Ageless Wisdom.

After we study the literature about the Self written by these different parties, we see that actually they do not contradict each other; they complete each other.

Let us take Buddhism. It says,

There is no Self. Self is delusion. Self is but a heap of composite qualities, and its world is empty like a fantasy. Self is an error, an illusion.[1]

Another passage from the same source reads,

Therefore, O Ananda, take the Self as a lamp; take the Self as a refuge. Betake yourselves to no external refuge. Hold fast as a refuge to the truth. Look not for refuge to anyone besides yourselves. Work out your own salvation with diligence.[2]

Self is the Lord of self and the goal of self. What other Lord can there be; Nirvana is the extinction of not-self in the completion of Self.[3]

---

[1] Humphreys, Christmas, *Buddhism.*

[2] Ibid., p. 93.

[3] Ibid., p. 88.

After reading the above passages and being familiar with Buddhist literature, we may say that in Buddhism there are various meanings for the Self. If a person does not know the different usages of the term, he gets lost.

1. One of the meanings of the Self is that we think each one of us is a separate being. Consequently our aim is to work for our separated self.

2. Self means selfishness, egotism.

3. Self means moods.

4. Self means complexes, engrams, commands in us, each of which presents itself as a self, or as an "I." If we observe ourselves, we see that most of these selves or "I's" are transient shadows, but they are strong enough to control our life and even to perform lasting deeds, good or bad.

But there is a True Self, too, which in the Ageless Wisdom is called the *Jewel*, the *Father*, the *One-and-Whole*. This is the Monad. And we are told that this divine presence in the human form is "unconscious on our plane." Through centuries the Monad is there, but man is not the Self. You are the Self when you become your Self *consciously*, and when you reach the Divinity in the form called *man*.

When Buddha says, "Take refuge in Self," he refers to this Monad, to the highest in you, which is the source of Life, Love, and Light. "Take" means to direct all your attention and activity to the Divinity in you, to the One in you who is everywhere as *Unity*. Raise all your consciousness and awareness to His level and to Him.

Actually man gradually is going toward Himself. He is becoming Himself which means that the shadow of the Monad, which is acting in a separate body, was glamored, illusioned, and had fallen asleep but now is awakening and becoming Himself.

Imagine an ocean, shining as a mirror. In one part of that ocean a bubble comes up and bursts, forming a very small concentric wave. Imagine it as a human being who thinks that he is a separate entity. Actually he is separate in his consciousness because of the limitations of his responses. Then gradually he gets bigger and bigger which means he unfolds his consciousness and responses and includes more and more. A "day" comes when this wave involves the ocean, becomes the ocean, and he realizes that He is the ocean.

Every step of expansion is a step of Self-realization. On every step he is a separate individuality due to his past, present, and future experiences and visions. At every expansion or unfoldment, he is a bigger and bigger self — but not the Real Self. He will be the Real Self when He is the ocean itself. The only existence is the SELF.

Every time a Son of God achieves that stage, He increases God, or He adds something to the ocean: his personal, individual experiences, collected throughout innumerable ages and ages on the path of outgoing and incoming.

During all this time the Real Self never loses Its individuality; It is not a separate being but an all-embracing awareness. This awareness shines all through the Path of the pilgrim as love, compassion, sense of unity, service, sacrifice, conscience, and so on and guides the shadow to the Reality within.

When the awareness or beingness of the man reaches to the "shoreless Shore," It, as a Monad, does not lose Its identity. It becomes the Ocean-Monad: a "separate" note in the one symphony, one with the whole of the symphony, as It has within Itself all the experiences which were gained through the seven planes of Its Father-Home, Himself.

The Monad, as a real Spark within, used thousands of personalities, vehicles, or forms of Its own as Its garments of expression. It collected experiences and learned how to master plane upon plane, and in the meantime caused radiation, radioactivity, and liberation in the substance through which it worked. It learned to create, to destroy, to transmute, and to use every bit of Its experience for the fulfillment of the Plan and the Purpose of the Supreme Self.

On the way back home, It gradually will take higher and higher offices: It will be a servant, a master, a savior, a member of the Hierarchy, an intermediary between the Hierarchy and Shamballa, a Planetary Logos, a Solar Logos, and so on, to carry on the Plan of all creation towards Its Real Self.

The true meaning of Nirvana is liberation, the destruction of the limitations which keep the shadow from becoming its Real Self. It is true that a process of annihilation occurs in the nirvanic state, but this is the annihilation of the separative thoughts, intentions, motives, and limitations.

Those who have entered into Nirvana are called *Nirvanis*. Some of them reappear again without losing consciousness of all the changes or experiences they had throughout the centuries. This means that they have the memory, and if there is memory, there is an individuality. But this does not mean that on this plane of existence memory limits them in any way; on the contrary, their memory becomes a tool in their hand to unlock more space, on any plane, at any time.

We may say that God, to Whom we are going, is an evolving Entity. He Himself is aspiring toward a greater One.

This is very beautifully put in *The Secret Doctrine*. It says,

> *The feeling of responsibility is inspired by the presence of the light of the Higher Ego. As the Ego in its cycle of rebirth becomes more and more individualized, it learns more and more by suffering to recognize its own responsibility, by which it finally gains Self-consciousness, the consciousness of all the Egos of the whole Universe. Absolute Being, to have the idea of sensation of all this, must pass through all experiences individually, not universally, so that when it returns it should be of the same omniscience as the Universal Mind plus the memory of all that it has passed through.*
>
> *At the Day "Be with Us" every Ego has to remember all the cycles of its past reincarnations for Manvantaras.... It sees the stream of its past reincarnations by a certain divine light. It sees all humanity at once, but still there is ever, as it were, a stream which is always the "I."*[1]

To conclude this part, we can say that we have a self that must pass away. We have another kind of Self which is the True Self. This Self is the Everlasting One.

The Tibetan Master summarizes all the foregoing in the following beautiful passage:

> *... All that remains is a point of light. This point is conscious, immutable and aware of the two extremes of*

---

[1] Blavatsky, H.P., *The Secret Doctrine*, Vol. III, p. 580.

the divine expression: the sense of individual identity and the sense of universality. These are fused and blended in the ONE. Of this ONE the divine Hermaphrodite is the concrete symbol — the union in one of the pairs of opposites, negative and positive, male and female. In the state of being which we call the monadic, no difference is recognised between these two because (if I can bring such ideas down to the level of the intelligence of the aspirant) it is realised that there is no identity apart from universality and no appreciation of the universal apart from the individual realisation, and this realisation of identification with both the part and the whole finds its point of tension in the will-to-be, which is qualified by the will-to-good and developed (from the consciousness angle) by the will-to-know.[1]

---

[1] Bailey, Alice A., *The Rays and the Initiations,* p. 106.

Chapter XXIV

THE SELF

More radiant than the sun,
purer than the snow,
subtler than the ether
is the Self,
the Spirit within my heart.
I am that Self,
that SELF am I.

Aham eva parabrahma
Verily I am the Boundless one.

Om tat sat
Om, that boundless Reality.

The Monadic Plane is the second cosmic-etheric plane. The Tibetan Master says that *Man is the Monad.* Upon this plane the remaining veils have disappeared, and the man *sees* himself as he is. In the *Bible* there is a mysterious verse which refers to this fact. St. John says,

> *My beloved, now we are the Sons of God, and as yet it has not been revealed what we shall be; but we know that when He shall appear, we shall be in his likeness, for we shall see Him as He is.*[1]

---

[1] I John 3:2

On this plane, the injunction of "Man, know Thyself" is superseded by the fact of *Being Himself.*

The Monad is our in-most Self, the source of Life and Light to the personality.[1]

The Monad cannot be called even Spirit; it is a ray, a breath of the Absolute, or the Absoluteness rather... having no relations with the conditioned and relative finiteness is unconscious on our plane.[2]

It would be very misleading to imagine a Monad as a Separate Entity trailing its slow way in a distinct path through the lower kingdoms and after an incalculable series of transformations flowering into a human being.[3]

It is the only immortal and eternal principle in us, being an indivisible part of the integral whole, the Universal Spirit, from which it emanates and into which it is absorbed to the end of the cycle.[4]

... The Monad relates the initiate to the Will of God, to the Council at Shamballa, to forces active on the planet Pluto, and on another planet which must remain nameless, and also to the Central Spiritual Sun.[5]

When we think about Self, about our inner, real individuality, we instinctively are inclined to think through forms. People think that to know something man must hear it, see it, smell it, touch it, or taste it. We want to compare the Self with something that we know we have experienced. Some people try to formulate or define the Self by some inner states; they think that the Self resembles happiness, joy, or bliss.

Very few people think about the Self as deeper states of consciousness, a state of wide awakeness, an inclusive, whole embracing consciousness. Still fewer people think about the Self as being Will, essentially one with absolute Space. G. de Purucker

---

[1] The Tibetan.

[2] Blavatsky, H. P., *The Secret Doctrine*, Vol. I, p. 267.

[3] Ibid., p. 178.

[4] Ibid., pp. 16-17.

[5] Bailey, Alice A., *The Rays and the Initiations*, p. 96.

says that the Self "starts out its cyclic journey as unself-conscious God Spark, and it ends as a Self-conscious God."[1]

People think all these ways about the Self, but the most essential and fundamental way of knowing is *the technique of Beingness.* You can truly know a given object only by being it.

The Self cannot be experienced with our senses. They are the instruments we are using to express our purpose. We are used to thinking that we are the form we see. This is so much impressed on our being that we cannot destroy that image and enter into the formless essence of our Selves. The Apostle says,

We see through a glass darkly, but the time will come when we will see our Selves face to face.[2]

"Face to face" means through beingness, through being our Self.

You must know the Self, the real You, as having no form. If you give any form to the Self, it means you are not yet yourself, but you are looking at yourself in the mirror of existence and interpreting yourself through the terms or codes you have upon the lower levels of existence. You cannot know your Self as a form.

Think about your eyes. They do see, but not themselves; however, they exist. In the same manner, the Self cannot see Itself for It does not have any visible, sensible, or cognizable nature. Yet you realize that you are the only central pivot or Lord in the body.

Once this is achieved, you will notice another mystery. You will see that you are not only the Lord in your body, but also the Lord of all those whose Lords are still sleeping. Then gradually you will notice that you are a real part of the creative power, everywhere present. This will start with flashes of cosmic consciousness. Then you will experience what Christ said, "I and My Father are one."

When the Self comes in contact with any level of substance, It appears as though It has a form. But this is only an impression upon the substance of a given plane and not the true reflection of the Self. So the Self has no form. It is a wave of life, a ripple in the ocean of life. And this life embraces the existence itself and palpitates in the hearts of all living forms and atoms, from the dust

---

[1] Purucker, G. de, *Fundamentals of the Esoteric Philosophy*, p. 103.
[2] I Corinthians 13:12

to man and to unknown galaxies. It is a part of Space; it is even Space Itself in Its absolute purity.

When this life vests itself with a pure atmic substance, it assumes some qualities which we call Will, Love, and Intelligence. The Tibetan Master says,

> ... the monad manifests essentially as a duality; it expresses itself as will and love, as atma-buddhi and these two energies when brought into relation with the point of mind, with the third aspect of divinity, produce the soul and then the tangible manifested world; then there is demonstrated in the planet will, love, and mind or intelligence; or atma-buddhi-manas.[1]

> ... the state of being of the Monad has naught to do with what we call consciousness.... It [Shamballa] is a world of pure energy, of light and of directed force; it can be seen as streams and centres of force, all forming a pattern of consummate beauty, all potently invocative of the world of the soul and of the world of phenomena....[2]

The Self is only an awareness, willingness, livingness. The monadic awareness is the true *consciousness*. Below that consciousness, all the rest are relative states of sleep. According to this, "to remember oneself" means to raise oneself to the Monadic Plane and see your Self as you are, and to see things on lower planes as they are.

People sometimes speak about self-observation. True Self-observation is not possible. You cannot observe yourself when you are in a monadic awareness because self-observation ceases once you reach there. You do not observe yourself; you *are*.

The so-called self-observation is the observation of the activities of lower sheaths, their automatic and mechanical reactions. The observer, in fact, observes the activities of a lower plane, while he himself is focussed a step higher than the plane he observes. "Observer" is a changing station or an imitation of the Self. However gradually, as the man continues to observe his lower self, a permanent observer emerges and observes. This observer is the presence of the True Self, or he is the future Self.

1 Bailey, Alice A., *Esoteric Healing*, p. 588.
2 Bailey, Alice A., *Discipleship in the New Age*, Vol. II, pp. 292-293.

The *Bhagavad Gita* says,

> *For the Self is the unmanifested One. No thought can conceive It, and It changes not. Knowing this fact, why mourn or grieve?*

> *And even if you think that the Self is ever-born, and constantly dying, you don't have reason to grieve, O mighty armed....*

> *Whoever is born in a body will leave the body. Whoever has left the body will take a new one. Then why grieve?*

> *All beings were in a state of unmanifestation at their beginning. At the mid-course, they came into manifestation. At the end, they will again enter into the unmanifested state. Then why grieve?*

> *For some, the Self is a marvel to look upon. For some, It is a marvel to speak about. For others, It is a marvel to hear about. But looking, speaking, and hearing, they do not understand It.*[1]

He is the Silent Watcher. Bodies act but not the Self. Heinrich Zimmer says in his *Philosophies of India*,

> *The supreme and characteristic achievement of the Brahman mind was its discovery of the Self, as an independent, imperishable entity, underlying the conscious personality and bodily frame. Everything that we normally know and express about ourselves belongs to the sphere of change, the sphere of time and space; but this Self is forever changeless, beyond time, beyond space, a veiling net of causality, beyond measure, beyond the dominion of the eye.*[2]

In the *Upanishads* we read,

> *The wise man, who, by means of concentration on the Self, realizes the ancient One, who is hard to be seen, unmanifest, hidden and who dwells in the buddhi and rests in the body, he indeed leaves joy and sorrow far behind.*[3]

---

[1] The *Bhagavad Gita* 2:25-29, translated by H. (Torkom) Saraydarian.

[2] Zimmer, Heinrich, *Philosophies of India*, p. 3.

[3] *Katha Upanishad*, p. 12.

The knowing Self is not born; it does not die; it has not sprung from anything; nothing has sprung from it. Birthless, it is eternal, everlasting and ancient. It is not killed when the body is killed.[1]

The Self, smaller than the small, greater than the great, is hidden in the hearts of all living creatures. A man who is free from desires beholds the majesty of the Self through tranquility of the senses and the mind, and becomes free from grief.[2]

Then the *Bhagavad Gita* gives the outward signs of those who have achieved the summit of light:

A man is called the knower of the Self who casts away all desires of the mind and is satisfied by the Self and in the Self alone.

A man is called enlightened by the Self whose mind is not disturbed by pain, whose cravings for pleasure have disappeared, who is free from passion, fear and anger, and who, under any condition, remains unattached. The good and evil cannot disturb him and he neither praises nor condemns nor hates. Thus he is well established in the light of Self-Knowledge.

He who is able to withdraw his senses from the objects of the senses, to refrain from receiving any impression from the objects, and focuses himself within the Self, as a tortoise which draws its limbs into its shell, such a man indeed is well established in the light of Self-Knowledge.[3]

For such a man the world and life are a field where he projects the inner treasures of Self, true arts, and sciences, putting meaning, significance, and purpose in all his creations and expressions.

In Christian literature the Self is called the *Father in Heaven.* Christ referred to it very beautifully in one of His parables when He said,

---

[1] *Katha Upanishad*, p. 18.

[2] Ibid., p. 20.

[3] The *Bhagavad Gita* 2:55-58, translated by H. (Torkom) Saraydarian.

The kingdom of Heaven is like a merchant who was seeking good pearls, and when he had found one costly pearl, he went and sold everything he had and bought it.[1]

The pearl is the Jewel in the Lotus, the Self. The man can attain his Self after he rejects and leaves behind everything that is not the Self. The words "bought it" mean that the man actually worked for it: he made sacrifices; he used discrimination; he had the needed spirit of aspiration, long-time preparation, and dedication.

Some people, after knowing all this, ask very sincerely, "If the Self was perfect in its origin, why did it come down and become limited and imperfect in its expressions and manifestation, and then, throughout centuries, try to reach the perfection it had?"

The answer is as follows. Look at an oak tree and at an acorn. See that the oak is perfect as an oak because it reached its destination as an oak. Then look at the acorn which rests on the earth and how it starts to sprout, to grow, and gradually, through the years, becomes a big, beautiful oak tree by itself.

We are Sparks of a great Sun. We are destined to become Suns. The way to become a Sun is to fall as a Spark into the darkest limitations and through overcoming the obstacles, grow, and bloom toward the Sun... and be a Sun.

In *The Secret Doctrine* we are told that,

> ... *the monad, having no relations with the conditioned and relative finiteness, is unconscious on our plane. Therefore, besides the material which will be needed for its future human form, the monad requires:*
>
> a. *A Spiritual model, or prototype, for that material to shape itself into.*
>
> b. *An intelligent consciousness to guide its evolution and progress, neither of which is possessed by the homogeneous monad, or by senseless though living matter.*[2]

We read again,

---

[1] Matthew 13:45-46

[2] Blavatsky, H.P., *The Secret Doctrine*, Vol. II, p. 267.

> *The doctrine teaches that, in order to become a divine, fully conscious God, the Spiritual Primeval Intelligences must pass through the human state.*[1]

Then in another place it says,

> *Man tends to become a God and then* — God, *like every other atom in the Universe.*[2]

In his book *Discipleship in the New Age* the Tibetan Master says,

> *The Lord of the World, through meditation, is carrying forward processes which He instituted in His original, creative meditation — back in the darkest night of time when He decided to create this planet of ours for strictly redemptive purposes. The whole creation is the result of His directed and controlled thought — a process of sustained thinking which sweeps all the creative energies into evolutionary and cyclic activity, in conformity to the pattern which He eternally visualises. He has organised a group which is responsive to His meditative intention; these Beings aid Him by Their* concentrated and realised Purpose *to bring into our planetary livingness certain extra-planetary energies which are needed to carry forward the planned work of the planetary Logos.*[3]

> *... the goal of evolution being to make the potential into the real, and the latent into the expressed. The work of the esotericist is just this very thing: to bring, out of latency, the hidden quality.*[4]

Throughout Its journey, the Monad builds that spiritual model *and* cultivates the intelligent consciousness in the man with the help of the Solar Angel,[5] until one day the man becomes fully conscious on all planes and becomes a high grade initiate into solar mysteries.

---

[1] Blavatsky, H.P., *The Secret Doctrine*, Vol. II, p. 132.

[2] Ibid., p. 183.

[3] Bailey, Alice A., *Discipleship in the New Age*, Vol. II, pp. 222-223.

[4] Bailey, Alice A., *Esoteric Psychology*, Vol. I, p. 27.

[5] See Saraydarian, Torkom, *The Hidden Glory of the Inner Man*, Ch. 3, and Saraydarian, Torkom, *The Solar Angel*.

The Monad is the source of Beauty, Goodness, and Righteousness. The man tries to express Beauty, Goodness, and Righteousness. He transforms life. He redeems, he heals, he bridges, he causes blooming and radioactivity. He himself becomes a conscious light-giver. He becomes a true leader for generations and generations. People look to him as a summit of Everest, and throughout centuries they try hard to reach the peak of the monadic awareness and repeat the words of Christ: "I and My Father are One."

Chapter XXV

A TEMPLE DRAMA

The relation of the Monad to the Soul and the state of the Monad in the arc of creation and evolution was very beautifully expressed in a temple dance which I saw in Asia.

There was a huge cave, and in it was a great stage where a king was sitting on his throne. He had long hair and a beautiful, ornamented coat. Light was focussed on him, but the corners of the big stage were dark.

As he was sitting, he decided to go into the darkness. So after removing his crown and stepping down from his throne, he started to walk. The beam of light still shone on the empty chair where the crown lay.

As he went down, he met a woman who gave him a cup of drink. He drank it, and his steps became confused. Then he met another woman, bowed to her, and touched his head to the earth. He went to another woman. As he went, he entered into more darkness and finally disappeared. There were seven women who gradually took him into darkness until he lost his light and king-ship.[1]

As he was in darkness and lying on the earth, a piercing voice tore the silence, calling him:

Where are you,

My Self —

the source of Beauty,

Righteousness, and Goodness?

And he started to move and to show signs of living again, walking as a blind or drunken man.

---

[1] In oriental tradition woman is the tempter.

In the meantime the seven women tried to prevent him from walking and finding his way back to the throne. As he was struggling to walk and find himself, he cried out:

Where am I?

Who am I?

Where are you — Me?

The women were confusing him, answering his call:

Here you are. Come and find yourself

in the wheel of the Seven Rivers of pleasure.

Here is body.

Here is glamor.

Here is illusion.

Here is pride, possession.

Here is hate.

Here is power, you!

He yielded himself often, but sometimes he endeavored to reject one of them or even two.

The conflict continued. While he was falling and getting up again, a radiant angel in a golden robe appeared and approached him. The angel touched him with his sword, giving him a shock. He turned to the angel with an expression of fear and adoration, but the next moment he turned toward the seven women. The angel gave him another shock. This time his adoration and attention lasted longer, but again he turned back.

This drama continued for a while until finally he jumped toward the angel and embraced him, saying:

My Self. Me!

After this moment, the Solar Angel, holding the man's hand, started to do rhythmic movements and dancing, forcing the man to do the same. As he became able to follow more and more the rhythm of the angel, the light increased until suddenly the man saw his throne. He made a cry which was both extremely sad and extremely joyful.

He went five steps toward the throne, and as he came closer, the angel disappeared in the light.

Eventually he reached his throne and sat there as a victor.

Seven virgins appeared and put a crown on his head which had a five-pointed star on the front. They knelt in front of him, and with one voice they said:

King!

Your glory is seven times more now.

You have overcome matter, the sea, and the red fire.

You have become a Soul. Now you are the SELF.[1]

---

[1] In the future, a great musician will write splendid music for this temple drama, and some spiritually developed artists will perform the drama, to awaken the glory hidden in man. This will be one of the dramas of initiation.

Chapter XXVI

THE BIRTH

... Every atom that draws, by its motion, toward the chain of the Cosmic Magnet, restores rhythm in the Cosmos. Each atom, in its motion, evokes a chain of other motions.[1]

Through scientific investigation we learn that an atom is a picture of a solar system. Centuries ago, Hermes, a Son of Heaven, said: "As above, so below." The small contains the large, and the large is reflected in the small.

The same is true for the whole existence. Whatever is happening in the world is the reflection of the things happening in the human being. And whatever is happening in the human being is the reflected picture of an inner world. The space age is not only the physical space of our visibility. The space age is also the reflected picture of what is happening in the inner space of the human being.

We are shooting toward other centers of energy in outer space. We are doing this because in our inner space a corresponding activity is taking place. We are building bridges between innumerable gaps within us.

Such was the story of Christ. He dramatized a great mystery which was going on very secretly in the hearts of the advanced sons of men.

According to the ancient mysteries and traditions, man is divided into two main parts: heaven and earth. Heaven is the spiritual side of man. Earth is the physical, emotional, and mental side of man. The spiritual side of man is feeding the earth side continuously with light, heat, and rain to make it grow. But throughout centuries the earth side of man became so materialized that a mas-

_____

[1] Agni Yoga Society, *Infinity I*, par. 158.

sive cloud of separation was created between heaven and earth. It obscured the true nature of heaven and cut the direct communication between them.

But the heaven side of man was not lost. It was there as before, making its presence felt by lightning, thunder, and penetrating rays of Saviors.

This is a symbolic or allegorical presentation of the relation between heaven and earth. Man was so close to heavenly states, but gradually he went down and down, merging with the lowest part of substance and becoming further and further removed from his own source as far as conscious communication was concerned. Days came where the dividing wall was so thick that he completely forgot his origin. We call such times "dark ages."

In the psychological world of man, his divine nature continuously tried to contact the brain consciousness through dreams and visions, with the voice of conscience, and with rare inspirations.

The birth of Christ and his three years of activity were the dramatization of the process of this inner descent from heaven to earth. Down the centuries, the sons of men who achieved the highest standing on the spiritual arc played out this drama *to lead humanity back to the Father.* This was the inner secret of the creation of so many mysteries, temples, rituals, ceremonies, and holy books.

But Christ came and revealed the mysteries openly in front of humanity, in a way that those who had eyes to see could see the science of redemption and take conscious steps toward the self-actualization of God within.

People generally have the idea that they are born into the physical world and are living a conscious life in the world. But a little self-examination will show that only their bodies are born. Their emotional, mental, and higher vehicles are still in the making. The Real Man, the Self, is awaiting the hour of birth.

The shadow of the Real Man is there like the reflection of the moon in the ocean, but the Self, the Monad, is not yet born and is not in Its full expression. As we know, all that such a man is doing is a sort of mechanical reaction on three levels according to the degree of development of the vehicles. The conscious act is not there. There is, of course, consciousness, but it is so limited and lost in the mess of mechanical reactions that we can really say that *man is living in sleep.* This is a strange idea, but many wise people spoke about this in the past and told us about the story of a second birth.

For example, Christ spoke to Nicodemus and said to him, "Except a man be born of water and spirit, he cannot enter the Kingdom of God." The church took this as a suggestion for baptism: man must be born anew in baptism and obtain the grace of the fire of the Holy Spirit and be born again. But there is a deeper meaning.

To be able to enter into the Kingdom of God — which is one of the highest levels of consciousness where the Will of God is obeyed — man must be born anew: first by water, then by Spirit. Water is the symbol of all our vehicles, the vehicles of the Monad, the planes about which we talked. They are always transient and flowing like water. Water is the symbol of matter, of substance. Things that flow, change. So man must be born of water or through the planes of expression and escape being the victim of the bodies. These bodies cannot give birth to the Real Man unless each of them is highly organized and mature.

Once these bodies are ready and pure enough, then the Real Man, the spiritual man, starts to express himself. He is a new-born baby because the reborn man appears completely different from the man he was before.

The former man was more or less an automaton, moving through the forces and energies acting upon him. But the new man is a conscious unit, acting as a creative source. He is his own master. He registers forces and energies, understands them, chooses them, and uses them according to what he wills and according to the Plan of the Greater Life.

The process of such a birth takes centuries and aeons. Life after life, the Inner Man comes down and gradually takes control of the vehicles.

At the first initiation which is called "The Birth in Bethlehem," Jesus was born, but in reality it was at the Transfiguration that the indwelling Divinity expressed Itself.

People sometimes think that the light of consciousness starts from the physical plane and goes up to the Divine Plane, but this is not the case. The Real Man is aware of Himself on the Divine Plane; he is aware of Himself on the Monadic Plane as a Monad in full relationship with the divine and monadic worlds. But there are gaps, and his full light does not penetrate down to the physical plane through the subtle bodies due to lack of receptivity or anchorages of the higher light. Light descends from high levels and gradually reaches the physical brain.

When the brain first registers the light, you get the first awakening, and suddenly you see that you exist. This is the first shock. You get a similar shock on the emotional plane when you start to work there. Years and ages later you could have other shocks on the mental, Intuitional, and Atmic Planes. But these shocks are only the anchorages of the higher light.

The conscious activity on each plane comes with hard work and self-exertion. Gradually the light penetrates, builds up the subtle mechanisms, and then creates responses from the lower bodies. As the responses increase, the light increases. As the light increases, the consciousness increases, the awareness increases, and then the Inner Man gradually reveals himself as he IS.

When this revelation occurs on the mental plane, you have the *Transfiguration* or *Illumination*. The mystery schools call this the *Third Initiation* or the *First Major Initiation*, when man contacts his own Essence. All the ancient ceremonies of initiation were the symbolic representation of the descent of light and of its fusion with the unfolding human soul.

Here we must make clear that the lower vehicles must be prepared and built by the light precipitating from above to be able to give birth to the higher man.

So it is a reciprocal process. From the higher pole comes the light of the Real Man to the lower pole. There it creates registration, reflection, and responses, and the mechanism builds itself. On the higher corresponding levels, the same process goes on with more responses, with less obstacles and refusals until one day the lower meets the higher, but the duality still prevails.

This duality gets less and less as the physical level man extends the thread of his consciousness higher and higher until it reaches to the Monadic Plane. Then the duality and plurality in man disappear. He is born now as a conscious, divine being with full glory and power.

There is a Virgin Mary in all religions. The Virgin Mary symbolizes the readiness of the bodies, purified, and flourishing in the fire of the experience of life. When the Virgin Mary is ready, then the process of Birth takes place.

We have all kinds of men around us. Through their works and motives we will know what percentage of the Real Man is born in them. Some of them are born only one percent Real Man, some three percent, four percent, or five percent. Only very few are born ninety percent, ninety-five percent, or one hundred percent Real Man. We call these men "Masters of Wisdom" or "The Hierarchy of Light." From such people came the great saviors and leaders of the world such as Hermes, Krishna, Zoroaster, Buddha, and Christ. Each of Them came down consciously, revealing the Divinity of Goodness, of Beauty, and of Righteousness.

Chapter XXVII

FREEDOM

The Monadic Plane is the plane of freedom. Those who function in that plane are free, great souls. In that plane, self-cognition and self-actualization are facts. This plane is the door through which the initiate passes to cosmic evolution.

Each initiation is a great step toward freedom, a great step toward compassion and unity. Freedom is the path of individual, planetary, and cosmic evolution. Evolution is the process of *becoming Oneself*. Step by step the Inner Spark becomes Itself.

Evolution is the process of the liberation of the Spirit from the prison of form. By this struggle for liberation, matter evolves and unfolds, producing more and more perfected mechanisms for the expression of the inner life. The phenomenal man is one of the mechanisms created through the process of liberation of the Spirit.

Evolution proceeds on three roads or in a triple way:

1. the outer evolution, the evolution of the atom and the form
2. the evolution of the Solar Angel
3. the evolution of the Spirit through liberation and individualization

These three resemble three wheels. They all turn, but they do not turn at the same speed. Sometimes evolution 1 turns faster, sometimes 2, and sometimes 3.

From the point of view of the Cosmos there is always progress. But from the human angle, when one or another of the wheels slows down or speeds up, we think that evolution is zigzagging. On the down side we call it *degeneration*, on the up side we call it *progress*. But this observation is from the narrow point of view of time and space. It is actually all progress.

Evolution 1 is the evolution of physical, astral, and mental matter. All the tiny lives in all these three planes are evolving.

This is an "unfolding of a continuously increasing power to respond."

Evolution 2 concerns the Thinker within us. It has its own evolution. Also it is an agent of evolution, serving as a center of communication between the higher and the lower.

It is our Solar Angel, the Ego, which aeons ago redeemed Itself from the chains of matter and saw the glory of the Self within Itself. Now It is working to unveil that greater beauty within Itself through continuous meditation. In the meantime It is trying to shed light on the tiny lives in the three bodies and cause them to unfold. Thus the human soul evolves.

Evolution 3 is the evolution of the human soul which is the "fallen" Spark going back Home. Man is in the process of becoming a soul and then his Real Self, the Spark. The evolving human soul, the unfolding Spark, senses its true picture in the Spark of Ego. For a while that Spark is its Home.

Afterward, when the human reaches the level of a Soul, he will see his own Jewel within himself.

Conscious evolution starts when the evolving human soul starts to respond to the light of the Inner Thinker and obeys consciously the pure ideas projected by the great Beings.

Our Planetary Life is a center in the greater Life of the Sun. This greater Life expresses Itself through seven planes. These planes are formed of tiny lives. Each life is progressing toward the Central Spiritual Sun. Man is a cell in the "body" of that greater Being, that greater Life. That greater Life is progressing; so are all the tiny lives and forms on the planet. This is *unconscious evolution*. There is no freedom in unconscious evolution.

Freedom begins when you start to become your Self, a conscious cell in that greater life. You become a co-worker for the great Purpose toward which that greater Life is progressing. The further you respond to the Purpose of that greater Life, the more freedom you obtain and the greater services you render. Beauty becomes your life expression and goodness your light.

Conscious evolution is a process of awakening and an increasing response to the higher ideas, to the Plan, and to the Purpose of our Solar Logos. No freedom is possible in sleep. No man starts to awaken unless he starts to respond consciously to the light of the Thinker within him.

Actually every step toward the Self is a step toward freedom.

Freedom is not a physical condition. Freedom is not an escape from our responsibilities and duties. Freedom is an inner radioactivity from which Beauty, Goodness, and Righteousness shine out and spread life everywhere in spite of all physical, emotional, and mental obstacles. In such a state of freedom, a prisoner can be the freest one, and the ruling king can be the most miserable slave.

The energy of freedom is the propelling power behind all creation. It is the energy behind all cultures and civilizations. It exists in each of us. It is the atmosphere in which the Real Self lives. That is why we cannot enjoy or experience full freedom until we become our Real Self.

Once you experience the energy of freedom, you become a living fire. When the ancients were keeping the fire perpetual; when they were worshiping the light, the lightning, the sun; when they were placing that fire upon their altars, they were actually worshiping the energy of freedom, the source of freedom.

This state of freedom is the result of conscious evolution, the result of long ages of suffering, detachment, and observation. Nothing in nature can be achieved easily. The path to freedom is hard work. On this path the petals of freedom slowly unfold and spread the fragrance of love, sincerity, respect, gratitude, harmlessness, sense of responsibility, creativity, service, and sacrifice.

Sometimes people think that a man who has a deep sense of responsibility and an intense will to serve is a slave. This is not true. The sense of responsibility and the will to serve are the first major signs that a man is now able to detach himself from the chains of his selfish interests; to refuse hindrances coming from his physical, emotional, and mental natures; to reject any personality response to the surrounding conditions and is now able to remain in the peace of the Soul, trying to live intelligently for the welfare of humanity.

Man's slavery starts when he begins to live for himself and forgets his responsibilities. This leads him into physical and psychological disorders or chains. You cannot free yourself and escape from your debts except by paying them. Albert Einstein once said,

The true value of a human being is determined primarily by the measure and the sense in which he has attained liberation for the self.[1]

We overcome our little self by living for others. If we are doing this wisely, we call it "sense of responsibility." As our sense of responsibility gets clearer and deeper, our true value appears because we release the hidden light within us, our TRUE SELF.

We have three thick walls around us. The first wall is the inertia of the body or the chaos of blind urges and drives in our etheric body.

We have the thick wall of our glamors. For example, there is the glamor of selfish personal ambition, the glamor of popularity, the glamor of being busy, the glamor of conflict with the objective of imposing righteousness and peace, the glamor of materiality, the glamor of adherence to forms and persons, the glamor of the mysterious and secret.[2]

We have also the wall of chaos of illusion in our mental plane. Illusion is created when the developing human soul starts to work on the mental plane, where many waves of ideas and thoughtforms are found. Because of his inexperience and the lack of clarity of vision, he cannot see these ideas and thoughtforms as they are. He tries to translate them, interprets them incorrectly, and thus creates illusions.

This creation of illusion continues until the evolving human soul expands his consciousness toward the greater Light within — the Solar Angel — and starts to see things as they are on the mental plane. That is why a man becomes more dangerous and sometimes more confused in his life when he starts to function on the mental plane.

Each illusion is a hindrance to freedom. Before a man steps to higher levels of the mental plane or enters into the freedom of the Intuitional Plane, he must cleanse himself of all his illusions through meditation and acts of will.

The Tibetan Master refers to another great obstacle on the path toward freedom. He calls it "the Dweller on the Threshold." This is a thick wall, a big thoughtform, built by the blind urges and

---

[1] Einstein, Albert, *Ideas and Opinions,* p. 12.
[2] See Bailey, Alice A., *Glamour: A World Problem,* pp. 120-123.

drives of the etheric body, by the glamors of the emotional nature, and by the illusions of the mental nature. A man who lives in the midst of these blind urges, glamors, and illusions cannot say that he is a free man. Such a man is a machine. He is in a state of dreaming. Any outer stimulus may create an unconscious response from the mechanism.

Freedom is a state of awareness. In that state, your True Self is not conditioned by any formula, doctrine, dogma, expression or by any physical, emotional, or mental form. You can penetrate through them and see things as they are.

Freedom is obedience to cosmic principles. Only through such an obedience can you destroy your limitations and hindrances. Obedience has an esoteric meaning. On the path to freedom, obedience becomes a ladder. On each step of the ladder, the traveler rejects the lower and accepts the higher.

Conscious obedience is a process of recognition and assimilation of the greater ideas, which are projected toward the human world as guiding lights on the path to freedom. They represent the true authority, the true experience. Man cannot reject them and be free. On the contrary, his freedom is achieved by the recognition of authority and experience and by his identification with them.

The goal of the cell is to obey the direction of the central life. The goal of all the tiny lives of our three worlds and up is to let the Will of the Inner Spark radiate through them. This is the meaning of obedience. When the cells or atoms resign their tiny wills and subject themselves consciously to the higher Will of the Inner Self, they have the possibility of being released from their limiting walls and of stepping into the freedom of a higher will.

Cosmic Intentions are sensed by and impressed upon the higher levels of the Spiritual Triad. Great Souls only can enter there, bring them out, and translate them for us. The Teachings of great Souls such as Buddha, Krishna, Zoroaster, and Christ were formulations of such Cosmic Intentions. Beauty, Goodness, Righteousness, Love, Unity, Purity, and Sacrifice are seven paths which lead us into the source of Cosmic Principles. Each step toward the source is a step toward freedom. Acts against these Cosmic Intentions are steps toward slavery. A slave is a man who obeys his body, glamors, and illusions, or he obeys the bodies, glamors, and illusions of his environment. He swims in the ocean of such slavery and calls it "freedom."

A free man is a man who tries to dispel attachment to matter, to the body, and to blind urges. He tries to dispel the glamors and illusions of society. He tries to eliminate the chains which were created through the attachment to matter, through glamor, and through separativeness. Such a man is a benefactor of humanity. He wants to find the causes of sickness, social misery, wars, hatred, revolution, ignorance, and slavery and eliminate them.

A man who wants to be free and to free others from such social hindrances strongly disciplines his body, cleanses his emotional world, and sharpens his mind. Only through such techniques can he reach the land of freedom and lift others toward that freedom. An artist cannot release the fire of his genius on an untuned violin. Great principles can only work out if the vehicles of expression are in the highest order of discipline and purity. Only through discipline and purity can one reach freedom. Actually the whole message of Christ is a message of freedom. The whole messages of Buddha, Krishna, and Zoroaster are the messages of freedom. All those who sacrificed their lives for freedom are heroes of the New Age, the Age of Freedom.

In the New Age the process of freedom is the process of appropriation, of fitting, of cooperation, of sharing, of right human relations with the above and the below. Freedom is not isolation. On the contrary, the highest freedom is total communication. Whenever you have a communication gap, there is your obstacle to freedom. Erase that obstacle and you are more free.

A synthesizing process is progress toward freedom. A separative process is a path toward slavery. Total freedom is freedom for the whole human race. No man can really achieve total freedom as long as slaves exist in the world — slaves of the body, emotions, and mind.

Those who once are charged with the energy of freedom become liberators on all levels. Thus liberated, they face the pressure of slavery, the hate, and the destructive forces of the physical, emotional, and mental slaves.

In sacrificing our lives for others, we are building the great temple of freedom. In using others for our little self, we are creating a prison for ourselves. In sharing we become more free; in grabbing we limit ourselves. In hating we are isolating ourselves; in loving we are becoming universal, even cosmic.

Freedom is the name of an energy which detaches us from limitations, pushes us into right human relations, into more sharing, into more communication and synthesis. The highest freedom is total sacrifice. Total sacrifice is absolute communication.

The Real Self is the fountain of the energy of freedom. That is why in the process of becoming oneself, man progressively enters into more freedom until he is released into the total freedom of his SELF.

Beauty, Goodness, and Righteousness are synthesized in freedom. But man cannot experience freedom until he expresses Beauty, Goodness, and Righteousness in all his life. Any act against Beauty, Goodness, or Righteousness leads man into slavery.

A free man is highly charged with energy. He is a man who releases you physically, emotionally, mentally, and spiritually because he creates in you harmony, integration, communication, and health.

Health is freedom. Sickness is slavery. Health is harmony. Sickness is chaos. Harmony is freedom. Knowledge is freedom. Ignorance is slavery.

Increasing knowledge is increasing freedom. Slavery starts when the knower stops knowing more, when the lover stops loving more, when the server stops serving more. Freedom is the expansion of the essence. Slavery is the expansion of the form instead of the essence.

Materialism is slavery. Totalitarianism is a big prison. A true disciple of wisdom rejects both materialism and totalitarianism in all their expressions in any field. A true disciple stands for freedom.

Franklin Delano Roosevelt was a great disciple. He formulated the four essential freedoms:

Freedom of speech

Freedom of worship

Freedom from want

Freedom from fear

These were given to humanity on January 6, 1941. A few months later, on August 14, 1941, another page of the gospel of freedom was given to humanity in the form of the Atlantic Charter. Later another page was given in the form of the Universal Declaration of Human Rights.

The new World Religion will have a major key. That key will be freedom. The gospel of the New Age will be the gospel of freedom — the gospel of Beauty, Goodness, and Righteousness.

Chapter XXVIII

JOY

... joy is a special wisdom.[1]

Joy is the fragrance of the Chalice, the Lotus. As the petals of the Lotus unfold, joy radiates out of the petals and gives vigor to the physical body, magnetism to the subtle body, and serenity to the mental body.

The Lotus is the permanent source of joy. As it unfolds, joy increases. Joy is not conditioned by outer circumstances; it is like a beacon, the foundation of which rests on ageless rocks.

Happiness is an effect of outer conditions. When favorable conditions change, happiness disappears, leaving the gloom of depression.

Joy never changes. It increases as the problems and conflicts increase in one's life. It grows in spite of conditions.

As the experience of the pilgrim increases, as the field of his service expands, as he wills to sacrifice more and more, as he conquers more territory in self-realization, the fragrance of the Lotus increases and spreads over vaster areas.

The most attractive energy of a server is his joy, radiating from his manners, from his voice, and through his eyes. Whatever he touches blooms and unfolds.

Joy is not a feeling, nor is it an emotion. It is a state of consciousness, a state which is detached from the domination of the three lower worlds. The problems of these three worlds cannot reach it. Knowledge, love, and the dynamic energy of the sacrificial petals are spread out, and they charge all the tiny lives of the lower vehicles with the energy of joy.

---

[1] Agni Yoga Society, *Fiery World II*, par. 258.

Joy is not the absence of hindrances, problems, and difficulties. On the contrary — joy is the flash springing out of each victory earned by the Inner Man through these obstacles. Joy grows in battle, in conflict, in service, in sacrifice. Real joy creates crises, tensions, and overcomes them; this is how it grows. It is joy that overcomes all hostilities, all doubts, and builds numberless bridges between the hearts.

Joy gives courage, inspiration, and vision. It purifies, heals, and sanctifies.

In the light of a joyful man, people see themselves as they are. All shadows of doubt disappear. They become inspired by a greater vision. The energy of courage starts to flow through their nerves. They make difficult decisions. Joy inflames their hearts toward greater beauties. Joy uplifts them and makes them more able, more free, and more radioactive. No one can hurt you if joy is there. Black arrows from visible or invisible worlds become powerless in front of the fortress of joy. Joy is harmony; that is why the black arrows cannot penetrate it.

Any attack against joy produces depression, gloom, darkness, and failure. Any communication with joy uplifts, exalts, and beautifies.

Joy is the alchemical stone. It is the path to life, to love, to light. It is the magnetism of the Sun. Locked doors and fenced paths open to the presence of joy. You can understand the expression of joy in any language. From any level you can translate it into your own.

A joyful man is the simplest man, the most straightforward man, and the most profound man. You always understand him, but always you find something deeper in him. When you unveil the depth, another depth opens. Through the simplicity of joy you are led into the mysteries of joy.

Success is the result of a labor which is carried on in joy. Start your work with joy, and the path of success will open in front of you. Communicate with joy. Work with joy. Be joyful in all your relationships. Even observe your failures with joy and in joy. Any failure observed in joy changes itself into success and victory. Any problems observed in joy dissolve. Joy is for infinity. Joy is for changelessness. Joy is the witness of the imperishability of the human flame.

The form of the warriors' salutation for the New Age will be, "*Rejoice!*"

This is not a hand-shake or a hello. This is not a kiss or an embrace. It is an act of charging people with the energy of joy. It is an act of uplifting them from the waves of the three worlds and holding them in beauty, in gratitude, in courage, in hope, in vision, in reality.

"*Rejoice!*" Joy is the fragrance rising out of the inner Chalice, an ever-singing melody.

In great humility, in great simplicity, enter into the inner sanctuary and see the Chalice. Look at the flame in the Chalice, the fire of bliss. Place your lips on the Chalice and taste. Then enter into the ecstacy of love, of joy, of bliss.

Chapter XXIX

THE TRUTH

For every need there is an answer. We have three factors in meeting our needs:

1. We have the need. The fact of the need is the fact of sensing one's own limitations and a mounting aspiration toward fullness, perfection, and freedom. It is actually the urge to grow and to expand on physical, emotional, and mental levels and into higher realms. The smallest need that man feels is a spark of invitation or a step toward the Self. Nature is created in a way that the needs of man expand as the inner nucleus of light — the nucleus of Goodness, Beauty, and Righteousness — starts to awaken. As his needs expand, his consciousness expands, and as his consciousness expands, proportionally his questions are answered. The evolution of a human being is a progressive path of surmounting limitations and hindrances and assimilating more energy of freedom.

2. The second factor is the bridge between our need and the answer. It is the transmitter or the link, the relation between, through which our need is met. This bridge can be in any form: an electric wire, a human body, a center, a mind, an intelligence, a soul, and so on. This bridge is the relation between the need and the answer. It presents the need to the source of the answer and brings the answer back to the level where the need of the human being is met.

3. The third factor is the answer itself.

So we have the formula $A = N + B$: answer is equal to need plus bridge. The need and the answer always exist together. They are the two faces of one coin. If there is a need, there is also an answer to that need. Often we do not see the answer because of the limitation of our bridge.

Our bridge is the result of the interchange or the dialogue between the need and the answer. If this bridge is not built sufficiently to carry the answer to us, we think there is no answer to our need. But the answer is there and will be ours as the process of bridge building is carried on.

The need actually is the reflection of the answer. It is the answer which causes the need. The answer is there; that is why we have the need.

The sign of progress and unfoldment is the increase of needs. Curiously enough, the sign of achievement is the "shortening" of the bridge between the need and the answer. All human progress is the action and the response of the need and the answer.

You have to walk two miles every day. You will need a good pair of shoes. Every time your need increases, you must go farther, farther, and farther. Now you need a donkey. Years later you need a horse, then a carriage, a car, an airplane, then, who knows, a space ship, or omnipresence! The line of communication between the two points — need and answer — increases in space, decreases in time.

All we know, have, and are is the answer to our needs. The need is the seed of a giant tree which we call the *Self*.

The process of changing the not-self into the Self is the process of need and answer. This means also that the answers we get for our needs, in their turn, create greater needs. As we go closer to the light, the speed of our search increases, and our horizon widens.

What is the source of the answers to our needs? And what is the bridge or the transmitter?

We may say that the source of all the answers to our needs is the Great Law, the Great Consciousness in which we live, move, and have our being. A part, a Spark of that Great Being, Law, or Consciousness is the essence of man, the Real Man himself. This Spark is also the need.

The bridge between the "need" and the "answer" can be the Solar Angel, Great Initiates, the Christ, the Hierarchy as a whole, the Law of Cause and Effect, and an expanding consciousness. Always man received the answers to his needs. As he progressed, greater answers came. But if man stopped in this process and rejected greater answers, he had conflict, war, crystallization, degeneration until he again started to formulate his own essential needs and invoke the answer.

His answers came from various levels and in different forms according to his needs and the transmitters. These answers brought fiery ideas. For a long period they became our ideals, our Path, our goal. The transmitters always emphasized that they were not the ends but the means, and that the progress of man is the result only of his own experience and mastery.

Age after age we saw that the answers to our questions or needs became our own limitations, our own prisons, when the dogmas, doctrines, and man-made laws settled themselves on our path of progress. Man built a cage out of these "truths," entered in, and called that cage "a religion" or "an ideology."

We know that our planet is an atom in the Cosmos and that man — with all his achievements and wisdom — is a momentary flash in a dark desert. Man in his physical, emotional, mental, and even spiritual limitations sees visions, senses glimpses from the Purpose of the Great Consciousness, and translates them according to his level and according to the conditions of his environment. He calls these visions "impressions" and these experiences "The Truth."

We can see how relative is the value of any truth by comparing it to the Unknown Reality. The founder of a religion saw only, let us say, twenty-five percent of that Great Unknown Reality and translated it in terms of wisdom, knowledge, or worship.

Out of this twenty-five percent of that truth, Christ's disciples grasped only five percent, and humanity grasped only one percent. Let us assume that the disciples of that Great One proclaimed that they are passing to humanity the absolute truth which can never be changed, added to, or cut because it presents the only way toward reality for a great cycle of manifestation. Such an expression would be the most limiting kind of hindrance to human progress and proves that the transmitter is caught in a self-made prison.

Divinity or Truth is an ever-revealing mystery. There are as many ways to Divinity as there exist human or super-human intelligences. This mystery is revealed according to the level of these beings, but always it is beyond the reach of human and superhuman intelligences.

Two thousand years ago, one of the great Sons of God was asked the question, "What is truth?" by a Roman. His answer was a defying silence. Christ stood silent with His beautiful eyes seeing beyond their ignorance. For He knew that Who was He to tell anyone what Truth is, while He was still climbing the ladder of evolution. Even the Gods in our cosmos are ever moving upward. Look at our planet, our solar system, our Milky Way, and other galaxies. Go beyond this in your imagination; time and space are beyond the comprehension of our minds. Yet from this vast Cosmos have come the energies and impressions that have filtered down into the consciousness of man. What is man in this scheme of the Cosmos? He is as invisible as the electron is in our physical world, but he is also as important to the Plan as the electron is to the atom.

Buddha was once asked by a crowd of people, "Is there a God?" He answered, "Did I say there is a God?" The crowd then asked, "Isn't there a God?" Again he answered, "Did I say there isn't?" Once again we have a son of God replying with the affirmation that we are but a speck in the Cosmos. Who are we to give the answer to the burning question, "What is Truth?"

Yet the various churches in the world are assuming the role that they are the truth and all other religions and churches are not the truth. An analogy would be this: you look at the sky through a magnifying glass and say, "The whole sky is shining." The whole sky is equated with the glass, but how is this possible when a speck of the sky is all you are seeing? All of us are a part in the Plan of God, just as all the religions are parts of the whole. If you hold to any one religion, you are rejecting what other religions have received as their interpretation of the truth.

All these religions started because they filled a *human need*. They represent an *answer* to the need. As the human mechanism advances or progresses, his needs increase. Thus the answer is created for all his needs. Look back over man's journey from the caves to the present day. Observe how his progress from walking to flying in jets parallels his progress in the development of his consciousness. His development produces the answer — but every time he has the answer, that answer becomes the need, which invokes another answer. As man's consciousness sensed a lack of something, the realization of a need, he began looking for the answer. This was the beginning of self-recognition. When the human factor is the bridge, then the quality of the answer is conditioned by the physical, emotional, and mental make-up. So how can man know what is truth when ninety-nine percent of us live mainly in the physical and emotional bodies? The energies and ideas coming from the Cosmos filter through the higher levels of being and consciousness and reach our physical brain. They cannot keep their original beauty, integrity, or their volume of energy. On each level they are deflected, mixed, and weakened. Only a small percentage is passed down to the next level.

All our knowledge is an echo of a higher one, which is passing through seven layers of atmosphere and impressing our brain. It is a reflection of the sun on a broken glass.

After knowing this, who will dare to call his teaching the absolute and unchangeable one? Who will dare to call it the absolute Truth?

All that we formulate and know are the steps of a ladder, leading us to the Great Unknown, the Truth. Every time we climb a new step, we feel the expansion of the Unknown. The steps taking us to the Great Unknown are the ways and means toward becoming Oneself. The ways and means change, but the Call of the Great Unknown, the Truth, the Self, remains and becomes our greatest need.

Man, know thyself.
Man, be thyself.

OM MANI PADME HUM

THE GREAT INVOCATION

From the point of Light within the Mind of God
Let light stream forth into the minds of men
Let Light descend on Earth.

From the point of Love within the Heart of God
Let love stream forth into the hearts of men
May Christ return to Earth.

From the center where the Will of God is known
Let purpose guide the little wills of men —
the Purpose which the Masters know and serve.

From the center which we call the race of men
Let the Plan of Love and Light work out
and may it seal the door where evil dwells.

Let Light and Love and Power
restore the Plan on Earth.

INDEX

A

absence
  two kinds of 92
absent-mindedness 92
acceptance 222
achievement
  sign of 300
acorn
  symbol of 273
action(s)
  basis of 29
  motivation of 148
  rela. to Chalice 116
activity
  conscious on each plane 284
adaptability 223
admiration 222, 251
  exercise of 67
  in marriage 252
A(a)ge
  Aquarian 7
  new, of the Spirit 20
  of release 7
  space 9, 10, 281
Aham eva parabrahma 267
Angel
  Solar 287, 300
    see also Thinker, The 288
    and etheric body 213
    rela. to mental plane 78
    thought rela. to 79
annihilation 263
answers
  source of all our 300
Antahkarana 134, 207, 212, 215
  see also bridge
  and blind commands 213
  and Self 210
  builder of 215
  building 215
    result of 211, 212, 213,
    215
    substance used for 215

contacts through 212
def. 211
group 210
meaning of 197, 201
meditation on 230
rela. to society 217
symbols of 197
Aquarian Age, see Age, Aquarian
archetypes 138, 162
art(s) 186
  def. 160
  endeavors in 70
  modern 162
  three elements of great 194
  true 191
artist(s) 86, 120, 208, 219
Aryan times 120
"As above, so below" 121
ascetic living 145
Ashrams 210
aspirations 83
assimilation
  def. 132
association 87
astral world, see world, astral
at-one-ment 50
Atlantean times 119
Atlantic Charter 293
atom(s) 139
  creation of 206
  Inner Core of 9
  permanent atom(s)/seed(s) 214
    affecting each other 111
    after death 111, 214
    and psychosomatic
      illnesses 112
    becoming radioactive 118
    bridge between mental unit
      and 119
    cause and result of dark
      shadows in 117
    contents 124
    dark
      releasing and
        annihilating 112
    effect of 118
    function of 109
    not always negative
      110
    result of 122
  currents through 117

305

F

G

I

P

W

Y

Z

OTHER WORKS BY
TORKOM SARAYDARIAN

BOOKS

The Aquarian Educational Group has published over forty-five books by Torkom Saraydarian. A few of them are:

The Ageless Wisdom
Cosmos in Man
Flame of Beauty, Culture, Love, Joy
Joy and Healing
Leadership
Other Worlds
The Psychology of Cooperation and Group Consciousness
The Purpose of Life
The Science of Meditation
The Sense of Responsibility in Society
Sex, Family and the Woman in Society
Talks on Agni
Thought and the Glory of Thinking

MUSIC

The following are a few selections on cassette and CD composed and performed by Torkom Saraydarian:

Far Horizons   *Infinity*
Fire Blossom   *Lily in Tibet*
A Touch of Heart   *Toward Freedom*

Write, call, or fax for additional information or to obtain any of the following:

- Catalog of author's books and music tapes
- Lectures on video and audio cassette by Torkom Saraydarian
- A list of available Correspondence Courses
- Seminars
- *Fiery Synthesis* (monthly newsletter with calendar of current events, classes and seminars)

T.S.G. Publishing Foundation, Inc.
Complete Line of Torkom Saraydarian's Works
P.O. Box 7068, Cave Creek, AZ 85327 USA
Tel: 480-502-1909 + Fax: 480-502-0713
www.tsgfoundation.org

ABOUT THE PUBLISHER

This book is published by the Aquarian Educational Group, an educational and religious tax-exempt organization dedicated to right human relations, goodwill, the enlightenment of the mind, and the development of the heart through education, the arts, and the study of world scriptures.

Classes are held at our Centers in Sedona, Arizona, and in Agoura, California. We also hold monthly seminars and Sun-sign festivals at both Centers. Our lectures, seminars, and festivals are dedicated to philosophy, psychology, science, and religion.

We offer home study courses on scientific meditation and world scriptures; we publish many educational and religious books and pamphlets. We also offer baptisms, weddings, Last Rites, and Holy Communion.

Special counseling and lectures are provided for those who need help in overcoming their habits of using marijuana, drugs, or those who need family counseling. Please contact us if we can be of service to you.

All our services are provided through contributions.

PUBLISHING FOUNDATION INC.

The Complete Line of Works by Torkom Saraydarian
P.O. Box 7068 • Cave Creek, AZ 85327
Phone: (480) 502-1909 • Fax: (480) 502-0713
www.tsgfoundation.org • info@tsgfoundation.org